This revised and updated edition incorporates many changes that refléct developments in language study over the past decade. There is an entirely new chapter on pragmatics, with an expansion of the chapter on semantics. The explosion of interest in many of the 'applied' areas of language study is also reflected in additional sections on speech recognition systems, sign languages, women's and men's language, input in language learning, and several other topics. The study questions and discussion topics following each chapter have also been thoroughly revised, with the addition of forty new tasks for students; and the further reading sections have been revised, updated and expanded, resulting in a comprehensive bibliography of contemporary thinking on language. The new edition also has many more illustrations, examples, and quotes from a wide range of commentators, from Groucho Marx to Gary Larson, and notes on new developments in contemporary English and other languages. The presentation retains the clear and lively style which made the first edition a widely used introduction to the study of language.

The study of language

Second edition

The study of language

Second edition

George Yule

CAMBRIDGE
UNIVERSITY PRESS

PUBLISHED BY THE PRESS SYNDICATE OF THE UNIVERSITY OF CAMBRIDGE
The Pitt Building, Trumpington Street, Cambridge, United Kingdom

CAMBRIDGE UNIVERSITY PRESS
The Edinburgh Building, Cambridge CB2 2RU, UK   http://www.cup.cam.ac.uk
40 West 20th Street, New York, NY 10011–4211, USA   http://www.cup.org
10 Stamford Road, Oakleigh, Melbourne 3166, Australia
Ruiz de Alarcón 13, 28014 Madrid, Spain

© Cambridge University Press 1985, 1996

First published 1985
Second edition first published 1996
Reprinted 1996, 1997, 1998, 1999, 2000

Printed in the United Kingdom at the University Press, Cambridge

A catalogue record for this book is available from the British Library

Library of Congress Cataloguing in Publication data
Yule, George, 1947–
   The Study of language / George Yule. – 2nd edn
     p.   cm.
   Includes bibliographical references and index.
   ISBN 0 521 56053 5 (hardback).   ISBN 0 521 56851 x (paperback)
     1. Language and languages.   2. Linguistics.   I. Title.
P 106.Y85   1996
410–dc20 95-44854 CIP

(First edition ISBN 0 521 30531 4 hardback
First edition ISBN 0 521 31877 7 paperback)

ISBN 0 521 56053 5 hardback
ISBN 0 521 56851 x paperback

TAG

Tutorial

7, 8, 9, 10

Contents

Preface xi
Preface to second edition xiii

1 The origins of language 1
The divine source; The natural-sound source; The oral-gesture source;
Glossogenetics; Physiological adaptation; Interactions and transactions;
Study questions; Discussion topics/projects; Further reading

2 The development of writing 9
Pictograms and ideograms; Logograms; Rebus writing; Syllabic writing;
Alphabetic writing; Written English; Study questions; Discussion topics/projects;
Further reading

3 The properties of language 19
Communicative versus informative; Unique properties; Displacement;
Arbitrariness; Productivity; Cultural transmission; Discreteness; Duality; Other
properties; Study questions; Discussion topics/projects; Further reading

4 Animals and human language 30
Chimpanzees and language; Washoe; Sarah and Lana; Nim Chimpsky; Hans, Buzz
and Doris; The controversy; Sherman, Austin and Kanzi; The barest rudiments;
Study questions; Discussion topics/projects; Further reading

5 The sounds of language 40
Phonetics; Articulation: voiced and voiceless; Place of articulation; Charting
consonant sounds; Manner of articulation; Vowels; Study questions; Discussion
topics/projects; Further reading

6 The sound patterns of language 53
Phonology; Phonemes; Phones and allophones; Minimal pairs and sets;
Phonotactics; Syllables and clusters; Co-articulation effects; Assimilation;
Elision; Study questions; Discussion topics/projects; Further reading

7 Words and word-formation processes   63

Word-formation processes; Coinage; Borrowing; Compounding; Blending; Clipping; Backformation; Conversion; Acronyms; Derivation; Prefixes and suffixes; Infixes; Multiple processes; Study questions; Discussion topics/projects; Further reading

8 Morphology   74

Morphology; Morphemes; Free and bound morphemes; Free morphemes; Bound morphemes; Derivational versus inflectional; Morphological description; Problems in morphological description; Morphs and allomorphs; Other languages; Study questions; Discussion topics/projects; Further reading

9 Phrases and sentences: grammar   86

Grammar; Types of grammar; The parts of speech; Traditional grammar; Traditional categories; Traditional analysis; The prescriptive approach; Captain Kirk's infinitive; The descriptive approach; Structural analysis; Immediate constituent analysis; Labeled and bracketed sentences; A Gaelic sentence; Study questions; Discussion topics/projects; Further reading

10 Syntax   100

Generative grammar; Some properties of the grammar; Deep and surface structure; Structural ambiguity; Different approaches; Symbols used in syntactic description; Labeled tree diagrams; Phrase structure rules; Back to recursion; Transformational rules; Study questions; Discussion topics/projects; Further reading

11 Semantics   114

Conceptual versus associative meaning; Semantic features; Semantic roles; Lexical relations; Synonymy; Antonymy; Hyponymy; Prototypes; Homophony, homonymy and polysemy; Metonymy; Collocation; Study questions; Discussion topics/projects; Further reading

12 Pragmatics   127

Invisible meaning; Context; Deixis; Reference; Anaphora; Presupposition; Speech acts; Politeness; Study questions; Discussion topics/projects; Further reading

13 Discourse analysis   139

Interpreting discourse; Cohesion; Coherence; Speech events; Conversational interaction; The Co-operative principle; Background knowledge; Study questions; Discussion topics/projects; Further reading

14 Language and machines   151

Speech synthesis and recognition; Artificial intelligence; Parsers; Understander systems; ELIZA, SHRDLU, PRAGMA; Study questions; Discussion topics/projects; Further reading

15 Language and the brain 162
Parts of the brain; Broca's area; Wernicke's area; The motor cortex; The arcuate fasciculus; The localization view; Other views; Tongue tips and slips; Aphasia; Broca's aphasia; Wernicke's aphasia; Conduction aphasia; Dichotic listening; The critical period; Genie; Study questions; Discussion topics/projects; Further reading

16 First language acquisition 175
Basic requirements; The acquisition schedule; Some controversies; Caretaker speech; Pre-language stages; The one-word or holophrastic stage; The two-word stage; Telegraphic speech; The acquisition process; Morphology; Syntax; Questions; Negatives; Semantics; Study questions; Discussion topics/projects; Further reading

17 Second language acquisition/learning 190
Acquisition barriers; Acquisition and learning; The affective filter; Focus on method; Grammar-translation method; Audiolingual method; Communicative approaches; Focus on the learner; Interlanguage; Motivation; Input and output; Communicative competence; Applied linguistics; Study questions; Discussion topics/projects; Further reading

18 Sign language 202
Alternate and primary sign languages; Oralism; Signed English; Origins of ASL; The structure of signs; The meaning of signs; Writing in ASL; ASL as a linguistic system; Study questions; Discussion topics/projects; Further reading

19 Language history and change 213
Family trees; Family relationships; Cognates; Comparative reconstruction; Language change; Old English; Middle English; Sound changes; Syntactic changes; Lexical changes; The process of change; Study questions; Discussion topics/projects; Further reading

20 Language varieties 226
The Standard Language; Accent and dialect; Regional dialects; Isoglosses and dialect boundaries; The dialect continuum; Bilingualism; Language planning; Pidgins and Creoles; The Post-Creole continuum; Study questions; Discussion topics/projects; Further reading

21 Language, society and culture 239
Sociolinguistics; Social dialects; Social class and education; Age and gender; Ethnic background; Idiolect; Style, register and jargon; Diglossia; Language and culture; Linguistic determinism; The Sapir-Whorf hypothesis; Language universals; Study questions; Discussion topics/projects; Further reading

Appendix *Suggested answers to study questions* 254

References 261

Index 286

Preface

In preparing this book, I have tried to present a survey of what is known about language and also of the methods employed by linguists in arriving at that knowledge. Many questions about the nature of language are still unanswered, and linguistics – often described as the scientific study of language – is a relatively new field. In fact, any individual speaker of a language has a more comprehensive 'unconscious' knowledge of how language works than any linguist has yet been able to describe. Consequently, as you read the following chapters, take a critical view of the effectiveness of the descriptions, the analyses, and the claims made, by measuring them against your own intuitions about how your language works. By the end of the book, you should feel that you do know quite a lot about both the internal structure of language (its form) and the varied uses of language in human life (its function), and also that you are ready to ask a lot of the kinds of questions that professional linguists ask.

To help you find out more about the issues covered in this book, each chapter ends with a set of further readings which will provide you with more detailed treatments than are possible in this introduction. Each chapter also has a set of study questions and a set of discussion topics/projects. The study questions at the end of each chapter are presented simply as a way for you to check that you understood some of the main points or important terms introduced in that chapter. They should be answered without difficulty and an appendix of suggested answers for each study question is provided at the end of the book. The set of discussion topics/projects provides an opportunity to apply some of the analytic procedures presented, to consider some of the controversies which exist in the study of individual topics, and to try to focus your own opinions on different language-related issues.

The origins of this book can be traced to introductory courses on language taught at the University of Edinburgh and the University of Minnesota, and to the suggestions and criticisms of several hundred students who forced me to present what I had to say in a way they could understand. An early version of the written material was developed for Independent Study students at the University of Minnesota, whose reactions prompted other changes in the direction of what I hope is greater relevance and clarity.

Naturally, a book like this does not come about without a lot of help from friends and colleagues. I would especially like to acknowledge my debt, for suggestions and advice, to Gill and Keith Brown, Penny Carter, Feride Erkü, Diana Fritz, Kathleen Houlihan, Tom McArthur, Jim Miller, Rocky Miranda, Eric Nelson, Sandra Pinkerton, Rich Reardon, Gerald Sanders, Elaine Tarone, Michele Trufant and, for my own introductory course, Willie and Annie Yule.

Preface to second edition

This revised and updated edition incorporates many changes that reflect developments in language analysis over the past decade. It also includes modifications and
additions prompted by comments from colleagues, students and many others who
have offered constructive criticism over the years. I would particularly like to
acknowledge the helpful suggestions provided by Hugh Buckingham, Louisiana
State University, Eric Nelson, University of Minnesota, and Maryann Overstreet,
University of Hawai'i. Actually getting the work into print was made possible
through the help of the staff of the Text Processing Center at Louisiana State
University and the support of Judith Ayling at Cambridge University Press.

1 The origins of language

The genesis of language is not to be sought in the prosaic, but in the poetic side of life; the source of speech is not gloomy seriousness, but merry play and youthful hilarity ... In primitive speech I hear the laughing cries of exultation when lads and lassies vied with one another to attract the attention of the other sex, when everybody sang his merriest and danced his bravest to lure a pair of eyes to throw admiring glances in his direction. Language was born in the courting days of mankind.   **Otto Jespersen (1921)**

Jespersen's proposal that human language originated while humans were actually enjoying themselves is one of the more endearing speculations concerning the origins of language. It remains, however, a speculation. We simply do not know how language originated. We do know that spoken language developed well before written language. Yet, when we uncover traces of human life on earth dating back half a million years, we never find any direct evidence relating to the speech of our distant ancestors. There are no dusty cassette-tape fragments among the ancient bones, for example, to tell us how language was back in the early stages. Perhaps because of this absence of direct physical evidence, there has been no shortage of speculation about the origins of human speech. In this chapter, we shall consider the merits of some of those speculations.

The divine source

According to one view, God created Adam and "whatsoever Adam called every living creature, that was the name thereof" (Genesis 2:19). Alternatively, following a Hindu tradition, language came from the goddess Sarasvati, wife of Brahma, creator of the universe. In most religions, there appears to be a divine source who provides humans with language. In an

I

attempt to rediscover this original, divine language, a few experiments have been carried out, with rather conflicting results. The basic hypothesis seems to have been that, if infants were allowed to grow up without hearing any language, then they would spontaneously begin using the original God-given language.

An Egyptian pharaoh named Psammetichus tried the experiment with two newborn infants around 600 BC. After two years in the company of goats and a mute shepherd, the children were reported to have spontaneously uttered, not an Egyptian word, but something reported to be the Phrygian word *bekos*, meaning 'bread'. The pharaoh concluded that Phrygian must be the original language. That seems unlikely. The children may not have picked up this 'word' from any human source, but, as several commentators have pointed out, they must have heard what the goats were saying. (Remove the *-kos* ending; can you hear the goats?)

James IV of Scotland carried out a similar experiment around AD 1500 and the children were reported to have started speaking Hebrew. It is unfortunate that all other cases of children who have been discovered living in isolation, without coming into contact with human speech, tend not to confirm the results of either of these 'divine-source' experiments. Children living without access to human speech in their early years grow up with no language at all. (We shall consider the case of one such child later, in Chapter 15.) If human language did emanate from a divine source, we have no way of reconstructing that original language, especially given the events in a city called Babel "because the Lord did there confound the language of all the earth" (Genesis 11:9).

The natural-sound source

A quite different view of the beginnings of human speech is based on the concept of 'natural sounds'. The suggestion is that primitive words could have been imitations of the natural sounds which early men and women heard around them. When an object flew by, making a CAWCAW sound, the early human imitated the sound and used it to refer to the object associated with the sound. And when another flying object made a CUCKOO sound, that natural sound was adopted to refer to that object. The fact that all modern languages have some words with pronunciations which seem to 'echo' naturally occurring sounds could be used to support this theory. In English, in addition to *cuckoo*, we have *splash*, *bang*, *boom*, *rattle*, *buzz*, *hiss*, *screech*, and forms such as *bow-wow*. In fact, this type of view has been called the "bow-wow theory" of language origin. While it is true that a number of words in any language are **onomatopoeic** (echoing natural sounds), it is hard to see how most of the soundless, not to mention abstract, entities in our world could have been referred to in a language that simply echoed natural sounds. We might also be rather skeptical about a view that seems to assume that a language is only a set of words which are used as 'names' for entities.

It has also been suggested that the original sounds of language came from natural cries of emotion, such as pain, anger and joy. By this route, presumably, *OUCH* came to have its painful connotations. Other interjections, often represented as *Ah!, Hey!, Wow!* or *Yuck!*, are not actually uttered via the consonants and vowels we use in trying to write them down. They also are often produced with sudden intakes of breath (the opposite of ordinary talk). Basically, the expressive noises people make in emotional reactions contain sounds that are not otherwise used in their language and, consequently, seem to be unlikely candidates as source-sounds.

One other 'natural sound' proposal has come to be known as the "yo-heave-ho" theory. The sounds of a person involved in physical effort could be the source of our language, especially when that physical effort involved several people and had to be coordinated. So, a group of early humans might develop a set of grunts, groans and swear words which they used when lifting and carrying bits of trees or lifeless mammoths. The appeal of this theory is that it places the development of human language in some social context. Human sounds, however produced, may have had some principled use within the social life of early human groups. This is an interesting idea which may relate to the use of humanly produced sounds. It does not, however, answer the question regarding the origins of the sounds produced. Apes and other primates have grunts and social calls, but they do not seem to have developed the capacity for speech.

The oral-gesture source

One suggestion regarding the origins of the sounds of language involves a link between physical gesture and orally produced sounds. It does seem reasonable that physical gesture, involving the whole body, could have been a means of indicating a wide range of emotional states and intentions. Indeed, many of our physical gestures, using body, hands and face, are a means of nonverbal communication still used by modern humans, even with developed linguistic skills.

The "oral-gesture" theory, however, proposes an extremely specific connection between physical and oral gesture. It is claimed that originally a set of physical gestures was developed as a means of communication. Then a set of oral gestures, specifically involving the mouth, developed, in which the movements of the tongue, lips and so on were recognized according to patterns of movement similar to physical gestures. You might think of the movement of the tongue (oral gesture) in a 'goodbye' message as representative of the waving of the hand or arm (physical gesture) for a similar message. This proposal, involving what was called "a specialized pantomime of the tongue and lips" by Sir Richard Paget (1930), does seem a bit outlandish now.

We can, indeed, use mime or specific gestures for a variety of communicative purposes, but it is hard to visualize the actual 'oral' aspect which would mirror many such gestures. Moreover, there is an extremely large number of linguistic messages which would appear to defy transmission via this type of gesturing. As a simple experiment, try to communicate, using only gesture, the following message to another member of your species: *My uncle thinks he's invisible*. Be prepared for a certain amount of misunderstanding.

Glossogenetics

A quite different level of speculation on the origins of human speech comes under the general heading of **glossogenetics**. This focuses mainly on the biological basis of the formation and development of human language. There is a concentration, in this approach, on some of the physical aspects of humans (past and present) that are not shared with any other creatures. It starts with the observation that, at some early stage, our human ancestors made the transition to an upright posture, with bipedal (two-legged) locomotion, and a revised role for the front limbs.

The effects of this change can be seen in the physical differences between the skull of a gorilla and that of Neanderthal man from around 60,000 BC. The reconstructed vocal tract of a Neanderthal suggests that some consonant-like sound distinctions would have been possible. We have to wait until about 35,000 BC for reconstructions of fossilized skeletal structures to begin to resemble those of modern humans. In the evolutionary development there are certain physical features, best thought of as partial adaptations, that appear to be relevant for speech. By themselves, such features would not lead to speech production, but they are good clues that a creature possessing such features probably has the capacity for speech.

Physiological adaptation

Human **teeth** are upright, not slanting outwards like those of apes, and they are roughly even in height. Such characteristics are not needed for eating, but they are extremely helpful in making sounds such as *f, v* and *th*. Human **lips** have much more intricate muscle interlacing than is found in other primates and their resulting flexibility certainly helps with sounds like *p, b* and *w.* The human **mouth** is relatively small, can be opened and closed rapidly, and contains a very flexible **tongue** which can be used to shape a wide variety of sounds.

The human **larynx**, or the 'voice box' (containing the vocal cords), differs significantly in position from that of monkeys. In the course of human physical development, the assumption of an upright posture moved the head forward and the larynx lower. This created a longer cavity, called the **pharynx**, above the vocal cords, which can act as a resonator for any sounds produced via the larynx. One unfortunate consequence is that the position of the human larynx makes it much more possible for the human to choke on pieces of food. Monkeys may not be able to use the larynx to produce speech sounds, but they do not suffer from the problem of getting food stuck in the windpipe. There must have been a huge survival advantage in getting this extra vocal power (i.e. a larger range of sound distinctions) to outweigh the potential disadvantage from increased risk of choking.

The human **brain** is **lateralized**, that is, it has specialized functions in each of the two hemispheres. Those functions which are analytic, such as tool-using and language, are largely confined to the left hemisphere of the brain for most humans. It may be that there is an evolutionary connection between the tool-using and language-using abilities of humans, and that both are related to the development of the human brain. Most of the other theories of the origin of speech have humans producing single noises or gestures to indicate objects in their environment. This activity may indeed have been a crucial stage in the development of language, but what it lacks is any 'manipulative' element. All languages, including sign language, require the organizing and combining of sounds or signs in specific constructions. This does seem to require a specialization of some part of the brain. (We shall return to this topic in Chapter 15.)

In the analogy with tool-using, it is not enough to be able to grasp one rock (make one sound); the human must also be able to bring another rock (other sounds) into proper contact with the first. In terms of linguistic structure, the human may have first developed the naming ability, producing a specific noise (e.g. *bEEr*) for a specific object. The crucial additional step which was then accomplished was to bring another specific noise (e.g. *gOOd*) into combination with the first to build a complex message (*bEEr gOOd*). Several thousand years of evolution later, humans have honed this message-building capacity to the point where, on Saturdays, watching a football game, they can drink a sustaining beverage and proclaim *This beer is good*. Other primates cannot do this.

Interactions and transactions

In developing speech, humans have obviously incorporated versions of naturally occurring sounds such as *cuckoo* and *bow-wow*. They have also incorporated cries of emotional reaction, such as *Wow*, *Ugh* and *Oops*, and accompany much of their speech with physical gestures such as pointing and raising of the hand in the shape of a fist, with middle finger pointing up. All this noise-making and gesturing, however, seems to be characteristic of only one of the major functions of language use, which we may describe as the **interactional** function. It has to do with how humans use language to inter-act with each other, socially or emotionally; how they indicate friendliness, co-operation or hostility, or annoyance, pain, or pleasure.

But there is another major function of language, the **transactional** func-tion, whereby humans use their linguistic abilities to communicate knowl-edge, skills and information. It is unfortunate that we tend to imagine our cave-dwelling ancestors solely as hairy, grunting, bonechewing individuals who mugged their mates, when a lot of that grunting may actually have been in the form of messages informing the junior caveboys and girls on the best way to hold the bones while chewing. The transactional function must have developed, in part, for the transfer of knowledge from one generation to the next. This transfer function of language remains fairly restricted in time and space as long as it can only be realized in speech. By its nature, speech is transient. The desire for a more permanent record of what was known must have been the primary motivation for the development of markings and inscriptions and, eventually, of written language.

Study questions

1 What is the basic idea behind the "yo-heave-ho" theory?
2 What specific type of claim is made by the "oral-gesture" theory?
3 What special features of human teeth and lips make them useful in the production of speech sounds?
4 What exactly happened with the larynx and why was it a disadvantage?
5 What are the two major functions of language, and how do they differ?

Discussion topics/projects

A   It has been claimed that the development of the young human child may offer insights into how language originally developed. For example, the reconstructed vocal tract of a Neanderthal and that of a newborn baby are remarkably similar. Are there any parallels between the behavior of infants and the proposals presented in this chapter about the behavior of early humans which leads to language use? (If you want to do some background reading, Bickerton, 1981, Lenneberg, 1967, and Lieberman, 1984, present some relevant arguments.)

B   The limitations of a purely gestural theory of language origin may be related to differences in the range of message types. Consider these two messages: *The dog is eating a chicken* and *My brother believes he's a chicken*. Which message would be easier to convey via gesture (plus primitive grunting, if required), and why?

   (You can try to discover an answer to this question by asking one friend to perform the 'message' for another who has to guess the meaning, as in the game of charades. Take notes! Or, you can spend some time in the library, reading the papers in Armstrong *et al.*, 1995. Take notes! Or, do both!)

C   Jeremy Campbell (1982: 156) has written: "The idea that tool making, the technology of subsistence, was the driving force behind the evolution of intelligence and language is open to serious question." Do you too have doubts about the proposal that the evolution of language can be tied to the evolution of tool-using skills? How does the concept of 'intelligence' fit into this discussion? (A good resource is the collection of papers in Gibson & Ingold, 1993.)

D   It has been suggested that speech is, in fact, an 'overlaid' function, employing physical attributes of the human which were developed for other, more basic, functions (e.g. breathing, eating). What evidence would you use to support or refute such a proposal?

E   A connection is sometimes proposed between language, tool-using and right-handedness in the majority of humans. The key is the left side of the human brain which has structures not found in any other creature. Is it possible that freedom to use the hands (in upright bipedal posture) created the manipulative skills that resulted in language structure? What kind of evidence would you need in order to test this hypothesis? (Two papers by MacNeilage *et al.*, 1988; 1993, will provide some ideas.)

Further reading

Some older texts provide surveys of this topic, as in Jespersen (1921), who is responsible for most of the funny names for the theories, or Diamond (1965) who explored ideas on the natural-sound source, or Paget (1930) who argued for the 'oral-gesture' view, also explored in Hewes (1973). Chapter 10 of Bolinger (1975) is an overview. A useful collection of readings edited by Salus (1969) contains selections from Plato (on 'natural sounds'), Rousseau (on 'cries of emotion'), Herder (against the 'natural cries' approach), plus an extract from Herodotus, describing the experiment conducted by Psammetichus. Another major eighteenth-century source of ideas is Condillac (1746/1947) whose perspective is given modern support in Wells (1987). A general review of these older philosophical approaches is presented in Stam (1976). On glossogenetics in general, see de Grollier (1983) or the contributions in Hawkins & Gell-Mann (1992). On the unique properties of the human, see Corballis (1991), Dingwall (1988) or Lieberman (1975; 1991). On the idea that language evolved via a gradual series of adaptations, see Pinker & Bloom (1990). Relevant evidence from fossil records is presented in Lieberman (1984) and Stringer & Andrews (1988). On the connection between tool-use and language, see Gibson & Ingold (1993). For a more anthropological perspective, try Marshack (1991) or Tobias (1991). Other diverse (and sometimes highly idiosyncratic) speculations are presented in Allott (1989), Bickerton (1990), Fano (1992) and Ruhlen (1994). The interactional–transactional distinction is described in Brown & Yule (1983a). Useful collections of papers, with a range of perspectives, can be found in Desmond (1991), Harnad *et al.* (1976), Landsberg (1988), von Raffler-Engel *et al.* (1991) and Wind *et al.* (1991).

2 The development of writing

When we consider the development of writing, we should bear in mind that a very large number of the languages found in the world today are used only in the spoken form. They do not have a written form. For those languages which do have writing systems, the development of writing, as we know it, is a relatively recent phenomenon. We may trace human attempts to represent information visually back to cave drawings which were made at least 20,000 years ago, or to clay tokens from about 10,000 years ago which appear to have been an early attempt at bookkeeping, but these artifacts are best described as ancient precursors of writing. Writing which is based on some type of alphabetic script can only be traced back to inscriptions dated around 3,000 years ago.

Much of the evidence used in the reconstruction of ancient writing systems comes from inscriptions on stone or tablets found in the rubble of ruined cities. If those ancients were using other elaborate scripts on wood, leather or other perishable materials, we have lost them. But those inscriptions we do have allow us to trace the development of one writing tradition going back a few thousand years with which the human has sought to create a more permanent record of what was thought and said.

Pictograms and ideograms

Cave drawings may serve to record some event (e.g. Humans 3, Buffaloes 1), but they are not usually thought of as any type of specifically linguistic message. They are normally considered as part of a tradition of pictorial art.

When some of the 'pictures' came to represent particular images in a consistent way, we can begin to describe the product as a form of picture-writing, or **pictograms**. Thus, a form such as ☀ might come to be used for the sun. An essential part of this use of a representative symbol is that everyone should use similar forms to convey roughly similar meaning. A conventional relationship must exist between the symbol and its interpretation. In time, this picture might take on a more fixed symbolic form, such as ⊙ , and come to be used for 'heat' and 'daytime', as well as for 'sun'. This type of symbol is considered to be part of a system of idea-writing, or **ideograms**. The distinction between pictograms and ideograms is essentially a difference in the relationship between the symbol and the entity it represents. The more 'picture-like' forms are pictograms, the more abstract, derived forms are ideograms. A key property of both pictograms and ideograms is that they do not represent words or sounds in a particular language. Modern pictograms, such as those represented in the accompanying illustration, are language-independent. It is generally thought that there are pictographic or ideo-

graphic origins for a large number of symbols which turn up in later writing systems. For example, in Egyptian hieroglyphics, the symbol ⊔ is used to refer to a house and derives from the diagrammatic representation of the floor-plan of a house. In Chinese writing, the character 川 is used for a river, and has its origins in the pictorial representation of a stream flowing between two banks. However, it should be noted that neither the Egyptian nor the Chinese written symbols are in fact pictures of a house or a river. There is an abstraction away from the form of the real-world entity in producing the symbol.

When the relationship between the symbol and the entity or idea becomes sufficiently abstract, we can be more confident that the symbol is being used to represent words in a language. In Egyptian writing, the ideogram for water was ≋ . Much later, the derived symbol ∼ came to be used for the actual word meaning 'water'. When symbols come to be used to represent words in a language, they are described as examples of word-writing, or 'logograms'.

Logograms

A good example of logographic writing is that used by the Sumerians, in the southern part of modern Iraq, between 5,000 and 6,000 years ago. Because of the particular shapes used in their symbols, these inscriptions are more generally described as **cuneiform** writing. The term 'cuneiform' means 'wedge-shaped' and the inscriptions used by the Sumerians were produced by pressing a wedge-shaped implement into soft clay tablets, resulting in forms like ⚟ .

The form of this symbol really gives no clue to what type of entity is being referred to. The relationship between the written form and the object it represents has become arbitrary, and we have a clear example of word-writing, or a **logogram**. The form above can be compared with a typical pictographic representation of the same fishy entity: ⚮ . We can also compare the ideogram for sun, presented earlier as ☉ , with the logogram used to refer to the same entity found in cuneiform writing: ⚞ .

So, by the time of the Sumerians, we have evidence that a writing system which was word-based had come into existence. In fact, it is Sumerian cuneiform inscriptions which are normally referred to when the expression "the earliest known writing system" is used.

A modern writing system which is based, to a certain extent, on the use of logograms can be found in China. Many Chinese written symbols, or **characters**, are used as representations of the meaning of words and not of the sounds of the spoken language. One of the advantages of such a system is that two speakers of very different dialects of Chinese, who might have great difficulty understanding each other's spoken forms, can both read the same written text. Chinese writing, with the longest continuous history of use as a writing system (i.e. 3,000 years), clearly has many other advantages for its users. One major disadvantage is that an extremely large number of different written symbols exists within this writing system, although basic literacy is possible with knowledge of only 2,000 characters. Remembering large numbers of different word-symbols, however, does seem to present a substantial memory load, and the history of most other writing systems illustrates a development away from logographic writing. To accomplish this, some principled method is required to go from symbols which represent words (i.e. a logographic system) to a set of symbols which represent sounds (i.e. a phonographic system).

Rebus writing

One way of using existing symbols to represent the sounds of language is via a process known as **Rebus writing**. In this process, the symbol for one entity is taken over as the symbol for the sound of the spoken word used to refer to that entity. That symbol then comes to be used whenever that sound occurs in any words. We can create an example, working with the sound of the English word *eye*. We can imagine how the pictogram ⬭ could have developed into the logogram ◠. This logogram is pronounced as *eye*, and with the Rebus principle at work, you should be able to refer to yourself as ◠ ("I"), to one of your friends as +◠ ("Crosseye"), combine this form with the logogram for 'deaf' and produce "defy", with the logogram for 'boat' and produce "bow-tie", and so on. Take another, non-English, example, in which the ideogram 🀫 becomes the logogram ⊔, for the word pronounced *ba* (meaning 'boat'). We can then produce a symbol for the word pronounced *baba* (meaning 'father') which would be ⊔⊔ . One symbol can thus be used in many different ways, with a range of meanings. What this process accomplishes is a sizeable reduction in the number of symbols needed in a writing system.

Syllabic writing

In the last example, the symbol which is used for the pronunciation of parts of a word represents a combination (*ba*) of a consonant (*b*) and a vowel (*a*). This combination is one type of syllable. When a writing system employs a set of symbols which represent the pronunciations of syllables, it is described as **syllabic writing.**

There are no purely syllabic writing systems in use today, but modern Japanese can be written with a set of single symbols which represent spoken syllables and is consequently often described as having a (partially) syllabic writing system, or a **syllabary.** In the nineteenth century, an American Indian named Sequoyah invented a syllabic writing system which was used by the Cherokee Indians to produce written messages from the spoken language. In these Cherokee examples, Ⱶ (*ho*), Ꮒ (*sa*) and Ꮇ (*ge*), note that the symbols do not correspond to single consonants or vowels, but to syllables.

Both the Egyptian and the Sumerian writing systems evolved to the point where some of the earlier logographic symbols were used to represent spoken syllables. However, the full use of a syllabic writing system does not appear until that used by the Phoenicians, inhabiting what is modern Lebanon, between 3,000 and 4,000 years ago. It is clear that many of the symbols which they used were taken from earlier Egyptian writing. The Egyptian form ⅃ , meaning 'house', was adopted, in a slightly reoriented form, as ᗡ .After being used logographically for the word pronounced *beth* (still meaning 'house'), it came to represent syllables beginning with a *b* sound. Similarly, the Egyptian form ∼ , meaning 'water', turns up as ᒐ , and is used for syllables beginning with an *m* sound. So, a word which might be pronounced *muba* could be written as ᗡ ᒐ , and the pronunciation *bima* as ᒐ ᗡ . Note that the direction of writing is from right to left. By about 1000 BC, the Phoenicians had stopped using logograms and had a fully developed syllabic writing system.

Alphabetic writing

If you have a set of symbols being used to represent syllables beginning with, for example, a *b* sound or an *m* sound, then you are actually very close to a situation in which the symbols can be used to represent single sound types in a language. This is, in effect, the basis of **alphabetic** writing. An alphabet is essentially a set of written symbols which each represent a single type of sound. The situation described above is generally what seems to have occurred in the origins of the writing systems of Semitic languages such as Arabic and Hebrew. The alphabets of these languages, even in their modern versions, largely consist of consonant symbols. This early form of alphabetic script, originating in the writing systems of the Phoenicians, is the general source of most other alphabets to be found in the world. A modified version can be traced to the East into Indian and South-East Asian writing systems and to the West through Greek.

Significantly, the early Greeks took the alphabetizing process a stage further by also using separate symbols to represent the vowel sounds as distinct entities, and so a remodeled alphabet was created to include these. This change produced a distinct symbol for the vowel *a* (*alpha*) to go with existing symbols for consonants such as *b* (*beta*). In fact, for some writers on the origins of the modern alphabet, it is the Greeks who should be given credit for taking the inherently syllabic system from the Phoenicians, and creating a writing system in which the single-symbol to single-sound correspondence was fully realized.

From the Greeks, this revised alphabet passed to the rest of Western Europe via the Romans and, of course, it underwent several modifications to fit the requirements of the spoken languages encountered. Another line of development took the same Greek writing system into Eastern Europe where Slavic languages were spoken. The modified version, called the **Cyrillic** alphabet (after St Cyril, a ninth century Christian missionary), is the basis of the writing system used in Russia today.

The actual form of a number of the letters in modern European alphabets can be traced, as in the illustration, from their origins in Egyptian hieroglyphics.

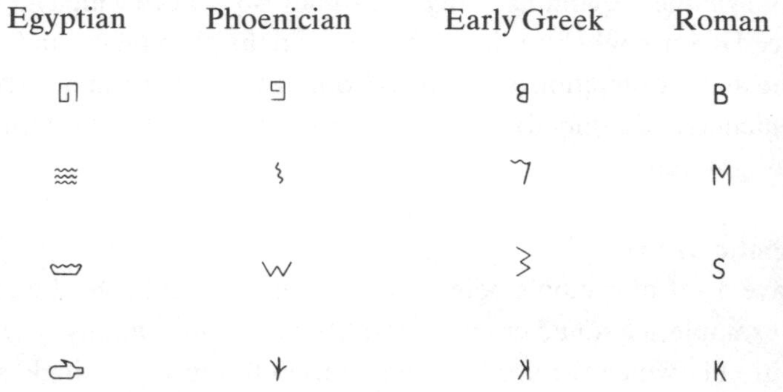
Egyptian
Phoenician
Early Greek
Roman
B
M
S
K

Written English

If indeed the origins of the alphabetic writing system were based on a correspondence between single symbol and single sound type, then one might reasonably ask why there is such a frequent mismatch between the forms of written English and the sounds of spoken English.

The answer to that question must be sought in a number of historical influences on the form of written English. The spelling of written English was very largely fixed in the form that was used when printing was introduced into fifteenth-century England. At that time, a number of conventions regarding the written representation of words derived from forms used in writing other languages, notably Latin and French. Moreover, many of the early printers were native Dutch speakers and could not make consistently accurate decisions about English pronunciations. Perhaps more important is the fact that, since the fifteenth century, the pronunciation of spoken English has undergone substantial changes. Thus, even if there had been a good, written-letter to speech-sound correspondence at that time, and the printers had got it right, there would still be major discrepancies for the present-day speakers of English. If one adds in the fact that a large number of older written English words were actually ‘recreated’ by sixteenth-century spelling reformers to bring their written forms more into line with what were supposed, sometimes erroneously, to be their Latin origins (e.g. *dette* became *debt*; *iland* became *island*), then the sources of the mismatch begin to become clear. How one goes about describing the sounds of English words in a consistent way, when the written forms provide such unreliable clues, is a problem we shall investigate in Chapter 5.

Study questions

1 Where will you find the writing system with the longest history of continuous use?
2 What is the name given to the writing system used for Russian?
3 Which modern language uses a partially syllabic writing system?
4 What are the disadvantages of a logographic writing system?
5 What is the process known as Rebus writing?

Discussion topics/projects

A Look at the standard keyboard used with a typewriter or computer. Clearly the majority of symbols (QWERTY) belong to an alphabetic system. But not all of them.

  (i) What about symbols such as = , + , & ; are they syllabic, logographic or ideographic?

  (ii) What kind of writing system has symbols such as %, @ and $?

  (iii) What about the role of the shift key? What exactly are CAPITAL LETTERS for in the English writing system? Is *conservative* different from *Conservative* and *now* distinct from *NOW*?

  (iv) Early alphabetic writing consisted of strings of letters with nospacesbetweenthem and no punctuation. What conventional uses of space and punctuation are characteristic of contemporary English writing? (Halliday, 1989 is a useful resource.)

B One point not considered in this chapter is the fact that not all the writing systems mentioned use the same linear direction for their scripts. Egyptian hieroglyphics are read in columns, for example. In Phoenician writing, like modern Arabic, the script has to be read from right to left. In Roman writing, like modern English, the script has to be read from left to right. This means that there must have been a period during which the development of alphabetic writing underwent a shift from right-to-left to left-to-right. Are there any clues in the chapter as to when this probably occurred? (You could look up the word *boustrophedon* in a dictionary for a further clue to how the transition took place. Or consult Jeffery, 1961 for some speculations on why the change occurred.)

C A rather specialized use of written language is found in graffiti (which also has a long history).

  (i) What is special or unusual about the actual written form of graffiti that makes it recognizable as graffiti?

(ii) A notorious problem with a lot of graffiti is that its interpretation is quite difficult because it depends on a great deal of specific knowledge about the immediate physical location, political issues of the time, special vocabulary, and much else. Find some examples of graffiti and consider what other knowledge, in addition to knowledge of language and writing, is needed in order to interpret the examples.

D You can encounter versions of different types of writing systems in everyday life (and you are often required by law to know what they mean). In the accompanying photograph (taken by Mary Sah on a country road in England), the signs are obviously intended to represent important information.

  (i) How would you write out, in English sentences, the 'message' being communicated by each of these signs?

 (ii) What kind of symbolic representation (e.g. ideographic) is being used in each?

(iii) Find examples of other street signs and try to work out what different writing-system conventions are most commonly used.

E Pictograms may be language-independent, but they do not seem to be culture-independent. In order to interpret many pictographic and ideographic representations, you have to be familiar with cultural assumptions about what the symbols 'mean'.

(i) As a simple exercise, show the twelve symbols illustrated below (from Ur, 1988) to some friends and ask them to decide what each means. (Be prepared for some unusual answers!)

(ii) Next, provide them with the following list of 'official meanings' and ask them to decide which symbol goes with which meaning.

(a) blood donors   (b) telegrams   (c) keep frozen   (d) agitate
(e) registration   (f) open door or lid   (g) lost child   (h) lock
(i) turning basin-manoeuvring (boats)   (j) dry, heat
(k) protection and safety equipment   (l) press, interview room

(iii) What kinds of cultural assumptions did you recognize in the process of attempting to interpret these symbols? (For example, first recognize the penguin, then what?)

Further reading
Older, fairly accessible accounts of the development of writing are available in Claiborne (1974), Chapter 7 of Hughes (1962), or Ullman (1969). More comprehensive treatments are provided by Diringer (1968), Gelb (1963) and Jensen (1969). A historical survey of the archaeological discoveries relevant to the study of writing is presented in Pedersen (1972). For an original account of the role of clay tokens in the development of writing, see Schmandt-Besserat (1991; 1992). A good facsimile edition of Egyptian writing can be found in

Budge (1913). A reproduction of the full Cherokee syllabary can be found in Gleason (1961). Illustrations of a wide range of contemporary scripts are presented in Nakanishi (1990). The origins of alphabetic writing (and its impact) are explored in Harris (1986), Healey (1990), Hooker (1990), Powell (1991), Senner (1989) and Thomas (1992). Several books provide linguistic analyses of different writing systems, as in Coulmas (1989), DeFrancis (1989), Miller (1994) and Sampson (1985), while the encyclopedic volume by Daniels & Bright (1995) is a comprehensive reference work. More specifically, on cuneiform see Walker (1987), on Egyptian hieroglyphics see Budge (1983) or Davies (1987), and on early Greek inscriptions see Cook (1987). The elaborate writing system developed by the Maya in central America is described in Houston (1989). On the differences between spoken and written language, try Biber (1991) or Halliday (1989). Considerations of writing often lead into concerns with literacy, which can be explored in Barton (1994), Downing, Lima & Noonan (1992), Goody (1986; 1987), Olson (1994), Olson & Torrance (1991), Scholes (1993) and Watt (1994).

3 The properties of language

I once knew a golden retriever named Newton who had a perverse sense of humor. Whenever I tossed out a Frisbee for him to chase, he'd take off in hot pursuit but then seem to lose track of it. Trotting back and forth only a yard or two from the toy, Newton would look all around, even up into the trees. He seemed genuinely baffled. Finally, I'd give up and head into the field to help him out. But no sooner would I get within ten feet of him than he would invariably dash straight over to the Frisbee, grab it and start running like mad, looking over his shoulder with what looked suspiciously like a grin.

Michael Lemonick (1993)

In Chapter 1 we considered some physiological properties of the human species as prerequisites for the production of language. The physical aspects of human teeth, larynx and so on are not shared by other creatures and may explain why only the human creature has the capacity for speech. However, we did not suggest that the human was the only creature which was capable of communicating. All creatures, from apes, bees, cicadas, dolphins, through to zebras, are capable of communicating with other members of their species. The range and complexity of animal communication systems are staggering and we could not hope even to summarize their diverse properties here. What we can do, as part of an investigation of language, is concentrate on those properties which differentiate human language from all other forms of signaling and which make it a unique type of communication system.

Communicative versus informative

In order to describe those properties, we should first distinguish what are specifically **communicative** signals from those which may be unintentionally **informative** signals. A person listening to you may become informed about you via a number of signals which you have not intentionally sent. She may note that you have a cold (you sneezed), that you aren't at ease (you shifted around in your seat), that you are untidy (unbrushed hair, rumpled clothing), that you are disorganized (non-matching socks), and that you are from some other part of the country (you have a strange accent). However, when you use language to tell this person, "I would like to apply for the vacant position of senior brain surgeon at the hospital," you are normally considered to be intentionally communicating something. By the same token, the blackbird is not normally taken to be communicating anything by having black feathers, perching on a branch and eating a worm, but is considered to be sending a communicative signal with the loud squawking to be heard when a cat appears on the scene. So, when we consider the distinctions between human language and animal communication, we are considering both in terms of their potential as a means of intentional communication.

Unique properties

There have been a number of attempts to determine the defining properties of human language, and different lists of features can be found. We shall take six of these features and describe how they are manifested in human language. We shall also try to describe in what ways these features are uniquely a part of human language and unlikely to be found in the communication systems of other creatures. We should remain aware, however, that our view of how other creatures communicate is essentially an outsider's view and may be inaccurate. It is possible that your pet has quite complex communication with other members of its species and frequently comments on how hard it is to get points across to the large clumsy bipeds who act as if they know it all. Bearing that caveat in mind, we can now consider some of the properties which the bipeds believe are unique to their linguistic system.

Displacement   超越時空   *Things may happen in the past* *happen now.*

When your pet cat comes home after spending a night in the back alleys and stands at your feet calling *meow*, you are likely to understand this message as relating to that immediate time and place. If you ask the cat where it was the night before and what it was up to, you may get the same *meow* response. It seems that animal communication is almost exclusively designed for this moment, here and now. It cannot effectively be used to relate events which are far removed in time and place. When your dog says *GRRR*, it is likely to mean *GRRR, right now*, because it does not appear capable of communicating *GRRR, last night, over in the park*. Now, human language-users are perfectly capable of producing messages equivalent to *GRRR, last night, over in the park*, and going on to say *In fact, I'll be going back tomorrow for some more*. They can refer to past and future time, and to other locations. This property of human language is called **displacement**. It allows the users of language to talk about things and events not present in the immediate environment. Animal communication is generally considered to lack this property.

However, it has been proposed that bee communication does have the property of displacement. For example, when a worker bee finds a source of nectar and returns to the hive, it can perform a complex dance routine to communicate to the other bees the location of this nectar. Depending on the type of dance (round dance for nearby and tail-wagging dance, with variable tempo, for further away and how far), the other bees can work out where this newly discovered feast can be found. This ability of the bee to indicate a location some distance away must mean that bee communication has at least some degree of displacement as a feature. The crucial consideration involved, of course, is that of degree. Bee communication has displacement in an extremely limited form. Certainly, the bee can direct other bees to a food source. However, it must be the most recent food source. It cannot be *that rose garden on the other side of town that we visited last weekend*, nor can it be, as far as we know, possible future nectar in bee heaven.

The factors involved in the property of displacement, as it is manifested in human language, are much more comprehensive than the communication of a single location. It enables us to talk about things and places whose existence we cannot even be sure of. We can refer to mythical creatures, demons, fairies, angels, Santa Claus, and recently invented characters such as Superman. It is the property of displacement that allows the human, unlike any other creature, to create fiction and to describe possible future worlds.

Arbitrariness 约定俗成

It is generally the case that there is no 'natural' connection between a linguistic form and its meaning. You cannot look at the Arabic word كلب, and from its shape, for example, determine that it has a natural meaning, any more than you can with its English translation form *dog*. The linguistic form has no natural or 'iconic' relationship with that four-legged barking object out in the world. Recognizing this general fact about language leads us to conclude that a property of linguistic signs is their arbitrary relationship with the objects they are used to indicate. The forms of human language demonstrate a property called **arbitrariness**: they do not, in any way, 'fit' the objects they denote. Of course, you can play a game with words to make them 'fit', in some sense, the property or activity they indicate, as in these examples from a child's game:

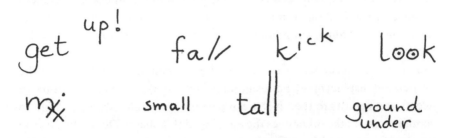

However, such a game only emphasizes how arbitrary the connection normally is between the linguistic form and its meaning.

There are, of course, some words in language which have sounds which seem to 'echo' the sounds of objects or activities. English examples might be *cuckoo*, *CRASH*, *slurp*, *squelch* or *whirr,* which are onomatopoeic, and which we have already noted (Chapter 1) as part of the 'natural sounds' theory of language origin. In most languages, however, these onomatopoeic words are relatively rare, and the vast majority of linguistic expressions are in fact arbitrary.

For the majority of animal signals, there does appear to be a clear connection between the conveyed message and the signal used to convey it. This impression we have of the non-arbitrariness of animal signaling may be closely connected with the fact that, for any animal, the set of signals used in communication is finite. That is, each variety of animal communication consists of a fixed and limited set of (vocal or gestural) forms. Many of these forms are used only in specific situations (e.g. establishing territory) and at particular times (e.g. during the mating season). As far as mating is concerned, the human seems to behave as if it is always open season, and the range and frequent novelty of linguistic expressions used in connection with that activity may provide evidence for another property of human language, normally described as 'productivity'.

Productivity 創新性

It is a feature of all languages that novel utterances are continually being created. A child learning language is especially active in forming and producing utterances which he or she has never heard before. With adults, new situations arise or new objects have to be described, so the language-users manipulate their linguistic resources to produce new expressions and new sentences. This property of human language has been termed **productivity** (or 'creativity', or 'open-endedness'). It is an aspect of language which is linked to the fact that the potential number of utterances in any human language is infinite.

Non-human signaling, on the other hand, appears to have little flexibility. Cicadas have four signals to choose from and vervet monkeys have about thirty-six vocal calls (including the noises for vomiting and sneezing). Nor does it seem possible for animals to produce 'new' signals to communicate novel experiences or events. The worker bee, normally able to communicate the location of a nectar source, will fail to do so if the location is really 'new'. In one experiment, a hive of bees was placed at the foot of a radio tower and a food source at the top. Ten bees were taken to the top, shown the food source, and sent off to tell the rest of the hive about their find. The message was conveyed via a bee dance and the whole gang buzzed off to get the free food. They flew around in all directions, but couldn't locate the food. (It is probably one way to make bees really mad.) The problem may be that bee communication regarding location has a fixed set of signals, all of which relate to horizontal distance. The bee cannot manipulate its communication system to create a 'new' message indicating vertical distance. According to Karl von Frisch, who conducted the experiment, "the bees have no word for *up* in their language". Moreover, they cannot invent one.

The problem seems to be that animal signals have a feature called **fixed reference**. Each signal is fixed as relating to a particular object or occasion. Among the vervet monkey's repertoire, there is one danger signal *CHUTTER*, which is used when a snake is around, and another *RRAUP*, used when an eagle comes by. These signals are fixed in terms of their reference and cannot be manipulated. What would count as evidence of productivity in the monkey's communication system would be the utterance of something like a *CHUTT–RRAUP* type of signal when a flying creature that looked like a snake came by. That is, the monkey would be capable of manipulating its 'language' to cope with the new situation. Unfortunately, we have no evidence that the monkey could produce a new danger signal. The human, given similar circumstances, is quite capable of creating a new 'signal', after initial surprise, by uttering something along the lines of *Wow, I don't believe it, an eagle-snake!*

Cultural transmission 文化承傳

While you may inherit brown eyes and dark hair from your parents, you do not inherit their language. You acquire a language in a culture with other speakers and not from parental genes. An infant born to Korean parents (who have never left Korea and speak only Korean), which is adopted and brought up from birth by English speakers in the United States, may have physical characteristics inherited from its natural parents, but it will inevitably speak English. A kitten, given comparable early experiences, will produce *meow* regardless.

This process whereby language is passed on from one generation to the next is described as **cultural transmission**. While it has been argued that humans are born with an innate predisposition to acquire language (discussed in more detail in Chapter 16), it is clear that they are not born with the ability to produce utterances in a specific language, such as English. The general pattern of animal communication is that the signals used are instinctive and not learned.

In the case of some birds, however, there is evidence that instinct has to combine with learning (or exposure) to produce the right song. If those birds spend their first seven weeks without hearing other birds, they will instinctively produce songs or calls, but these songs will be abnormal in some way. Human infants, growing up in isolation, produce no 'instinctive' language. Cultural transmission of a specific language is crucial in the human acquisition process.

Discreteness 不連續性

The sounds used in language are meaningfully distinct. For example, the difference between a *b* sound and a *p* sound is not actually very great, but when these sounds are part of a language like English, they are used in such a way that the occurrence of one rather than the other is meaningful. The fact that the pronunciation of the forms *pack* and *back* leads to a distinction in meaning can only be due to the difference between the *p* and *b* sounds in English. This property of language is described as **discreteness**. Each sound in the language is treated as discrete. It is possible, in fact, to produce a range of sounds in a continuous stream which are all generally like the *p* and *b* sounds. These physically different sounds could be conceived of as the spoken counterpart of a written set such as:

$$P \quad P \quad P \quad p \quad b \quad b \quad B \quad B$$

However, that continuous stream will only be interpreted as being either a *p* sound, or a *b* sound (or, possibly, as a non-sound) in the language. We have a very discrete view of the sounds of our language and wherever a pronunciation falls within the physically possible range of sounds, it will be interpreted as a linguistically specific and meaningfully distinct sound.

Duality 双属組織

Language is organized at two levels or layers simultaneously. This property is called **duality**, or 'double articulation'. In terms of speech production, we have the physical level at which we can produce individual sounds, like *n*, *b* and *i*. As individual sounds, none of these discrete forms has any intrinsic meaning. When we produce those sounds in a particular combination, as in *bin*, we have another level producing a meaning which is different from the meaning of the combination in *nib*. So, at one level, we have distinct sounds, and, at another level, we have distinct meanings. This duality of levels is, in fact, one of the most economical features of human language, since with a limited set of distinct sounds we are capable of producing a very large number of sound combinations (e.g. words) which are distinct in meaning.

It is obvious that, although your dog may be able to produce *woof*, it does not seem to be a feature of the canine repertoire that the *w*, *oo* and *f* elements can be separated out as a distinct level of production. If your dog could operate with the double level (i.e. duality), then you might expect to hear *oowf* and even *foow*, each with different meanings.

Other properties

These six properties of displacement, arbitrariness, productivity, cultural transmission, discreteness and duality may be taken as the core features of human language. Human language does of course have many other properties, but these are not uniquely human characteristics.

The use of the **vocal-auditory channel**, for example, is certainly a feature of human speech. Human linguistic communication is typically generated via the vocal organs and perceived via the ears. Linguistic communication, however, can also be transmitted without sound, via writing or via the sign languages of the deaf. Moreover, many other species (e.g. dolphins) use the vocal-auditory channel. Thus, this property is not a defining feature of human language.

Similar points can be made about **reciprocity** (any speaker/sender of a linguistic signal can also be a listener/receiver); **specialization** (linguistic signals do not normally serve any other type of purpose, such as breathing or feeding); **non-directionality** (linguistic signals can be picked up by anyone within hearing, even unseen); and **rapid fade** (linguistic signals are produced and disappear quickly). Most of these are properties of the spoken language, but not of the written language. They are also not present in many animal communication systems which characteristically use the visual mode or involve frequent repetition of the same signal. Such properties are best treated as ways of describing human language, but not as a means of distinguishing it from other systems of communication.

Study questions

1 Can you briefly explain what the term 'arbitrariness' means as it is used to describe a property of human language?
2 Which term is used to describe the ability of human language-users to discuss topics which are remote in space and time?
3 Is the fact that linguistic signals do not normally serve any other type of purpose, such as feeding, a good reason to consider this a unique property of human language?
4 What is the term used to describe the fact that, in a language, we can have different meanings for the three words *tack*, *act* and *cat*, yet, in each case, use the same basic set of sounds?
5 What kind of evidence supports the idea that language is culturally transmitted?

Discussion topics/projects

A Lying and deception, which appear to be particularly human traits, may have prompted Charles Hockett (1963) to include them (in technical terms, as *prevarication*) as a possible property of human language. In discussing this property, he claimed that "linguistic messages can be false" while "lying seems extremely rare among animals". Keeping this in mind, consider the following report (from Jolly, 1985) of an event involving two female chimpanzees named Matata and Lorel.

Matata returned to the social group for breeding and found herself subordinate to Lorel, a female she had easily dominated in earlier years. The situation lasted for some days, until Matata happened to be alone in the outer cage with Lorel and the child of a still more dominant female. Matata reached up and yanked on the child's leg where it dangled on the net above her. The little chimp squealed, of course. All the other animals came pounding out of the inside cage, including the adult male and the child's bristling mother. As they emerged Matata glared at

Lorel and barked. The dominant mother swung round and attacked innocent Lorel. From that day on, Matata again lorded it over Lorel whenever there was food to take or babies to groom.

(i) Is this an example of prevarication? If yes, does this mean that prevar-ication cannot be treated as a key property of human language? If no, then what is it?

(ii) If you can accept the idea that animals are capable of prevarication, what must it mean for our concept of intelligence or cognitive ability in animals? Are there other indications of highly developed intelli-gence in non-humans?

B An attempt was made, at the beginning of this chapter, to create a simple distinction between 'communicative' and 'informative' signals. The basic element in that distinction was the idea of intention. However, whether something is done 'intentionally', or not, may not always be so easily identified.

(i) What about choice of clothing? Can what you wear be communica-tive?

(ii) Is body language communicative or informative? How about hand-shakes and facial expressions?

(iii) Are all gestures interpreted in the same way by all cultures? Is it possible to distinguish intentional (i.e. communicative) gestures from those that are unintentional? Or is the actual concept of 'intentional behavior' something that differs from one cultural group to another?

C The properties of 'non-directionality' and 'reciprocity' are not consid-ered unique to human language. In what other communication systems are they present and are they present in all forms of human communica-tion via language?

D In this chapter the set of properties is simply enumerated and described. There was no discussion of whether a communication system having these properties would provide its users with advantages in terms of survival or development. Can a case be made for these unique properties of language being viewed as advantageous for the human creature? (For background reading, Hockett, 1963, has some speculations on this subject.)

E   In presenting the property of arbitrariness, we placed little value on
    the iconic aspects of language (where form echoes meaning). We did
    mention onomatopoeia, also known as 'sound symbolism', which some
    people believe is actually quite common in language. They point to the
    "unpleasant" sense of words beginning with the sound combination *sl-*,
    as in *slithering slimy slugs*. From this perspective, any assumption of the
    arbitrariness of language forms needs to be reconsidered.

   (i) Is the 'unpleasant' sense actually true of all, or even most,
       words beginning with *sl-* in English?

  (ii) Are there any other sounds or sound combinations that you
       associate with particular meanings?

 (iii) How about the vowel sounds in words that identify near-to-speaker
       concepts (*this*, *near*, *here*) versus far-from-speaker concepts (*that*,
       far, *there*)? What is this difference? Is it a general pattern distin-
       guishing terms for things that are near versus far?

 (iv) Is there a possible correspondence between size of word and com-
       mon or frequent usage (e.g. the more common the word, the smaller
       it is)? If true, is this evidence against the idea of arbitrariness?
       (A useful resource might be the papers in Hinton *et al.*, 1994.)

Further reading

An introductory treatment of the properties of language and a discussion
of the communication systems of bees, birds and primates can be found in
Akmajian *et al.* (1990) or in Chapter 14 of O'Grady *et al.* (1993). The fullest
treatment of the topic is to be found in the work of Hockett (1958; 1960; 1963).
Other accessible reviews of the issues are provided by Demers (1988) and
Dingwall (1988). More specifically, on the distinction between communicative
and informative signals see Chapter 2 of Lyons (1977) which also has, in
Chapter 3, a summary of views on the properties of language. For different perspectives on 'communicating', see Mellor (1990). On animal communication,
see Wilson (1991), and for a much more balanced view of how instinct and
learning integrate, see Gould & Marler (1991). On the vocal signals of vervet
monkeys, see Cheney & Seyfarth (1990) or Seyfarth & Cheney (1992). For the
original studies on bee communication, see von Frisch (1962; 1967). The source
of the term 'double articulation', used sometimes in place of 'duality', is
Martinet (1964). On the significance of 'productivity' and a discussion of what
might be 'innate' about human language, consult Chomsky (1965; 1983; 1988)
or Aitchison (1989), which also has an extended discussion of human versus

animal language. On animal thinking (and deception), try Cheney & Seyfarth (1991), Griffin (1984), and the contributions in Parker & Gibson (1990) or Whiten (1991).

4 Animals and human language

My principal Endeavour was to learn the Language, which my Master and his Children, and every Servant of his House were desirous to teach me. For they looked upon it as a Prodigy, that a brutal Animal should discover such Marks of a rational Creature. I pointed to everything, and enquired the Name of it, which I wrote down in my Journal Book when I was alone, and corrected my bad Accent, by desiring those of the Family to pronounce it often. In this Employment, a Sorrel Nag, one of the under Servants, was ready to assist me.

Jonathan Swift (1726)

In the preceding chapter, we concentrated on the ways in which human language is distinct from the 'languages' of other creatures. If human language is indeed such a unique form of communication, then it would seem inconceivable that other creatures would be able to develop an understanding of this specialized human mode of expression. Some humans, however, do not behave as if this is the case. There is, after all, a lot of spoken language directed by humans to animals, apparently under the impression that the animal follows what is being said. Riders can say *Whoa* to horses and they stop (or so it seems), we can say *Heel* to dogs and they will follow at heel (well, sometimes), and, in circus rings, a variety of animals go *Up*, *Down* and *Roll over* in accordance with spoken commands. Should we use these examples as evidence that non-humans can understand human language? Surely not. As far as animal behavior is concerned, the standard explanation is that the animal produces a particular behavior in response to a particular sound-stimulus, but does not actually 'understand' the meaning of the words uttered.

If it seems difficult to conceive of animals 'understanding' human language, then it appears to be even less likely that an animal would be capable of 'producing' human language. After all, we do not generally observe animals of one species learning to produce the signals of another species. You could keep your horse in a field of cows for years, but it still won't say *Moo*. And, in many households, a new baby and a puppy may arrive at the same time. Baby and puppy grow up in the same environment, hearing mostly the same things, but about two years later, the baby is making human noises and the puppy is not.

But perhaps a puppy is a poor example. Wouldn't it be better to work with a closer relative, such as a chimpanzee? After all, the chimpanzee does have 99% of its basic genetics in common with the human.

Chimpanzees and language

The idea of raising a chimp and a child together may seem like a nightmare, but this is basically what was done in an early attempt to teach a chimpanzee to use human language. In the 1930s, two scientists (Luella and Winthrop Kellogg) reported on their experiences of raising an infant chimpanzee together with their infant son. The chimpanzee, called Gua, was reported to be able to understand about a hundred words, but did not 'say' any of them. In the 1940s, a chimpanzee named Viki was reared by another scientist couple (Catherine and Keith Hayes) in their own home, exactly as if she were a human child. These foster parents spent five years attempting to get Viki to 'say' English words by trying to shape her mouth as she produced sounds. Viki eventually managed to produce some 'words', rather poorly articulated versions of *mama*, *papa* and *cup*. In retrospect, this was a remarkable achievement since it has become clear that non-human primates do not have a physically structured vocal tract which is suitable for producing human speech sounds. Apes and gorillas can, like chimpanzees, communicate with a wide range of vocal calls, but they just cannot speak.

Washoe

Recognizing that a chimpanzee was a poor candidate for spoken-language learning, Beatrix and Allen Gardner set out to teach a female chimpanzee called Washoe to use a version of American Sign Language. This sign language, used by the deaf, has all the properties described earlier as basic features of human language and is learned by many congenitally deaf children as their natural first language. (It is discussed in greater detail in Chapter 18.)

Beginning in June 1966, the Gardners and their research assistants raised Washoe like a human child in a comfortable domestic environment. Sign language was always used when Washoe was around and she was encouraged to use signs, even her own incomplete 'baby-versions' of the signs used by adults. In a period of three and a half years, Washoe came to use signs for more than a hundred words, ranging from *airplane*, *baby* and *banana* through to *window*, *woman* and *you*. Even more impressive was Washoe's ability to take these forms and combine them to produce 'sentences' of the type *gimme tickle*, *more fruit* and *open food drink* (to get the refrigerator opened). Some of the forms used appear to have been inventions by Washoe, as in her novel sign for *bib* and in the combination *water bird* (referring to a swan), which would seem to indicate that her linguistic system had the potential for productivity. Moreover, Washoe demonstrated understanding of a much larger number of signs than she actually produced. She also seemed capable of holding rudimentary conversations, mainly in the form of question–answer sequences. A similar conversational ability with sign language was reported for a gorilla named Koko not long after.

Sarah and Lana

At the same time as Washoe was learning sign language, another chimpanzee named Sarah was being taught (by Ann and David Premack) to use a set of plastic shapes for the purposes of communicating with humans. These plastic shapes represented 'words' which could be arranged (Sarah preferred a vertical order) in sequence to build 'sentences'. The basic approach was quite different from that of the Gardners. Sarah was systematically trained to associate these shapes with objects or actions. She remained an animal in a cage, being trained with food rewards to manipulate a set of symbols. Once she had learned to use a large number of these plastic shapes, Sarah was capable of getting an apple by selecting the correct plastic shape (a blue triangle) from a large array. Notice that this symbol is arbitrary, since it would be hard to argue for any natural connection between an apple and a blue plastic triangle. Sarah was also capable of producing 'sentences' such as *Mary give chocolate Sarah*, and had the impressive capacity to understand complex structures such as *If Sarah put red on green, Mary give Sarah chocolate*. Sarah got the chocolate.

lexigram
↓
word diagram

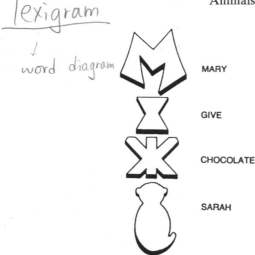

MARY

GIVE

CHOCOLATE

SARAH

A similar training technique with a similar artificial language was used (by Duane Rumbaugh) to train a chimpanzee called Lana. The language she learned was called Yerkish and consisted of a set of symbols on a large keyboard linked to a computer. When Lana wanted some water, she had to press four symbols, in the correct sequence, to produce the message *please machine give water*.

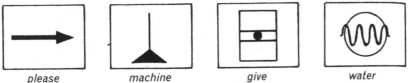

please   *machine*   *give*   *water*

Both Sarah and Lana demonstrated an ability to use what look like logographic codes and basic structures in ways which superficially resemble the use of language. There was, however, a lot of skepticism regarding these apparent linguistic skills. It was pointed out that when Lana used the symbol for 'please', she did not have to understand the meaning of the English word *please*. There was no choice involved, as, for example, in omitting *please*, as we often do, in order to produce a different, but nevertheless meaningful, 'utterance'. The symbol for 'please' on the computer keyboard was the equivalent of a button on a vending machine and, so the argument goes, we can learn to operate vending machines without necessarily knowing language. The strongest arguments against accepting the achievements of Washoe, Sarah and Lana as evidence of linguistic abilities have been put forward by the psychologist Herbert Terrace, who worked with a chimpanzee called Nim.

Nim Chimpsky

The name given to this chimpanzee, Nim Chimpsky, was a deliberate play on the name of the linguist Noam Chomsky, who had claimed that language is an innate ability and unique to the human species. Perhaps Nim would show that Noam was mistaken.

Beginning in 1973, a concentrated effort was made to teach Nim American Sign Language under controlled conditions, with careful records and video-taping of Nim's classroom activities. Over a two-year period, Nim produced a large number of single-word signs, developed two-word combinations such as *more drink* and *give banana*, and used them in appropriate circumstances. The initial impression was that Nim, like Washoe, was developing an ability to use language in much the same way as human children. However, this impression did not survive some close inspection of the videotaped record. The structure of Nim's longer 'utterances' was simply a repetition of simpler structures, not an expansion into more complex structures, as produced by human children. Moreover, in contrast to the human child, Nim only rarely used sign language to initiate interaction with his teachers. In general, he produced signs in response to their signing and tended to repeat signs they used.

This type of finding prompted Terrace to reinvestigate the filmed record of Washoe's use of sign language and led him to argue that both Nim and Washoe only appeared to use signs as language. In fact, he argued, they were simply producing prompted repetitions of their teachers' signs, yet being interpreted as if they were taking part in 'conversations'. His conclusion was that chimpanzees are clever creatures who learn to produce a certain type of behavior (signing) in order to get rewards, and who are essentially per-forming sophisticated 'tricks'. Consequently, their signing is not linguistic behavior at all.

Hans, Buzz and Doris

The arguments presented by Terrace are very similar to those which have been used in the past to discredit claims that any animal was capable of understanding and using any form of linguistic communication. At the turn of the century, a German horse called Clever Hans astounded many by using hoofbeats to answer arithmetical questions and to tap out the letters of the alphabet. However, it was demonstrated that Hans was actually responding to subtle visual cues provided by those asking him questions. If the questioner didn't know the answer to the question, he couldn't uncon-sciously indicate that Hans had tapped the correct number of hoofbeats and consequently Hans got the answers wrong.

In the 1960s, two dolphins called Buzz and Doris were reported to have developed a means of signaling, across an opaque barrier, which enabled one of them to 'tell' the other how they could both get a fish snack. When Doris saw a flashing light, she had to press a paddle on the left-hand side and 'tell' Buzz (who couldn't see the light or Doris) to press his left-hand paddle. When the light was kept steady, Doris had to press the right-hand paddle and 'tell' Buzz to press his right-hand paddle. Over thousands of trials, these dolphins inevitably got the fish. However, it turned out that Doris would continue to 'tell' Buzz when Buzz could see the light himself and even when Buzz was taken out of the tank. The conclusion was that Doris's behavior consisted of conditioned responses to the different light signals and Buzz's behavior was conditioned to responding to Doris's calls.

The controversy

These two phenomena, the unwitting cues provided by human trainers and the conditioned response behavior of animals, are usually cited as the explanation of language-like behavior in animals generally, and of chimpanzees in particular. However, those foster parents of Washoe, the Gardners, have argued that they were not 'animal trainers', nor were they inculcating and then eliciting conditioned responses from Washoe. In a complex experiment, designed to eliminate any possible provision of cues, they showed that, in the absence of any human, Washoe could produce correct signs to identify objects in pictures. They also emphasize what they consider to be a major advantage of their approach over most other work with chimpanzees. They note that Terrace carefully instructed his research assistants to remember that Nim was a research animal and not a child. Most of Nim's training took place in a bare windowless cell and the majority of research assistants involved were not fluent in American Sign Language. The Gardners point out that a deaf human child might not develop into a fully interactive and sociable user of sign language under comparable circumstances.

In sharp contrast, the Gardners have stressed the need for a domestic environment, without cages, in which the chimpanzee has a lot of opportunity for imaginative play and interaction with fluent sign language users who use the language normally with each other. They report that a group of younger chimpanzees (Moja, Pili, Tatu and Dar) not only learned sign language, but used it with each other and with Washoe, even when there were no humans present. In a later development, an infant chimpanzee named Loulis was adopted by Washoe and, without any human training at all, developed a signing vocabulary of more than fifty signs.

Sherman, Austin and Kanzi

The idea of chimpanzees developing language-like skills with other chimpanzees was also crucial in the case of Sherman and Austin. As reported by Sue Savage-Rumbaugh, these two chimpanzees became the first to communicate with each other using a version of the printed symbols of Yerkish (developed initially for Lana). But the most exciting development in this area came about almost by accident.

While Savage-Rumbaugh was attempting to train a bonobo (a kind of chimpanzee) called Matata how to use the symbols of Yerkish, Matata's nursing baby, Kanzi, was always with her. Although Matata did not do very well, her son Kanzi spontaneously started using the symbol system with great ease. He had learned not by being taught, but by being exposed to, and observing, language in use. Kanzi eventually developed a large symbol vocabulary (over 250 forms). By the age of eight, he had become capable, via associations of symbols with spoken words, of understanding spoken English at a level comparable to a two-and-half-year-old human child. He had also become capable of asking to watch his favorite movies, *Quest for Fire* (about primitive humans) and *Greystoke* (about the Tarzan legend).

The barest rudiments

Based on experiment human found

There are important lessons which have been learned from attempts to teach chimpanzees to use some forms of language. We have answered some questions. Were Washoe and Kanzi capable of taking part in interaction by using a symbol system which was chosen by humans and not chimpanzees? The answer is clearly "Yes". Did Washoe and Kanzi perform linguistically on a level comparable to a human child of the same age? The answer is just as clearly "No". In addition, one of the most important lessons for those who study the nature of language is the realization that we clearly do not have a totally objective and non-controversial definition of what counts as 'using language'. We assume that when young human children make 'language-like' noises we are witnessing language development, but when young chimpanzees produce 'language-like' signs in interaction with humans, many scientists are very unwilling to classify this as language use. Yet, the criteria we use in each case do not seem to be the same.

This problem remains, as does the controversy among different psychologists over the reported abilities of chimpanzees to use language. However, given the mass of evidence from the studies described here, we might suggest that the linguist Noam Chomsky should revise his claim that "acquisition of even the barest rudiments of language is quite beyond the capacities of an otherwise intelligent ape". We may not have had reports on the chimpanzee view of linguistic theory, but on their obvious capacity to cope with "the barest rudiments of language" we certainly have.

Study questions

1　Have any chimpanzees ever been taught to produce human speech sounds? What's been the problem?
2　In Sarah's vocabulary, the color 'red' was represented by a grey plastic shape. If Sarah could use this plastic shape to convey the meaning 'red', which property does her language have?
3　What was the basis of Terrace's conclusion that the chimpanzee's use of sign language is not true language?
4　How did the Gardners try to show that Washoe was not necessarily repeating signs made by interacting humans?
5　What was the key element in Kanzi's language learning?

Discussion topics/projects

A　The most persistent criticism of the chimpanzee language-learning projects is that the chimpanzees simply make responses like trained animals for rewards and are consequently not using language to express anything. Read over the following reports (from Rimpau et al., 1989) and try to decide how the different chimpanzees' behaviors should be characterized. (Signs are represented by capital letters.)

Greg was hooting and making other sounds, to prevent Dar from falling asleep. Dar put his fist to Greg's lips and made kissing sounds. Greg asked, WHAT WANT? and Dar replied, QUIET, placing the sign on Greg's lips.

After her nap, Washoe signed OUT. I was hoping for Washoe to potty herself and did not comply. Then Washoe took my hands and put them together to make OUT, and then signed OUT with her own hands, to show me how.

Moja signed DOG on Ron and me, and looked at our faces, waiting for us to "woof". After several rounds, I made a "meeow" instead. Moja signed DOG again, I repeated "meeow" again, and Moja slapped my leg harder. This went on. Finally, I woofed and Moja leapt on me and hugged me.

Moja stares longingly at Dairy Queen as we drive by. Then for a minute or more signs NO ICE CREAM many times, by shaking her head while holding fist to mouth, index edge up.

B   What do you think is meant by "the Clever Hans phenomenon" and how
could it be avoided in studies of linguistic behavior in animals? (A good
resource is the collection of papers in Sebeok & Rosenthal, 1981.) When
people tell stories of how intelligent their pets are, does it typically
sound like yet another version of Clever Hans, or are other explanations
possible?

C   What are the advantages and disadvantages of the different symbol
systems (plastic shapes, keys on a computer console, sign language)
which have been used with chimpanzees? Which system (one of these or
one of your own invention) would you use if you were given the opportunity to try to teach language to a chimpanzee?

D   Here are some examples of (i) the earliest two-word combinations of a
typical child and some examples of (ii) the two-sign combinations from
Washoe. On the basis of this evidence, do you think that the child and
Washoe are doing essentially the same linguistic thing?

(i) red book   (ii) baby mine
     mommy lunch   go flower
     go store   drink red
     hit ball   tickle Washoe
     book table   more fruit

E   Among those who are critical of even the idea of chimpanzees having
the capacity for language, a common argument is based on differences in
evolutionary biology, as exemplified in the following paragraph from
Wallman (1992: 109). What additional arguments can you provide for or
against this point of view?

Is it absurd to consider the linguistic incompetence of apes as something
requiring explanation? After all, no one would think to pose the question of,
say, why *Homo sapiens* cannot fly, or why birds cannot swim. These questions
are not asked because it is assumed that taxa separated by millions of years
of evolution will differ in their adaptations, the extent of the divergence corresponding roughly to the length of that separation, barring parallel or conver-
gent evolution. Given that our lineage diverged from the most closely related
hominoid at the very least four million years ago, which separates us by eight
million years of independent evolution, why is it thought likely by some that an
ape species would possess a human faculty, especially an unused form of it?

Further reading

Some basic background on the topic can be found in Linden (1976) and
Sebeok & Sebeok (1980). More recent overviews are presented in Linden
(1987), Premack (1986) – which are favorable, and Wallman (1992) – which is
highly critical. For more general background, such as the extent to which
humans and chimpanzees have nearly identical genetic make-up, see Deninger
& Schmid (1976) or King & Wilson (1975); on the features of natural primate
communication, see Snowdon *et al.* (1982); and on the vocalizations of apes, see
Goodall (1986). More specifically, life with Gua is described in Kellogg &
Kellogg (1933), life with Viki in Hayes (1951). On the original Washoe project,
see Gardner & Gardner (1969); on later developments, see Gardner &
Gardner (1978) and, more recently, see Gardner *et al.* (1989). On Washoe and
Loulis, see Fouts *et al.* (1989). On Koko, see Patterson & Linden (1981). On
Sarah, see Premack & Premack (1983; 1991), and on Lana, see Rumbaugh
(1977). For Nim's experiences, see Terrace (1979) which is reviewed very
critically by Gardner (1981). On Sherman and Austin, read Savage-Rumbaugh
(1986) and on Kanzi, read Savage-Rumbaugh & Lewin (1994). On Clever
Hans, see Pfungst (1911) and Sebeok & Rosenthal (1981), and on Buzz and
Doris, check Evans & Bastain (1969). The quotation regarding 'the barest
rudiments' is from Chomsky (1972).

5 The sounds of language

I take it you already know
Of tough and bough and cough and dough?
Others may stumble but not you
On hiccough, thorough, lough and through.
Well done! And now you wish, perhaps,
To learn of less familiar traps?

Beware of heard, a dreadful word,
That looks like beard and sounds like bird.
And dead: it's said like bed, not bead –
For goodness sake don't call it 'deed'!
Watch out for meat and great and threat
(They rhyme with suite and straight and debt). **T. S. W. (1970)**

Imagine that a restaurant manager who has always had trouble with the spelling of English words places an advertisement for a new *SEAGH*. You see the advertisement and your confusion leads you to ask how he came to form this unfamiliar word. It's very simple, he says. Take the first sound of the word *SURE*, the middle sound of the word *DEAD*, and the final sound of the word *LAUGH*. You will, of course, recognize that this form conveys the pronunciation usually associated with the word *chef*.

This tale, however unlikely, may serve as a reminder that the sounds of spoken English do not match up, a lot of the time, with letters of written English. If we cannot use the letters of the alphabet in a consistent way to represent the sounds we make, how do we go about describing the sounds of a language like English? One solution is to produce a separate alphabet with symbols which represent sounds. Such a set of symbols does exist and is called the 'phonetic alphabet'. We will consider how these symbols are used to represent both the consonant and vowel sounds of English words and what physical aspects of the human vocal tract are involved in the production of those sounds.

Phonetics

The general study of the characteristics of speech sounds is called **phonetics**. Our primary interest will be in **articulatory phonetics**, which is the study of how speech sounds are made, or 'articulated'. Other areas of study within phonetics are **acoustic phonetics**, which deals with the physical properties of speech as sound waves 'in the air', and **auditory** (or perceptual) **phonetics**, which deals with the perception, via the ear, of speech sounds. One other area, called **forensic phonetics**, has applications in legal cases involving speaker identification and the analysis of recorded utterances.

Articulation: voiced and voiceless

In articulatory phonetics, we investigate how speech sounds are produced using the fairly complex oral equipment we have. We start with the air pushed out by the lungs up through the trachea (the 'windpipe') to the larynx. Inside the larynx are your vocal cords which take two basic positions.

(1) When the vocal cords are spread apart, the air from the lungs passes between them unimpeded. Sounds produced in this way are described as **voiceless**.

(2) When the vocal cords are drawn together, the air from the lungs repeatedly pushes them apart as it passes through, creating a vibration effect. Sounds produced in this way are described as **voiced**.

The distinction can be felt physically if you place a fingertip gently on the top of your 'Adam's apple' (i.e. part of your larynx) and produce sounds like Z-Z-Z-Z or V-V-V-V. Because these are voiced sounds, you should be able to feel some vibration. Keeping your fingertip in the same position, make the sounds S-S-S-S or F-F-F-F. Because these are voiceless sounds, there should be no vibration. Another trick is to put a finger in each ear, not too far, and produce the voiced sounds (e.g. Z-Z-Z-Z) to hear some vibration, whereas no vibration will be heard if the voiceless sounds (e.g. S-S-S-S) are produced in the same manner.

Place of articulation

Once the air has passed through the larynx, it comes up and out through the mouth and/or the nose. Most consonant sounds are produced by using the tongue and other parts of the mouth to constrict, in some way, the shape of the oral cavity through which the air is passing. The terms used to describe many sounds are those which denote the place of articulation of the sound: that is, the location, inside the mouth, at which the constriction takes place.

What we need is a slice of head. If you crack a head right down the middle, you will be able to see which parts of the oral cavity are crucially involved in speech production. To describe the place of articulation of most consonant sounds, we can start at the front of the mouth and work back. We can also keep the voiced–voiceless distinction in mind and begin using the symbols of the phonetic alphabet to denote specific sounds. These symbols will be enclosed within square brackets [ ].

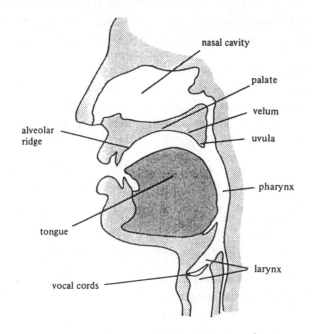

Bilabials. These are sounds formed using both (= bi) upper and lower lips (= labia). The initial sounds in the words *pat*, *bat* and *mat* are all bilabials. They are represented by the symbols [p], which is voiceless, and [b] and [m], which are voiced. The [w] sound found at the beginning of *way*, *walk* and *world* is also a bilabial.

Labiodentals. These are sounds formed with the upper teeth and the lower lip. The initial sounds of the words *fat* and *vat* and the final sounds in the words *safe* and *save* are labiodentals. They are represented by the symbols

[f], which is voiceless, and [v], which is voiced. Notice that the final sounds of *laugh* and *cough*, and the initial sound of *photo*, despite the spelling differences, are all pronounced as [f].

Dentals. These sounds are formed with the tongue tip behind the upper front teeth. The term **interdental** is sometimes used to describe a manner of pronunciation with the tongue tip between (=inter) the upper and lower teeth. The initial sound of *thin* and the final sound of *bath* are both voiceless dentals. The symbol used for this sound is [θ], usually referred to as 'theta'. It's the symbol you would use for the first and last sounds in the phrase *three teeth*.

The voiced dental is represented by the symbol [ð], usually called 'eth'. This sound is found in the pronunciation of the initial sound of common words like *the*, *there*, *then* and *thus*. It's also the middle sound in *feather* and the final sound of *bathe*.

Alveolars. These are sounds formed with the front part of the tongue on the alveolar ridge, which is the rough, bony ridge immediately behind the upper teeth. The initial sounds in *top*, *dip*, *sit*, *zoo* and *nut* are all alveolars. The symbols for these sounds are quite easily remembered - [t], [d], [s], [z], [n]. Of these, [t] and [s] are voiceless, whereas [d], [z] and [n] are voiced.

It may be clear that the final sounds of the words *bus* and *buzz* have to be [s] and [z] respectively, but what about the final sound of the word *raise*? The spelling is misleading because the final sound in this word is voiced, and so must be represented by [z]. Notice also that despite the different spelling of *knot* and *not*, both of these words are pronounced with [n] as the initial sound.

Other alveolars are the [l] sound found at the beginning of words such as *lap* and *lit*, and the [r] sound at the beginning of *right*, *write* and *rip*.

Alveo-palatals. If you feel back behind the alveolar ridge, you should find a hard part in the roof of your mouth. This is called the palate. Sounds which are produced with the tongue at the very front of the palate, near the alveolar ridge, are called alveo-palatals. Examples are the initial sounds in the words *shout* and *child*, which are voiceless.

Although there are two letters in the spelling of 'sh' and 'ch', the sounds are represented by the single phonetic symbols [š] and [č] respectively. The small mark above the symbols is called 'wedge'. So, the word *shoe-brush* begins and ends with the voiceless alveo-palatal sound [š] and the word *church* begins and ends with the voiceless alveo-palatal sound [č].

One of the voiced alveo-palatal sounds, represented by the symbol [ž], is not very common in English, but can be found as the middle consonant sound in words like *treasure* and *pleasure*, or the final sound in *rouge*. The other voiced alveo-palatal sound is represented as [ǰ] and is the initial sound in words like *joke* and *gem*. The word *judge* and the name *George* both begin and end with the sound [ǰ], despite the obvious differences in spelling.

One sound which is produced with the tongue in the middle of the palate is the [y] sound to be found at the beginning of words like *you* and *yet*. This sound is usually described as a **palatal**.

Velars. Even further back in the roof of the mouth, beyond the hard palate, you will find a soft area which is called the soft palate, or the velum. Sounds produced with the back of the tongue against the velum are called velars. There is a voiceless velar sound, represented by the symbol [k], which occurs not only in *kid* and *kill*, but is also the initial sound in *car* and *cold*. Despite the variety in spelling, this [k] sound is both the initial and final sound in the words *cook*, *kick* and *coke*. The voiced velar sound to be heard at the beginning of words like *go*, *gun* and *give* is represented by [g]. This is also the final sound in words like *bag*, *mug* and, despite the spelling, *plague*.

The velum can be lowered to allow air to flow through the nasal cavity and thereby produce another voiced velar which is represented by the symbol [ŋ], typically referred to as 'angma'. In written English, this sound is normally spelled as the two letters 'ng'. So, the [ŋ] sound is at the end of *sing*, *sang* and, despite the spelling, *tongue*. It would occur twice in the form *ringing*. Be careful not to be misled by the spelling – the word *bang* ends with the [ŋ] sound only. There is no [g] sound in this word.

Glottals. There is one other sound that is produced without the active use of the tongue and other parts of the mouth. It is the sound [h] which occurs at the beginning of *have* and *house*, and, for most speakers, as the first sound in *who* and *whose*. This sound is usually described as a voiceless glottal. The 'glottis' is the space between the vocal cords in the larynx. When the glottis is open, as in the production of other voiceless sounds, but there is no manipulation of the air passing out through the mouth, the sound produced is that represented by [h].

Charting consonant sounds

Having described in some detail the place of articulation of English consonant sounds, we can summarize the basic information in the following chart. Along the top of the chart are the different labels for places of articulation and, under each, the labels −V (= voiceless) and +V (= voiced). Also included in this chart, on the left-hand side, is a set of terms used to describe 'manner of articulation' which we will discuss in a later section.

	Bilabial −V +V	Labio-dental −V +V	Dental −V +V	Alveolar −V +V	Alveo-palatal −V +V	Velar −V +V	Glottal −V +V
Stops	p b			t d		k g	
Fricatives		f v	θ ð	s z	š ž		
Affricates					č ǰ		
Nasals	m			n		ŋ	
Approximants	w			l,r	y		h

Notes on the chart. This chart is far from complete. It does contain the majority of consonant sounds used in the basic description of English pronunciation. There are, however, several differences between this basic set of symbols and the much more comprehensive chart produced by the International Phonetic Association (IPA). The most obvious difference is in the range of sounds covered.

The IPA aims to describe the sounds of all languages and includes, for example, symbols for the velar fricative sound you may have heard in the German pronunciation of the "ch" part of *Bach* or *Achtung*. It also includes sounds made with the back of the tongue and the uvula (below the velum) which represents the "r" parts of the French pronunciation of *rouge* and *lettre*. Uvular sounds also occur in many American Indian languages. Other, non-English sounds such as pharyngeals (produced in the pharynx) occur in Semitic languages such as Arabic. There are many more.

Another shortcoming of the chart above is the single entry covering *r* sounds in English. There can be a lot of variation among speakers in the pronunciation of the initial sound in *raw* and *red*, the medial sound in *very*, and the final sound in *hour* and *air*. Different symbols (e.g. [ɹ], [R]) may be encountered in transcriptions where the different *r* sounds are distinguished.

Finally, the IPA uses different symbols for a few of the sounds represented here. These alternatives are [ʃ] = [š]; [ʒ] = [ž]; [tʃ] = [č]; [dʒ] = [ǰ] and [j] = [y]. For a fuller discussion of the use of IPA symbols, see Ladefoged (1992).

Manner of articulation

So far, we have concentrated on describing consonant sounds in terms of where they are articulated. We can, of course, describe the same sounds in terms of how they are articulated. Such a description is necessary if we wish to be able to differentiate between some sounds which, in the preceding discussion, we have placed in the same category. For example, we can say that [t] and [s] are both voiceless alveolar sounds. How do they differ? They differ in their manner of articulation, that is, in the way they are pronounced. The [t] sound is one of a set of sounds called 'stops' and the [s] sound is one of a set called 'fricatives'.

Stops. Of the sounds we have already mentioned, the set [p], [b], [t], [d], [k], [g] are all produced by some form of complete 'stopping' of the airstream (very briefly) and then letting it go abruptly. This type of consonant sound resulting from a blocking or stopping effect on the airstream is called a stop (or a 'plosive'). A full description of the [t] sound at the beginning of a word like *ten* is as a 'voiceless alveolar stop'. On occasion, only the manner of articulation is mentioned, as when it is said that the word *bed*, for example, begins and ends with 'voiced stops'.

Fricatives. The manner of articulation used in producing the set of sounds [f], [v], [θ], [ð], [s], [z], [š], [ž] involves almost blocking the airstream, and having the air push through the narrow opening. As the air is pushed through, a type of friction is produced and the resulting sounds are called fricatives. If you put your open hand in front of your mouth when making these sounds, [f] and [s] in particular, you should be able to feel the stream of air being pushed out. A word like *fish* will begin and end with 'voiceless fricatives'. The word *those* will begin and end with the 'voiced fricatives' [ð] and [z].

Affricates. If you combine a brief stopping of the airstream with an obstructed release which causes some friction, you will be able to produce the sounds [č] and [ǰ] These are called affricates and occur at the beginning of the words *cheap* and *jeep*. In the first of these, there is a 'voiceless affricate', and in the second a 'voiced affricate'.

Nasals. Most sounds are produced orally, with the velum raised, preventing airflow from entering the nasal cavity. However, when the velum is lowered and the airstream is allowed to flow out through the nose to produce [m], [n] and [ŋ], the sounds are described as nasals. These three sounds are all voiced. Words like *morning*, *knitting* and *name* begin and end with nasals.

Approximants. In the set of sounds called approximants, the articulation of each is strongly influenced by the following vowel sound. Indeed, the sounds

[w] and [y] are sometimes called 'semi-vowels' or 'glides', because they are typically produced with the tongue moving, or 'gliding', to or from the position of a nearby vowel. Both [w] and [y] are voiced, occurring at the beginning of *we*, *wet*, *you* and *yes*.

Also voiced are the two initial approximants in *led* and *red*. The [l] sound is formed by letting the airstream flow around the sides of the tongue as it makes contact with the alveolar ridge. The type of sound for which we are using the [r] symbol is formed with the tongue tip raised and curled back behind the alveolar ridge. The [l] and [r] sounds are also sometimes called 'liquids'.

The sound [h] is a voiceless approximant which, in common words like *Hi* or *hello*, simply begins the pronunciation of the following vowel as if it was voiceless.

The glottal stop and the flap. Two common terms used to describe ways of pronouncing consonants are not included in the chart presented earlier.

The **glottal stop**, represented by the symbol [ʔ], occurs when the space between the vocal cords (the glottis) is closed completely, very briefly, and then released. Try saying the expression *Oh oh!*. Between the first *Oh* and the second *oh*, people typically produce a glottal stop. Some people do it in the middle of *Uh-uh* (meaning 'no'), and others put one in place of 't' in pronouncing *Batman*. You can also produce a glottal stop if you try to say the words *butter* or *bottle* without pronouncing the *-tt-* part in the middle. This sound is considered to be characteristic of Cockney (London) speech, but it is also used by Scottish speakers and New Yorkers.

If, however, you are an American English speaker who pronounces the word *butter* in a way that is close to 'budder', then you are making a **flap**. It is represented by [D] or sometimes [ɾ]. This flap is produced by the tongue tip being thrown against the alveolar ridge for an instant. Many Americans tend to flap the [t] and [d] consonants between vowels so that, in casual speech, the pairs *latter* and *ladder*, *writer* and *rider*, *metal* and *medal* do not have distinct middle consonants. They all have flaps. The student who was told about the importance of 'Plato' in class and reported it as 'play-dough' was clearly a victim of a misinterpreted flap.

This rather lengthy list of the phonetic features of English consonant sounds is not presented as a challenge to your ability to memorize a lot of terminology and symbols. It is presented as an illustration of how a thorough description of the physical aspects of speech production will allow us to characterize the sounds of spoken English, independently of the vagaries of spelling found in written English. There are, however, some sounds which we have not yet investigated. These are the types of sounds known as vowels and diphthongs.

Vowels

While the consonant sounds are mostly articulated via closure or obstruction in the vocal tract, vowel sounds are produced with a relatively free flow of air. They are all typically voiced. To describe vowel sounds, we consider the way in which the tongue influences the 'shape' through which the airflow must pass. To talk about place of articulation, we think of the space inside the mouth as having a front versus a back and a high versus a low area. Thus, in the pronunciation of *heat* and *hit*, we talk about 'high, front' vowels, because the sound is made with the front part of the tongue in a raised position.

In contrast, the vowel sounds in *hot* and *hat* are produced with the tongue in a relatively lower position and are described as 'low, back' vowels. The next time you're facing the bathroom mirror, try saying *heat, hit, hot, hat*. For the first two, your mouth will stay fairly closed, but for the last two, your tongue will move lower and cause your mouth to open wider. (You may also notice that the sounds of relaxation and pleasure, if you're getting any, typically contain back vowels.)

The terminology for describing vowels is usually presented in the form of a chart, as shown below, which provides a means of classifying the most common vowel sounds of English.

	Front	Central	Back
	i		
High			u
	I		ʊ
	e	ə	o
Mid	ɛ		ɔ
		ʌ	
Low	æ		a

The easiest way to become familiar with the distinctions within the set of vowel sounds is to have some examples of familiar words which for a lot of American English speakers, most of the time, contain those sounds. The following list goes from the high front vowels through to the low back vowel and ends with three diphthongs:

[i]	*see, eat, key*	[ʊ]	*put, could, foot*
[I]	*hit, myth*	[o]	*no, know, though*
[e]	*tail, great, weight*	[ɔ]	*raw, fall, caught*
[ɛ]	*pet, said, dead*	[a]	*cot, father, body*
[æ]	*sat, ban*	[ay]	*my, buy, eye*
[ə]	*above, sofa*	[aw]	*cow, loud*
[ʌ]	*putt, blood, tough*	[ɔy]	*boy, void*
[u]	*move, two, glue*		

Diphthongs. The last three symbols in the list above contain two sounds. These 'combined' vowel sounds are called diphthongs. Note that in each case they begin with a vowel sound and end with a glide. With the majority of single vowel sounds, the vocal organs remain relatively steady, but in pronouncing diphthongs, we move from one vocalic position to another.

This process of **diphthongization** can actually happen with a wide range of vowel sounds and is more common in some varieties of English (e.g. Southern British) than in others. Most Americans pronounce the word *say* as [sey], with a diphthong rather than a single vowel. You will also hear the pronouns *they* as [ðey], *you* as [yuw] and *we* as [wiy], all diphthongized. If you try to pronounce the consonants and diphthongs in the following transcription, you should recognize a traditional speech training exercise: [haw naw brawn kaw].

Notes on the vowel chart. Vowel sounds are notorious for varying between one variety of English and the next, often being a key element in what we recognize as different accents. So, you may find that some of the words offered here as examples are not normally encountered with the vowel sounds as listed. Also, some of the sounds shown here may not be commonly used in your dialect. It may be, for example, that you make no distinction between the vowels in the words *caught* and *cot*. Some transcriptions only use [a] for this back vowel sound.

Or, you may not make a significant distinction between the central vowels [ə] and [ʌ]. If not, then just use the symbol [ə], called 'schwa'. In fact, in casual speech, we all use schwa more than any other single sound. It is the unstressed vowel in the everyday use of words like *afford*, *collapse*, *oven*, *photograph*, *wanted*, and in the common words *a* and *the*.

There are many other variations in the actual physical articulation of the sounds we have considered here. The more we focus on the subtle differences of the actual articulation of each sound, the more likely we are to find ourselves describing the pronunciation of small groups or even individual speakers. Such subtle differences allow us to identify individual voices. But those differences don't help us understand how we know what total strangers with unfamiliar voices are saying. To make sense of that, we need to look at the more general sound patterns of a language, also known as 'phonology'.

Study questions

1 Try pronouncing the initial sounds of the following words and then determine the place of articulation (e.g. bilabial, alveolar, etc.) of each:

(a) hand _____   (b) foot _____   (c) toe _____
(d) belly _____   (e) chin _____   (f) thigh _____
(g) calf _____   (h) knee _____

2 Which of the following words end with voiceless (–V) sounds and which end with voiced (+V) sounds?

(a) crash _____   (b) bang _____   (c) smack _____
(d) thud _____   (e) wham _____   (f) splat _____

3 Identify the manner of articulation (e.g. stop, fricative, etc.) of the initial sounds in the following words:

(a) silly _____   (b) crazy _____   (c) jolly _____
(d) merry _____   (e) dizzy _____   (f) happy _____
(g) loony _____   (h) funny _____

4 Which written English words are usually pronounced as transcribed here?

(a) klŋ _____   (b) fes _____   (c) šip _____
(d) ðə _____   (e) hu _____   (f) bæk _____
(g) bɔt _____   (h) haw _____

5 Produce a phonetic transcription of the most common pronunciation you hear of the following words:

(a) she _____   (b) tape _____   (c) dope _____
(d) walk _____   (e) sigh _____   (f) fell _____
(g) these _____   (h) thought _____

Discussion topics/projects

A (ii) Below is a set of English words with different written forms representing the same sounds in a number of ways. Can you identify the alternative spellings of the sounds [i], [f] and [e]?

elephant, rare, marines, pear, hay, feet, quay, air, suite, weigh, giraffe, pier, tough, keys, meat, Sikh.

(ii) How many different ways of spelling the sounds [s], [k], [š] and [ɛ] can you discover in English words?

B (i) Using the first two examples as a guide, can you provide a description, in terms of manner of articulation and voicing (if necessary), of your pronunciation of the initial consonants of the following English words?

(a) mist (NASAL)	(g) thin
(b) bat (VOICED STOP)	(h) near
(c) far	(i) tall
(d) wall	(j) joke
(e) rope	(k) shop
(f) zoo	(l) gun

(ii) What criteria did you use to decide if the voicing aspect was 'necessary' or not?

C Two other distinctions used in describing the articulation of vowels are called 'rounded versus unrounded' and 'tense versus lax'.
(i) The description 'rounded' applies to the shape of the lips. With the help of a mirror or a co-operative friend, try to decide which English vowels are normally rounded and which are not. Is there any other term that you would use to describe a common recognizable shape of the lips for some vowels?

(ii) The term 'tense' means that the vowels are produced with extra muscular effort whereas 'lax' vowels do not require this effort. Can you identify which of the English vowels are easily identifiable as 'tense' or 'lax'? Are there any contexts (e.g. presence or absence of other sounds) that make this identification easier?
(You can consult any of the Phonetics texts in the Further reading section for help with this one.)

D Consider the following set of transcribed 'words'. Can you divide the set into those forms which are English words, those which could not possibly be English words, and those which are not English words at this time, but might possibly become English words? How do you make the decision regarding what goes in the second or third group?

(1)	flem	(5)	ksln	(9)	črls
(2)	ərlnz	(6)	šlop	(10)	blʌnk
(3)	ɵiətər	(7)	kwlk	(11)	fɛrt əm
(4)	sɔng	(8)	zun	(12)	bɔyllŋ

E   English has a number of expressions such as chit-chat and flip-flop which never seem to occur in the reverse order (i.e. chat-chit, flop-flip). Perhaps you can add examples to the following list?

criss-cross	hip-hop	riff-raff
dilly-dally	knick-knacks	see-saw
ding-dong	mish-mash	sing-song
fiddle-faddle	ping-pong	tick-tock
flim-flam	pitter-patter	zig-zag

(i)   Can you think of a phonetic description of the regular pattern in these expressions?

(ii)   What kind of phonetic description might account for these other common pairings?

fuddy-duddy	hocus-pocus	namby-pamby
fuzzy-wuzzy	hurly-burly	razzle-dazzle
hanky-panky	lovey-dovey	roly-poly
helter-skelter	mumbo-jumbo	super-duper

Further reading

Introductory chapters on phonetics can be found in all linguistics textbooks, such as Chapter 3 of Akmajian *et al.* (1990), Chapter 2 of Finegan & Besnier (1989), Chapter 5 of Fromkin & Rodman (1993), or Chapter 2 of O'Grady *et al.* (1993). The standard textbook is Ladefoged (1992). Other texts are Calvert (1992), Catford (1988), Clark & Yallop (1995), Edwards (1992), MacKay (1987) and Roach (1991). More specialized discussion of the issues can be found in Abercrombie (1967), Fromkin (1985), Hardcastle & Laver (1995), Ladefoged & Maddieson (1995), Laver (1994), Levelt (1989) and Ramsaran (1990). Pullum & Ladusaw (1986) is a useful guide to phonetic symbols and Crystal (1991) is a dictionary. Section 17 of Crystal (1995) provides information on regional variants of pronunciation. Texts with a greater emphasis on describing pronunciation are Gimson (1994) and Kreidler (1989), and on teaching pronunciation (mainly to learners of English), see Avery & Ehrlich (1992), Celce-Murcia *et al.* (1996), Prator & Robinett (1985) or Dalton & Seidlhofer (1994). On auditory and acoustic phonetics, see Denes & Pinson (1993), Fry (1979) or Lieberman & Blumstein (1988). On forensic phonetics, try Baldwin & French (1990) or Hollien (1990). The closely related area of speech science is described in Borden *et al.* (1994).

6 The sound patterns of language

Ever on the search for legal jokes not necessarily connected with the death penalty, I consulted a friend who is still practising. She said a member of her chambers was in court one Monday morning when the judge said, "I'm afraid we'll have to adjourn this case, I have written my judgment out, but I left it in my cottage in Devon and I can't get it sent here until tomorrow." "Fax it up, my Lord," the helpful barrister suggested, to which his Lordship replied, "Yes, it does rather." **Quoted in Crystal (1995)**

In the preceding chapter, we investigated the physical production of speech sounds in terms of the articulatory mechanisms of the human vocal tract. That investigation was possible because of some rather amazing facts about the nature of language. When we considered the human vocal tract, we did not have to specify whether we were talking about a fairly large male, over six feet tall, weighing over 200 pounds, or about a rather small female, about five feet tall, weighing 100 pounds. Yet those two physically different individuals would inevitably have physically different vocal tracts, in terms of size and shape. In a sense, every individual has a physically different vocal tract. Consequently, in purely physical terms, every individual will pronounce sounds differently. There are, then, potentially thousands of physically different ways of saying the simple word *me*.

In addition, each individual will not pronounce the word *me* in a physically identical manner on every occasion. Obvious differences occur when the individual is shouting, is asking for a sixth martini, or is suffering from a cold. Given this vast range of potential differences in the actual physical production of a speech sound, how do we manage consistently to recognize all those versions of *me* as the form [mi], and not [ni], or [si], or [ma], or [mo], or something else entirely? The answer to that question is provided to a large extent by the study of phonology.

Phonology

Phonology is essentially the description of the systems and patterns of speech sounds in a language. It is, in effect, based on a theory of what every speaker of a language unconsciously knows about the sound patterns of that language. Because of this theoretical status, phonology is concerned with the abstract or mental aspect of the sounds in language rather than with the actual physical articulation of speech sounds. Phonology is about the underlying design, the blueprint of the sound type, that serves as the constant basis of all the variations in different physical articulations of that sound type in different contexts.

Thus, when we think of the [t] sound in the words *tar*, *star*, *writer* and *eighth* as being 'the same', we actually mean that, in the phonology of English, they would be represented in the same way. In actual speech, these [t] sounds are all very different.

However, all those articulation differences in [t] sounds are less important than the distinction between the [t] sounds in general and the [k] sounds, or the [f] sounds, or the [b] sounds, because there are meaningful consequences related to the use of one rather than the others. These sounds must be distinct meaningful sounds, regardless of which individual vocal tract is being used to pronounce them, because they are what make the words *tar*, *car*, *far* and *bar* meaningfully distinct. Considered from this point of view, we can see that phonology is concerned with the abstract set of sounds in a language which allows us to distinguish meaning in the actual physical sounds we say and hear.

Phonemes

Each one of these meaning-distinguishing sounds in a language is described as a **phoneme**. When we considered the basis of alphabetic writing in Chapter 2, we were actually working with the concept of the phoneme as the single sound type which came to be represented by a single symbol. It is in this sense that the phoneme /t/ is described as a sound type, of which all the different spoken versions of [t] are tokens. Note that slash marks are conventionally used to indicate a phoneme, /t/, an abstract segment, as opposed to the square brackets, as in [t], used for each phonetic, or physically produced, segment.

An essential property of a phoneme is that it functions contrastively. We know that there are two phonemes /f/ and /v/ in English because they are the only basis of the contrast in meaning between the forms *fat* and *vat*, or *fine* and *vine*. This contrastive property is the basic operational test for determining the phonemes which exist in a language. If we substitute one sound for another in a word and there is a change of meaning, then the two sounds represent different phonemes. The consonant and vowel charts presented in Chapter 5 can now be seen as essentially a mapping out of the phonemes of English.

The terms which were used in creating that chart can be considered 'features' which distinguish each phoneme from the next. If the feature is present, we mark it with a plus (+) sign; if it's not present, we use a minus (–) sign. Thus, /p/ can be characterized as [–voice, +bilabial, +stop] and /k/ as [–voice, +velar, +stop]. Because these two sounds share some features, they are sometimes described as members of a natural class of sounds. The prediction would be that sounds which have features in common would behave phonologically in some similar ways. A sound which does not share those features would be expected to behave differently.

For example, /v/ has the features [+voice, +labiodental, +fricative] and so cannot be in the same 'natural class' as /p/ and /k/. Although other factors will be involved, this feature-analysis could lead us to suspect that there may be a good phonological reason why words beginning with /pl-/ and /kl-/ are common in English, but words beginning /vl-/ are not. Could it be that there are some definite sets of features required in a sound in order for it to occur word-initially before /l/? If so, then we will be on our way to producing a phonological account of permissible sound sequences in the language.

Phones and allophones

While the phoneme is the abstract unit or sound-type ('in the mind'), there are many different versions of that sound-type regularly produced in actual speech ('in the mouth'). We can describe those different versions as **phones**. Phones are phonetic units and will appear in square brackets. When we have a set of phones, all of which are versions of one phoneme, we refer to them as the **allophones** of that phoneme.

For example, the [t] sound in the word *tar* is normally pronounced with a stronger puff of air than is present in the [t] sound of the word *star*. If you put the back of your hand in front of your mouth as you say *tar*, then *star*, you should have some physical evidence of the **aspiration** (the puff of air) accompanying the [t] sound in the initial position of *tar* (but not in *star*). This aspirated version is represented more precisely as [tʰ]. That's one phone. In the last chapter, we noted that the [t] sound between vowels in a word like *writer* often becomes a 'flap', which we represented as [D]. That's another phone. In the pronunciation of a word like *eighth*, the influence of the final dental [θ] sound causes a dental articulation of the [t] sound. This would be represented more precisely as [t̪]. That's yet another phone. There are other variations of this sound which, like [tʰ], [D] and [t̪], can be represented differently in a detailed, or narrow, phonetic transcription. Because these variations form a set of phones, they would typically be referred to as allophones of the phoneme /t/.

The crucial distinction between phonemes and allophones is that substituting one phoneme for another will result in a word with a different meaning (as well as a different pronunciation), but substituting allophones only results in a different (and perhaps odd) pronunciation of the same word.

Let's take another brief example. In English, there is a difference in pronunciation of the /i/ sound in words like *seed* and *seen*. In the second word, the effect of the nasal consonant [n] makes the [i] sound nasalized. This nasalization can be represented by a diacritic [~], called 'tilde', over the symbol [ĩ] in narrow phonetic transcription. So, there are at least two phones, [i] and [ĩ], used in English to realize a single phoneme. They are allophones of /i/ in English.

It is possible, of course, for two languages to have the same pair of phonetic segments, but to treat them differently. In English, the effect of nasalization on a vowel is treated as allophonic variation because the nasalized version is not meaningfully contrastive. In French, however, the pronunciation [mɛ] is used for one word *mets*, meaning 'dish', and [mɛ̃] for a different word *main*, meaning 'hand'. Also, [so] for *seau*, meaning 'pail', contrasts with [sõ] for *son*, meaning 'sound'. Clearly, in these cases, the distinction is phonemic.

Minimal pairs and sets

Phonemic distinctions in a language can be tested via pairs and sets of words. When two words such as *pat* and *bat* are identical in form except for a contrast in one phoneme, occurring in the same position, the two words are described as a **minimal pair**. More accurately, they would be classified as a minimal pair in the phonology of English. (Arabic does not have this contrast between the two sounds.) Other examples of English minimal pairs are *fan – van, bet – bat, site – side*. Such pairs have been used frequently in tests of English as a second language to determine non-native speakers' ability to understand the contrast in meaning resulting from the minimal sound contrast.

When a group of words can be differentiated, each one from the others, by changing one phoneme (always in the same position), then we have a **minimal set**. Thus, a minimal set based on the vowel phonemes of English would include *feat, fit, fat, fate, fought, foot,* and one based on consonants could have *big, pig, rig, fig, dig, wig*.

Phonotactics

This type of exercise involving minimal sets also allows us to see that there are indeed definite patterns to the types of sound combinations permitted in a language. In English, the minimal set we have just listed does not include forms such as *lig* or *vig*. As far as I know, these are not English words, but they can be viewed as possible English words. That is, your phonological knowledge of the pattern of sounds in English words would allow you to treat these forms as acceptable if, at some future time, they came into use. They represent 'accidental' gaps in the vocabulary of English.

It is, however, no accident that forms such as [fsIg] or [rnIg] do not exist or are unlikely ever to exist. They have been formed without obeying some constraints on the sequence or position of English phonemes. Such constraints are called the **phonotactics** of a language and are obviously part of every speaker's phonological knowledge. Because these constraints operate on units larger than the single segment, or phoneme, we have to consider the basic structure of that larger phonological unit called the syllable.

Syllables and clusters

A **syllable** must contain a vowel (or vowel-like) sound. The most common type of syllable in language also has a consonant before the vowel, often represented as CV. Technically, the basic elements of the syllable are the **onset** (one or more consonants) and the **rime**. The rime (also written as 'rhyme') consists of the vowel, which is treated as the **nucleus**, plus any following consonant(s), treated as the **coda**.

Thus, syllables like *me, to* or *no* have an onset and a nucleus, but no coda. They are known as 'open' syllables. When a coda is present, as in the syllables *up, cup, at* or *hat*, they are called 'closed' syllables. The basic structure of the kind of syllable found in English words like *green* (CCVC), *eggs* (VCC), *and* (VCC), *ham* (CVC), *I* (V), *do* (CV), *not* (CVC), *like* (CVC), *them* (CVC), *Sam* (CVC), *I* (V), *am* (VC), is shown in the accompanying diagram.

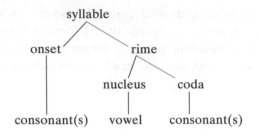

Both the onset and the coda can consist of more than one consonant, also known as a **consonant cluster**. The combination *st* is a consonant cluster (CC) as onset in the word *stop*, and as coda in the word *post*. There are many CC onset combinations permitted in English phonotactics, as in b̲l̲ack, b̲r̲ead, t̲r̲ick, t̲w̲in, f̲l̲at and t̲h̲r̲ow, with approximants (/w/, /r/, /l/) frequently appearing in second position. (Note that *throw* begins with only two consonants, /θ r/, once again showing that spelling is not a good guide in phonology.)

English actually can have larger onset clusters, as in *stress* and *splat*, consisting of three consonants (CCC). The phonotactics of these larger onset consonant clusters in English is not difficult to describe. The first consonant must always be /s/, followed by one of the voiceless stops (/p/, /t/, /k/) and then one of the approximants (/r/, /l/, /w/). You can check if this description is adequate for the combinations in *splash*, *spring*, *strong*, *scream* and *square*. Does the description also cover the second syllable in the pronunciation of *exclaim*? How about /ɛk-skleym/? Remember that it is the onset of the syllable that is being described, not the beginning of the word.

It is quite unusual for languages to have consonant clusters of this type. Indeed, the syllable structure of many languages (e.g. Hawaiian or Japanese) is predominantly CV. It is also noticeable in English that large consonant clusters are frequently reduced in casual conversational speech, particularly if they occur in the middle of a word. This is just one example of what is often discussed in terms of 'co-articulation effects'.

Co-articulation effects

In much of the preceding discussion, we have been describing the speech sounds as if they are always pronounced carefully and deliberately, almost in slow motion. Speech isn't like that very often. Mostly our talk is fast and spontaneous, and it requires our articulators to move from one sound to the next without stopping. The process of making one sound almost at the same time as the next is called **co-articulation**. There are two well-known co-articulation effects, called 'assimilation' and 'elision'.

Assimilation

When two phonemes occur in sequence and some aspect of one phoneme is taken or 'copied' by the other, the process is known as **assimilation**. In terms of the physical production of speech, one might assume that this regular process is occasioned by ease of articulation in everyday talk. In isolation, you would probably pronounce /I/ and /æ/ without any nasal quality at all. However, in saying words like *pin* and *pan*, the anticipation of forming the final nasal consonant will make it 'easier' to go into the nasalized articulation in advance and consequently the vowel sounds in these words will be, in precise transcription, [Ĩ] and [æ̃]. This is a very regular feature of English speakers' pronunciation. So regular, in fact, that a phonological rule can be stated in the following way: 'Any vowel becomes nasal whenever it immediately precedes a nasal.'

This type of assimilation process occurs in a variety of different contexts. It is particularly noticeable in ordinary conversational speech. By itself, you may pronounce the word *can* as [kæn], but, if you tell someone *I can go*, the influence of the following velar [g] will almost certainly make the preceding nasal sound come out as [ŋ] (a velar) rather than [n] (an alveolar). The most commonly observed 'conversational' version of the phrase is [aykəŋgo]. Notice that the vowel in *can* has also changed to schwa [ə] from the isolated-word version [æ]. In many words spoken carefully, the vowel receives stress, but in the course of ordinary talk, that vowel may no longer receive any stress and reduce to schwa. For example, you may pronounce *and* as [ænd] in isolation, but in the casual use of the phrase *you and me*, you almost certainly say [ən], as in [yuənmi].

Elision

Note that in the last example, in the environment of preceding and following nasals, the [d] sound of *and* has simply disappeared. The [d] sound is also commonly 'omitted' in the pronunciation of a word like *friendship*, [frɛnšIp]. This 'omission' of a sound segment which would be present in the deliberate pronunciation of a word in isolation is technically described as **elision**. In consonant clusters, especially in coda position, /t/ is a common casualty in this process, as in the typical pronunciation [æspɛks] for *aspects*, or in [himəsbi] for *he must be*. You can, of course, slowly and deliberately pronounce the phrase *we asked him*, but the process of elision in casual speech is likely to produce [wiæstIm]. Vowels also disappear, as in [εvri] for *every*, [IntrIst] for *interest*, [kæbnIt] for *cabinet*, and [spowz] for *suppose*.

These two processes of assimilation and elision occur in everyone's speech and should not be treated as a form of sloppiness or laziness in speaking. In fact, consistently avoiding the regular patterns of assimilation and elision used in a language would result in extremely artificial-sounding talk. The point of investigating phonological processes (only a very small number of which have been explored here) is not to arrive at a set of rules about how a language should be pronounced, but to try to come to an understanding of the regularities and patterns which underlie the actual use of sounds in language.

Study questions

1 What is the test used for determining phonemes in a language?
2 Which of the following words would be treated as minimal pairs?
   pat, pen, more, heat, tape, bun, fat, ban, chain, tale, bell, far, meal, vote, bet, pit, heel
3 How does an allophone differ from a phoneme?
4 What's the difference between an open and a closed syllable?
5 Which segments are most likely to be affected by elision in the pronunciation of the following words?

   (i) *postman*　(ii) *government*　(iii) *sandwich*　(iv) *pumpkin*

Discussion topics/projects

A (i) In all of the following English words there is an onset consonant cluster with /r/ in second position. Is there any way (using voice, place and manner features) to describe the kind of consonant that can appear before /r/ in these clusters, and to exclude any other consonants?
        brave, crash, freak, growl, pray, shriek, three, trick

   (ii) When the second part of an onset cluster is /l/, as in *black* and other words, which features are required in the first consonant?

B English words like *audible* and *edible* can be made negative by adding *in-* to produce *inaudible* and *inedible*.
   (i) What types of assimilation processes appear to have been involved in the pronunciation of the following negatives?
        impossible, illegal, irresponsible, immature, indecent, incomplete, ingratitude, insane

(ii) Can you think of any reason why these assimilation processes do not happen with *un-* in words like *unpleasant* or *unreal*? (You can consult chapter 1 of Harris, 1994, for some suggestions.)

C In this chapter, aspiration of a stop consonant in word-initial position was illustrated.

(i) Can you work out, by testing how /p/ is pronounced in the following words, whether "word-initial" is in fact the most accurate description of that phenomenon?
personal, rapid, desperate, computer, competition, special, description, empathy, peculiar

(ii) If you can identify the stressed syllable in each of these words, does that help you arrive at a different phonological description?

D The use of plural *-s* in English has three different, but very regular, phonological alternatives. You add:
/s/ to words like *ship, bat, book* and *cough*
/z/ to words like *cab, lad, cave, rag* and *thing*
/əz/ to words like *bus, bush, judge, church* and *maze*

(i) Can you work out the set of sounds which regularly precedes each of these alternatives?

(ii) What features do each of these sets have in common?

E There seems to be some phonological rule involved in the different pronunciations of the past tense *-ed* form in English. It is /t/ at the end of *walked* and *passed*; it is /d/ at the end of *jogged* and *played*; it is /əd/ at the end of *bounded* and *vaulted*.

(i) What is the phonological pattern in these words (and any others you can add) that determines which *-ed* version is used?

(ii) Do you think that one of these phonological forms for *-ed* is more basic, with the others being derived from it in a regular way? Which, and how?

Further reading

All basic texts in linguistics have a chapter on phonology, as in Chapter 4 of Akmajian *et al.* (1990), Chapter 3 of Finegan & Besnier (1989), Chapter 6 of Fromkin & Rodman (1993) and Chapter 3 of O'Grady *et al.* (1993). Many of the other texts listed at the end of the previous chapter, on phonetics, also deal with phonology, particularly Clark & Yallop (1995), Ladefoged (1992) and Roach (1991). For a useful set of basic exercises in phonology, see Halle &

Clements (1983). Well-established reference works are Chomsky & Halle
(1991), Hyman (1975) and Lass (1984). A different perspective is offered in
Hogg & McCully (1987). Other relatively accessible treatments are in Carr
(1993), Halle (1990), Hawkins (1984), Katamba (1989) and Maddieson (1984).
Edwards & Shriberg (1983) and Lowe (1994) address phonological issues in
speech therapy. Specifically focusing on the phonology of English are
Giegerich (1992), Jensen (1993), Lodge (1984) and Wolfram & Johnson (1982).
Brown (1990) presents an extended treatment of assimilation and elision.
Historical perspectives are provided by Anderson (1985) and Jones (1989).
Other theoretical treatments are available in Goldsmith (1994), Harris (1994)
and Kaye (1988).

7 Words and word-formation processes

When, in about 1820, a congressman named Felix Walker was accused of speaking drivel - which, evidently, he was – he replied that he was speaking to the people of Buncombe County, North Carolina, his district. Almost immediately his congressional colleagues began referring to any political claptrap or bombast as *speaking to Buncombe*. Soon the phrase had spread beyond Washington and was being abbreviated to *buncombe*, often respelled *bunkum*, and eventually further contracted to *bunk*. *Debunk* did not come until 1927. *Bunkum* in turn begat *hokum* – a blend of *hocus* and *bunkum*. Thus with a single fatuous utterance, the forgotten Felix Walker managed to inspire half a page of dictionary entries.   **Bill Bryson (1994)**

Around 1900, in New Berlin, Ohio, a department-store worker named J. Murray Spangler invented a device which he called an *electric suction sweeper*. This device eventually became very popular and could have been known as a *spangler*. People could have been *spanglering* their floors or they might even have *spanglered* their rugs and curtains. The use could have extended to a type of person who droned on and on (and really sucked), described as *spanglerish*, or to a whole style of behavior called *spanglerism*. However, none of that happened. Instead, Mr Spangler sold his new invention to a local businessman called William H. Hoover whose Hoover Suction Sweeper Company produced the first 'Hoover'. Not only did the word *hoover* (without a capital letter) become familiar all over the world, but in Britain, people still talk about *hoovering* (and not *spanglering*) their carpets.

The point of this small tale is that, although you had never heard of Mr. Spangler before, you really had no difficulty coping with the new words: *spangler*, *spanglering*, *spanglered*, *spanglerish* or *spanglerism*. That is, you can very quickly understand a new word in your language (a **neologism**) and accept the use of different forms of that new word. This ability must derive in part from the fact that there is a lot of regularity in the word-formation processes in your language. In this chapter, we shall explore some of those basic processes by which new terms are created.

Word-formation processes

In some respects, the study of the processes whereby new words come into being in a language like English seems relatively straightforward. This apparent simplicity, however, masks a number of controversial issues, some of which we shall consider in the following chapter. Despite the disagreements among scholars in this area, there do seem to be some regular processes involved, and in the following sections we shall cover the technical terms used to describe those processes and identify examples currently in use which are the result of those processes.

It should be remembered that these processes have been at work in the language for some time and many words in daily use today were, at one time, considered barbaric misuses of the language. It is difficult now to understand the views expressed in the early nineteenth century over the "tasteless innovation" of a word like *handbook*, or the horror expressed by a London newspaper in 1909 over the use of the newly coined word *aviation*. Yet many terms of recent currency cause similar outcries. Rather than act as if the language is being debased, we might prefer to view the constant evolution of new terms and new uses of old terms as a reassuring sign of vitality and creativeness in the way a language is shaped by the needs of its users. Let us consider the ways.

Coinage

One of the least common processes of word-formation in English is **coinage**, that is, the invention of totally new terms. The most typical sources are invented trade names for one company's product which become general terms (without initial capital letters) for any version of that product. Older examples are *aspirin*, *nylon* and *zipper*; more recent examples are *kleenex*, *teflon* and *xerox*. It may be that there is an obscure technical origin (e.g. *te*(tra)-*fl*(uor)-*on*) for such invented terms, but after their first coinage, they tend to become everyday words in the language.

Borrowing

One of the most common sources of new words in English is the process simply labeled **borrowing**, that is, the taking over of words from other languages. Throughout its history, the English language has adopted a vast number of loan-words from other languages, including *alcohol* (Arabic), *boss* (Dutch), *croissant* (French), *lilac* (Persian), *piano* (Italian), *pretzel* (German), *robot* (Czech), *tycoon* (Japanese), *yogurt* (Turkish) and *zebra* (Bantu). Other languages, of course, borrow terms from English, as can be observed in the Japanese use of *suupaamaaketto* ('supermarket') and *rajio* ('radio'), or Hungarians talking about *sport, klub* and *futbal*, or the French discussing problems of *le stress*, over a glass of *le whisky*, during *le weekend*.

A special type of borrowing is described as **loan-translation**, or **calque**. In this process, there is a direct translation of the elements of a word into the borrowing language. An interesting example is the French term *un gratte-ciel*, which literally translates as 'a scrape-sky', or the German *Wolkenkratzer* ('cloud scraper'), both of which were used for what, in English, is normally referred to as a *skyscraper*. The English word *superman* is thought to be a loan-translation of the German *Übermensch*, and the term *loan-word* itself is believed to have come from the German *Lehnwort*. Nowadays, some Spanish speakers eat *perros calientes* (literally 'dogs hot'), or *hot dogs*. The American concept of 'boyfriend' was a borrowing, with sound modification, into Japanese as *boyifurendo*, but as a calque into Chinese as 'male friend' or *nan pengyu*.

Compounding

In some of those examples we have just considered, there is a joining of two separate words to produce a single form. Thus, *Lehn* and *Wort* are combined to produce *Lehnwort* in German. This combining process, technically known as **compounding**, is very common in languages like German and English, but much less common in languages like French and Spanish. Obvious English examples would be *bookcase, fingerprint, sunburn, wallpaper, doorknob, textbook, wastebasket* and *waterbed*.

This very productive source of new terms has been well documented in English and German, but can also be found in totally unrelated languages, such as Hmong, in South East Asia, which combines *hwj* ('pot') and *kais* ('spout') to produce *hwjkais* ('kettle'). The forms *pajkws* ('flower' + 'corn' = 'popcorn') and *hnabloojtes* ('bag' + 'cover' + 'hand' = 'glove') are recent creations.

Blending

This combining of two separate forms to produce a single new term is also present in the process called **blending**. However, blending is typically accomplished by taking only the beginning of one word and joining it to the end of the other word. In some parts of the United States, there's a product which is used like *gasoline*, but is made from *alcohol*, so the 'blended' term for referring to this product is *gasohol*. If you wish to refer to the combined effects of *smoke* and *fog*, there's the term *smog*. In places where they have a lot of this stuff, they can jokingly make a distinction between *smog*, *smaze* (smoke + haze) and *smurk* (smoke + murk). Some other commonly used examples of blending are *bit* (binary/digit), *brunch* (breakfast/lunch), *motel* (motor/hotel), *telecast* (television/broadcast) and the *Chunnel* (Channel/tunnel), connecting England and France.

The recent phenomenon of fund-raising on television that feels like a marathon is typically called a *telethon* and if you are excessively crazy about video, you may be called a *videot*. *Infotainment* (information/entertainment) and *simulcast* (simultaneous/broadcast) are also new blends from life with television. To describe the mixing of languages, people refer to *Franglais* (French/English) and *Spanglish* (Spanish/English). In order to send information fast, you may use a *telex* (teleprinter/exchange) or, via computer, a *modem* (modulator/demodulator), or you may decide to send a *fax*. But that's not a blend. It's an example of our next category.

Clipping

The element of reduction which is noticeable in blending is even more apparent in the process described as **clipping**. This occurs when a word of more than one syllable (*facsimile*) is reduced to a shorter form (*fax*), often in casual speech. The term *gasoline* is still in use, but occurs much less frequently than *gas*, the clipped form. Common examples are *ad* ('advertisement'), *bra* ('brassiere'), *cab* ('cabriolet'), *condo* ('condominium'), *fan* ('fanatic'), *flu*, *perm*, *phone*, *plane*, *pram*, *pub* and *sitcom* ('situation comedy'). English speakers also like to clip each other's names, as in *Al*, *Ed*, *Liz*, *Mike*, *Ron*, *Sam*, *Sue* and *Tom*.

There must be something about educational environments that encourages clipping because just about every word gets reduced, as in *chem*, *exam*, *gym*, *lab*, *math*, *phys-ed*, *poly-sci*, *prof* and *typo*.

Backformation

A very specialized type of reduction process is known as **backformation**. Typically, a word of one type (usually a noun) is reduced to form another word of a different type (usually a verb). A good example of backformation is the process whereby the noun *television* first came into use and then the verb *televise* was created from it. Other examples of words created by this process are: *donate* (from 'donation'), *opt* (from 'option'), *emote* (from 'emotion'), *enthuse* (from 'enthusiasm'), *liaise* (from 'liaison') and *babysit* (from 'babysitter'). Indeed, if you *backform* anything, you have used a backformation.

One very regular source of backformed verbs in English is based on the pattern: *worker – work*. The assumption seems to have been that if there is a noun ending in *-er* (or something close in sound), then we can create a verb for what that noun-*er* does. Hence, an *editor* must *edit*, a *sculptor* must *sculpt* and *burglars*, *peddlers* and *swindlers* must *burgle*, *peddle* and *swindle*.

A particular type of backformation, favored in Australian and British English, produces forms technically known as **hypocorisms**. First, a longer word is reduced to a single syllable, then *-y* or *-ie* is added to the end. Perhaps the most familiar versions of this process are the words *movie* ('moving pictures') and *telly* ('television'). It has also produced *Aussie* ('Australian'), *barbie* ('barbecue'), *bookie* ('bookmaker'), *brekky* ('breakfast') and *hankie* ('handkerchief'). You can probably guess what *Chrissy pressies* are.

Conversion

A change in the function of a word, as, for example, when a noun comes to be used as a verb (without any reduction), is generally known as **conversion**. Other labels for this very common process are 'category change' and 'functional shift'. A number of nouns, such as *paper*, *butter*, *bottle*, *vacation*, can, via the process of conversion, come to be used as verbs, as in the following sentences: *He's papering the bedroom walls*; *Have you buttered the toast?*; *We bottled the home-brew last night*; *They're vacationing in France*. These conversions are readily accepted, but some examples, such as the noun *impact* being used as a verb, seem to *impact* some people's sensibilities rather negatively.

The conversion process is particularly productive in modern English, with new uses occurring frequently. The conversion can involve verbs becoming nouns, with *guess*, *must* and *spy* as the sources of *a guess*, *a must* and *a spy*. Phrasal verbs (*to print out*, *to take over*) also become nouns (*a printout*, *a takeover*) One complex verb combination (*want to be*) has become a very useful noun as in *He isn't in the group, he's just a wannabe.*

Verbs (*see through, stand up*) also become adjectives, as in *see-through material* or *a stand-up comedian.* Or adjectives, such as *dirty, empty, total, crazy* and *nasty,* can become the verbs *to dirty, to empty, to total,* or the nouns *a crazy* and *a nasty.* You may even hear of people *doing the nasty.*

Some compound nouns have assumed adjectival or verbal functions, exemplified by *the ball park* appearing in a *ball-park figure* or asking someone to *ball-park an estimate of the cost.* Other nouns of this type are *carpool, mastermind, microwave* and *quarterback,* which are all regularly used as verbs. Other forms, such as *up* and *down,* can also become verbs, as in *They up the prices* or *We down a few brews.*

It is worth noting that some converted forms shift substantially in meaning when they change category. The verb *to doctor* often has a negative sense, not normally associated with the source noun *a doctor.* A similar kind of reanalysis of meaning is taking place with respect to the noun *total* and the verb *run around,* which do not have negative meanings. However, after conversion, if you *total* your car (= verb), and your insurance company gives you *the runaround* (= noun), then you will have a double sense of the negative.

Acronyms

Some new words, known as **acronyms**, are formed from the initial letters of a set of other words. These can remain essentially 'alphabetisms' such as *CD* ('compact disk') or *VCR* ('video cassette recorder') where the pronunciation consists of the set of letters. More typically, acronyms are pronounced as single words, as in *NATO, NASA* or *UNESCO.* These examples have kept their capital letters, but many acronyms lose their capitals to become everyday terms such as *laser* ('light amplification by stimulated emission of radiation'), *radar* ('radio detecting and ranging'), *scuba* ('self contained underwater breathing apparatus') and *zip* ('zone improvement plan') code. You might even hear talk of a *snafu* which is reputed to have its origins in 'situation normal, all fouled up', though there is some dispute about the f-word in there.

Names for organizations are often designed to have their acronym represent an appropriate term, as in 'mothers against drunk driving' (*MADD*) and 'women against rape' (*WAR*). Some new acronyms come into general use so quickly that many speakers do not think of their component meanings. Recent innovations in banking such as the *ATM* ('automatic teller machine') and the required *PIN* ('personal identification number') are regularly heard with one of their elements repeated, as in *I sometimes forget my PIN number when I go to the ATM machine.*

Derivation

In our list so far, we have not dealt with what is by far the most common word-formation process to be found in the production of new English words. This process is called **derivation**, and it is accomplished by means of a large number of small 'bits' of the English language which are not usually given separate listings in dictionaries. These small 'bits' are called **affixes** and a few examples are the elements *un-*, *mis-*, *pre-*, *-ful*, *-less*, *-ish*, *-ism*, *-ness* which appear in words like *unhappy*, *misrepresent*, *prejudge*, *joyful*, *careless*, *boyish*, *terrorism* and *sadness.*

Prefixes and suffixes

In the preceding group of words, it should be obvious that some affixes have to be added to the beginning of a word (e.g. *un-*). These are called **prefixes**. The other affix forms are added to the end of the word (e.g. *-ish*) and are called **suffixes**. All English words formed by this derivational process use either prefixes or suffixes, or both. Thus, *mislead* has a prefix, *disrespectful* has both a prefix and a suffix, and *foolishness* has two suffixes.

Infixes

There is a third type of affix, not normally to be found in English, but fairly common in some other languages. This is called an **infix** and, as the term suggests, it is an affix which is incorporated inside another word. It is possible to see the general principle at work in certain expressions, occasionally used in fortuitous or aggravating circumstances by emotionally aroused English speakers: *Hallebloodylujah!*, *Absogoddamlutely!* and *Unfuckingbeliev-able!.* In the movie *Wish You Were Here*, the main character expresses her aggravation (at another character's trying to contact her) by screaming *Tell him I've gone to Singabloodypore!* The expletive may even have an infixed element, as in *godtripledammit!.* We could view these 'inserted' forms as a special version of infixing. However, a much better set of examples can be provided from Kamhmu, a language spoken in South East Asia. These examples are taken from Merrifield *et al.* (1962):

('to drill')	*see-srnee*	('a drill')
('to chisel')	*toh-trnoh*	('a chisel')
('to eat with a spoon')	*hiip-hrniip*	('a spoon')
('to tie')	*hoom-hrnoom*	('a thing with which to tie')

It can be seen that there is a regular pattern whereby the infix -*rn* is added to verbs to form corresponding nouns. If this pattern is generally found in the language and you know that the form *krnap* is the Kamhmu word for 'tongs', then you should be able to work out what the corresponding verb 'to grasp with tongs' would be. It is *kap*.

Multiple processes

Although we have concentrated on each of these word-formation processes in isolation, it is possible to trace the operation of more than one process at work in the creation of a particular word. For example, the term *deli* seems to have become a common American English expression via a process of first 'borrowing' *delicatessen* (from German) and then 'clipping' that borrowed form. If you hear someone complain that *problems with the project have snowballed*, the final term can be noted as an example of 'compounding', whereby *snow* and *ball* have been combined to form the noun *snowball*, which has then undergone 'conversion' to be used as a verb. Forms which begin as 'acronyms' can also undergo other processes, as in the use of *lase* as a verb, the result of 'backformation' from *laser*. In the expression, *waspish attitudes*, the form *WASP* ('white Anglo-Saxon Protestant') has lost its capital letters and gained a suffix (-*ish*) in the 'derivation' process.

An acronym that never seems to have had capital letters comes from 'young urban professional', plus the -*ie* suffix, as in hypocorism, to produce the word *yuppie* (first recorded in 1984). The formation of this new word, however, was helped by a quite different process, known simply as **analogy**, whereby words are formed to be similar in some way to existing words. *Yuppie* was made possible as a new word by the earlier existence of *hippie* and the other short-lived analogy *yippie*. The term *yippie* also had an acronym basis ('youth international party'), but was generally used for students protesting the Vietnam war in the United States. One joke has it that *yippies* just grew up to be *yuppies*. And the process continues. Another analogy, with the word *yap* ('making shrill noises'), has recently helped label some of those noisy young professionals as *yappies*.

Many such forms can, of course, have a very brief life-span. Perhaps the generally accepted test of the 'arrival' of recently formed words in a language is their published appearance in a dictionary. However, even this may not occur without protests from some, as Noah Webster found when his first dictionary, published in 1806, was criticized for citing words like *advocate* and *test* as verbs, and for including such 'vulgar' words as *advisory* and *presidential*. It would seem that Noah had a keener sense than his critics of which new word-forms in the language were going to last.

Study questions

1   Which of the following expressions is an example of 'calque'?
How would you describe the others?

(a) *luna de miel* (Spanish) – *honeymoon* (English)
(b) *mishin* (Japanese) – *machine* (English)
(c) *tréning* (Hungarian) – *training* (English)

2   The term *vaseline* was originally created as a trade name for a product,
but has become an ordinary English word. What is the technical term
used to describe this process?

3   Identify the affixes used in the words *unfaithful*, *carelessness*, *refillable*
and *disagree*, and decide whether they are prefixes or suffixes.

4   Can you identify the word-formation processes involved in producing
the italicized forms in these sentences?

(a) Laura *parties* every Saturday night.
(b) Tom was worried that he might have *AIDS*.
(c) Zee described the new toy as *fantabulous*.
(d) Eliza exclaimed, "*Absobloominglutely!*"

5   More than one process was involved in the creation of each of the forms
indicated below. Can you identify them?

(a) I just got a new *car-phone*.
(b) Shiel wants to be a *footballer*.
(c) The negotiators *blueprinted* a new peace proposal.
(d) Another *carjacking* has just been reported.

Discussion topics/projects

A   The compound word *birdcage* is formed from a noun *bird* plus another
noun *cage*, while the word *widespread* is formed from an adjective *wide*
and a verb *spread*. So, compounds differ in terms of the types of elements
which are combined. Can you identify the different elements involved in
each of the following compounds?
*bedroom, blackbird, brainwash, catfish, clean-shaven, crybaby, haircut,
heartbeat, hothouse, house-sit, hovercraft, leadfree, madman, ready-
made, seasick, sunflower, sunrise, telltale, threadbare, watchdog, well-
dressed, wetsuit*

B   The work of Bruce Downing and Judy Fuller (at the University of
Minnesota) in a study of the language of Hmong refugees now living in
the United States has produced some interesting examples of new word-

formations designed to cope with new objects and experiences. If you are given the translation equivalents of some Hmong terms, can you work out the English equivalents of the Hmong compounds which follow?

kws ('artisan'); *kev* ('way'); *ntaus* ('hit', 'mark'); *ntoo* ('tree'); *nqaj* ('rail'); *ntawv* ('paper'); *niam* ('mother'); *hlau* ('iron'); *tshuaj* ('medicine'); *tsheb* ('vehicle'); *kho* ('fix'); *hniav* ('teeth'); *mob* ('sick'); *cai* ('right', 'law'); *dav* ('bird', 'hawk'); *daim* ('flat'); *muas* ('buy').

niam hlau ('mother iron' = a magnet)		*kev kho mob*
kws ntawv	*kws ntaus ntawv*	*kws kho tsheb*
kws tshuaj	*kws hlau*	*kev cai*
kev nqaj hlau	*tsheb nqaj hlau*	*kws kho hniav*
kws ntoo	*dav hlau*	*daim ntawv muas tshuaj*

C   A number of interesting word-formation processes can be discerned in some of the following examples. Can you identify what is going on in these, and have you come across any comparable examples?
   When I'm ill, I want to see a doc, not a vet.
   I was a deejay before, but now I emcee in a nightclub.
   That's a-whole-nother problem.
   The deceased's cremains were scattered over the hill.
   He's always taking pills, either uppers or downers

D   Only a handful of the English words borrowed from other languages are presented in this chapter
   (i) Can you find out, by consulting a dictionary (an etymological dictionary if possible), which of the following words are borrowings and from which languages they came?
       advantage, assassin, caravan, cash, child, clinic, cobalt, cockroach, crime, have, laundry, measles, physics, pony, ranch, scatter, slogan, violent, wagon, yacht, zero

   (ii) While you have that dictionary, try to discover the source of the following 'eponyms' (words derived from names of people or places):
       biro, blurb, boycott, cardigan, denim, diesel, fahrenheit, nicotine, sandwich, saxophone, watt

E   In deriving new words via a suffix such as *-able*, there seems to be some constraint on what is permitted. The words in the first column below are 'acceptable' (that's one!) formations, but the forms in the other columns are not. Can you work out what the rule(s) might be for making new adjectives with the suffix -*able*? (Hint: if X is *fixable*, then someone can fix X.)

breakable	*?carable*	*?dieable*
doable	*?chairable*	*?downable*
inflatable	*?deskable*	*?oldable*
movable	*?hairable*	*?redable*
understandable	*?housable*	*?runable*
wearable	*?pencilable*	*?sleepable*

Further reading

There are a number of general treatments of word-formation in English, such as the textbooks by Adams (1973) and Bauer (1983). Espy (1978) and Levi (1978) are other traditional presentations. More technical treatments are offered by Aronoff (1976) and Di Sciullo & Williams (1987). Comprehensive reference works are Marchand (1969) or Quirk *et al.* (1985), Appendix 1, which is mainly based on British English. For American English, the journal *American Speech* regularly carries articles on new word-formations and Algeo (1991) presents a collection from that source. Other collections are Green (1991), Le May *et al.* (1988), Barnhart *et al.* (1990) and Mish (1986). Books with a more social (and entertaining) perspective are Bryson (1994) for American English and Howard (1990) or Hughes (1988) for British English. Carver (1991) presents a historical perspective, Randall (1991) explains the distinctions between many confused terms and Allan & Burridge (1991) explore why some words are considered better than others. Aitchison (1994), Allan (1986), Lipka (1990) and Miller (1991) all include discussions of word-formation, with Allan (1986) illustrating many hypocorisms. McArthur (1992) is a good resource, as are Barnhart (1988) on etymology and Mossman (1933) for acronyms. Volume 3 of Shopen (1985) contains several papers on word-formation processes in different languages. For an exhaustive survey of contemporary examples of conversion, see Clark & Clark (1979) and on infixing in English, see McMillan (1980). A survey of English words in other languages is presented in Viereck & Bald (1986).

8 Morphology

BAMBIFICATION:The mental conversion of flesh and blood living creatures into cartoon characters possessing bourgeois Judeo-Christian attitudes and morals.
Douglas Coupland (1991)

Throughout the preceding chapter, we approached the description of processes involved in word-formation as if the unit called the 'word' was a regular and easily identifiable form. This doesn't seem unreasonable when we look at a text of written English, since the 'words' in the text are, quite obviously, those sets of things marked in black with the bigger spaces separating them. Unfortunately, there are a number of problems with using this observation as the basis of an attempt to describe language in general, and individual linguistic forms in particular.

Morphology

In many languages, what appear to be single forms actually turn out to contain a large number of 'word-like' elements. For example, in Swahili (spoken throughout East Africa), the form *nitakupenda* conveys what, in English, would have to be represented as something like *I will love you*. Now, is the Swahili form a single word? If it is a 'word', then it seems to consist of a number of elements which, in English, turn up as separate 'words'. A very rough correspondence can be presented in the following way:

ni	*-ta*	*-ku*	*-penda*
'I	will	you	love'

It seems as if this Swahili 'word' is rather different from what we think of as an English 'word'. Yet, there clearly is some similarity between the languages, in that similar elements of the whole message can be found in both. Perhaps a better way of looking at linguistic forms in different languages would be to use this notion of 'elements' in the message, rather than to depend on identifying 'words'. The type of exercise we have just performed is an example of investigating forms in language, generally known as **morphology**. This term, which literally means 'the study of forms', was originally used in biology, but, since the middle of the nineteenth century, has also been used to describe that type of investigation which analyzes all those basic 'elements' which are used in a language. What we have been describing as 'elements' in the form of a linguistic message are more technically known as **morphemes**.

Morphemes

free
bound

We do not actually have to go to other languages such as Swahili to discover that 'word-forms' may consist of a number of elements. We can recognize that English word-forms such as *talks*, *talker*, *talked* and *talking* must consist of one element *talk*, and a number of other elements such as *-s*, *-er*, *-ed*, *-ing*. All these elements are described as morphemes. The definition of a morpheme is "a minimal unit of meaning or grammatical function". Let's clarify this definition with some examples. We would say that the word *reopened* in the sentence *The police reopened the investigation* consists of three morphemes. One minimal unit of meaning is *open*, another minimal unit of meaning is *re-* (meaning 'again'), and a minimal unit of grammatical function is *-ed* (indicating past tense). The word *tourists* also contains three morphemes. There is one minimal unit of meaning, *tour*, another minimal unit of meaning *-ist* (meaning 'person who does something'), and a minimal unit of grammatical function *-s* (indicating plural).

Free and bound morphemes

From these two examples, we can make a broad distinction between two types of morphemes. There are **free morphemes**, that is, morphemes which can stand by themselves as single words, e.g. *open* and *tour*. There are also **bound morphemes**, that is, those which cannot normally stand alone, but which are typically attached to another form, e.g. *re-*, *-ist*, *-ed*, *-s*. You will recognize this last set as a group of what we have already described in Chapter 7 as affixes. So, all affixes in English are bound morphemes. The free morphemes can be generally considered as the set of separate English word-forms. When they are used with bound morphemes, the basic word-form involved is technically known as the **stem**. For example:

undressed			*carelessness*		
un-	*dress*	*-ed*	*care*	*-less*	*-ness*
prefix	stem	suffix	stem	suffix	suffix
(bound)	(free)	(bound)	(free)	(bound)	(bound)

It should be noted that this type of description is a partial simplification of the morphological facts of English. There are a number of English words in which the element which seems to be the 'stem' is not, in fact, a free morpheme. In words like *receive, reduce, repeat* we can recognize the bound morpheme *re-*, but the elements *-ceive, -duce* and *-peat* are clearly not free morphemes. There is still some disagreement over the proper characterization of these elements and you may encounter a variety of technical terms used to describe them. It may help to work with a simple distinction between those forms like *-ceive* and *-duce* as 'bound stems' and other forms like *dress* and *care* as 'free stems'.

Free morphemes

What we have described as free morphemes fall into two categories. The first category is that set of ordinary nouns, adjectives and verbs which we think of as the words which carry the 'content' of messages we convey. These free morphemes are called **lexical morphemes** and some examples are: *boy, man, house, tiger, sad, long, yellow, sincere, open, look, follow, break*. We can add new lexical morphemes to the language rather easily, so they are treated as an 'open' class of words.

The other group of free morphemes are called **functional morphemes**. Examples are: *and, but, when, because, on, near, above, in, the, that, it*. This set consists largely of the functional words in the language such as conjunctions, prepositions, articles and pronouns. Because we almost never add new functional morphemes to the language, they are described as a 'closed' class of words.

Bound morphemes

The set of affixes which fall into the 'bound' category can also be divided into two types. One type we have already considered in Chapter 7, the **derivational morphemes**. These are used to make new words in the language and are often used to make words of a different grammatical category from the stem. Thus, the addition of the derivational morpheme *-ness* changes the adjective *good* to the noun *goodness*. The noun *care* can become the adjectives *careful* or *careless* via the derivational morphemes *-ful* or *-less*. A list of derivational morphemes will include suffixes such as the *-ish* in *foolish*, the

-*ly* in *badly* and the -*ment* in *payment*. It will also include prefixes such as *re-*, *pre-*, *ex-*, *dis-*, *co-*, *un-* and many more.

The second set of bound morphemes contains what are called **inflectional morphemes**. These are not used to produce new words in the English language, but rather to indicate aspects of the grammatical function of a word. Inflectional morphemes are used to show if a word is plural or singular, if it is past tense or not, and if it is a comparative or possessive form. English has only eight inflectional morphemes, illustrated in the following:

> *Let me tell you about Jim **'s** two sister**s**.*
> *One like**s** to have fun and is always laugh**ing**.*
> *The other lik**ed** to study and has always tak**en** things seriously.*
> *One is the loud**est** person in the house and the other is quiet**er** than a mouse.*

From these examples, we can see that two of the inflections, -*'s* (possessive) and -*s* (plural) are attached to nouns. There are four attached to verbs, -*s* (3rd person present singular), -*ing* (present participle), -*ed* (past tense) and -*en* (past participle). There are two inflections, -*est* (superlative) and -*er* (comparative) attached to adjectives. Note that, in English, all inflectional morphemes listed here are suffixes.

Noun +	-*'s*, -*s*
Verb +	-*s*, -*ing*, -*ed*, -*en*
Adjective +	-*est*, -*er*

There is some variation in the form of these inflectional morphemes, with, for example, the possessive sometimes occurring as -*s'* (*those boys' bags*) and the past participle as -*ed* (*they have finished*).

Derivational versus inflectional

The difference between derivational and inflectional morphemes is worth emphasizing. An inflectional morpheme never changes the grammatical category of a word. For example, both *old* and *older* are adjectives. The -*er* inflection (from Old English -*ra*) simply creates a different version of the adjective. However, a derivational morpheme can change the grammatical category of a word. The verb *teach* becomes the noun *teacher* if we add the derivational morpheme -*er* (from Old English -*ere*). So, the suffix form -*er* can be an inflectional morpheme as part of an adjective and also a distinct derivational morpheme as part of a noun. Just because they (-*er*) look the same doesn't mean they do the same kind of work. In both cases, they are bound morphemes.

Whenever there is a derivational suffix and an inflectional suffix attached to the same word, they always appear in that order. First the derivational -er attaches to *teach*, then the inflectional -s is added to yield *teachers*.

Morphological description

Armed with all these terms for the different types of morphemes, you can now take most sentences of English apart and list the 'elements'. As an example, the English sentence *The girl's wildness shocked the teachers* contains the following elements:

The	girl	- 's	wild	-ness
(functional)	(lexical)	(inflectional)	(lexical)	(derivational)

shock	-ed	the
(lexical)	(inflectional)	(functional)

content word

teach	er	s
(lexical)	(derivational)	(inflectional)

As a useful way to remember the different categories of morphemes, the following chart can be used:

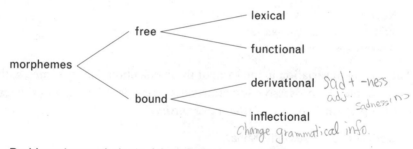

sad + -ness
adj. *sadness (n)*

change grammatical info.

Problems in morphological description

The rather neat chart presented above conceals a number of outstanding problems in the analysis of English morphology. So far, we have only considered examples of English words in which the different morphemes are easily identifiable as separate elements. Thus, the inflectional morpheme -s is added to *cat* and we get the plural *cats*. What is the inflectional morpheme which makes *sheep* the plural of *sheep*, or *men* the plural of *man*? A related question concerns the inflection which makes *went* the past tense of *go*. And yet another question concerns the derivation of an adjective like *legal*. If -al is the derivational suffix, as it is in forms like *institutional*, then what is the stem? No, it isn't *leg*.

These problematic issues, and many others which arise in the analysis of different languages, have not been fully resolved by linguists. The solutions to these problems are clearer in some cases than in others. The relationship between *law* and *legal* is a reflection of the historical influence of other languages on English word-forms. The modern form *law* is a result of a borrowing into Old English from Old Norse, over 1,000 years ago. The modern form *legal* is a borrowing from the Latin form *legalis* ('of the law'). Consequently, there is no derivational relationship between the two forms in English, nor between the noun *mouth* (an Old English form) and the adjective *oral* (a Latin borrowing). It has been pointed out that an extremely large number of English forms owe their morphological patterning to languages like Latin and Greek. Consequently, a full description of English morphology will have to take account of both historical influences and the effect of borrowed elements.

[handwritten: morpheme   plural morpheme]

Morphs and allomorphs

The solution to other problems remains controversial. One way to treat differences in inflectional morphemes is by proposing variation in morphological realization rules. In order to do this, we draw an analogy with some processes already noted in phonology (Chapter 6). If we consider 'phones' as the actual phonetic realization of 'phonemes', then we can propose **morphs** as the actual forms used to realize morphemes. Thus, the form *cat* is a single morph realizing a lexical morpheme. The form *cats* consists of two morphs, realizing a lexical morpheme and an inflectional morpheme ('plural'). Just as we noted that there were 'allophones' of a particular phoneme, then we can recognize **allomorphs** of a particular morpheme.

Take the morpheme 'plural'. Note that it can be attached to a number of lexical morphemes to produce structures like 'cat + plural', 'sheep + plural', and 'man + plural'. Now, the actual forms of the morphs which result from the single morpheme 'plural' turn out to be different. Yet they are all allomorphs of the one morpheme. It has been suggested, for example, that one allomorph of 'plural' is a zero-morph, and the plural form of *sheep* is actually 'sheep + ø'. Otherwise, those so-called 'irregular' forms of plurals and past tenses in English are described as having individual morphological realization rules. Thus, 'man + plural' or 'go + past', as analyses at the morpheme-level, are realized as *men* and *went* at the morph-level.

[handwritten notes:
morph   girl + |pl| → girls   {-s} plural morpheme
church + |pl| → churches   {-es / -ø / -en} morphs
allomorphs refer to set of morphs with the same meaning]

Other languages

This type of analytic approach is not without its critics, particularly when applied to other languages. Yet, the absence of a comprehensive analytic system should not discourage us from exploring and describing some of the morphological features of other languages. Some patterns appear to be describable in terms of the basic categories we listed earlier. The first example below is from English and the second is from Aztec:

Stem	Derivational	Inflectional	
DARK	+-EN ('make')	+-ED ('past')	= DARKENED
MIC ('die')	+ TIA ('cause to')	+-S ('future')	= MICTIAS ('will kill')

Different patterns occur in other languages. Let's look at some sample data, adapted from examples originally presented in Gleason (1955), and try to work out which morphological features can be identified. The first is from Kanuri, a language spoken in Nigeria.

Kanuri

('excellent')	karite	- nəmkarite	('excellence')
('big')	kura	- nəmkura	('bigness')
('small')	gana	- nəmgana	('smallness')
('bad')	dibi	- nəmdibi	('badness')

From this set, we can propose that the prefix *nəm-* is a derivational morpheme which can be used to derive nouns from adjectives. Discovering a regular morphological feature of this type will enable us to make certain predictions when we encounter other forms in the language. For example, if the Kanuri word for 'length' is *nəmkurugu*, then we can be reasonably sure that 'long' is *kurugu*.

Different languages also employ different means to produce inflectional marking on forms. Here are some examples from Ganda, a language spoken in Uganda:

Ganda

('doctor')	omusawo	- abasawo	('doctors')
('woman')	omukazi	- abakazi	('women')
('girl')	omuwala	- abawala	('girls')
('heir')	omusika	- abasika	('heirs')

From this small sample, we can observe that there is an inflectional prefix *omu-*, used with singular nouns, and a different inflectional prefix *aba-*, used with the plural of those nouns. If you are told that *abalenzi* is a Ganda plural, meaning 'boys', you should be able to determine the singular form, meaning 'boy'. It is, of course, *omulenzi*.

The following data from Ilocano, a language of the Philippines, will serve to illustrate a quite different method for marking plurals:

Ilocano

('head')	úlo	- ulúlo	('heads')
('road')	dálan	- daldálan	('roads')
('life')	bíag	- bibíag	('lives')
('plant')	múla	- mulmúla	('plants')

In these examples, there seems to be repetition of the first part of the singular form. When the first part is *bi-* in the singular, the plural begins with this form repeated, *bibi-*. The process involved here is technically known as **reduplication** and several languages use this repetition device as a means of inflectional marking. Having seen how plurals differ from singular forms in Ilocano, you should be able to take this plural form *taltálon* ('fields') and work out what the singular ('field') would be. If you follow the pattern observed, you should get *tálon*.

Finally, here are some intriguing data provided by Lisa Miguel, who speaks Tagalog, another language of the Philippines:

Tagalog

basa ('read')	tawag ('call')	sulat ('write')
bumasa ('Read!')	tumawag ('Call!')	sumulat ('Write!')
babasa ('will read')	tatawag ('will call')	susulat ('will write')

If we assume that the first form in each set is some type of stem, then it appears that in the second member of each set an element *-um-* has been inserted after the first consonant. It must be an example of an infix. In the third member of each set, note that the change in form involves, in each case, a repetition of the first syllable. So, the marking of future reference in Tagalog appears to be accomplished via reduplication. If you know that *lapit* is the verb meaning 'come here' in Tagalog, how would you expect the expressions 'Come here!' and 'will come here' to be realized? How about *lumapit* and *lalapit*? And if you hear *lalakad* ('will walk'), you can guess that *lakad* will translate as 'walk'.

It may have occurred to you as we were exploring all these features of morphology that the discussion often seemed to be connected to what was traditionally called 'grammar'. That would have been an accurate observation and we shall continue the exploration in the following chapter.

Study questions

1 (a) List the 'bound' morphemes to be found in these words:
       misleads, previewer, shortened, unhappier, fearlessly.
   (b) In which of the following examples should the 'a' be treated as a
       bound morpheme: *a boy, apple, atypical, AWOL?*
2 What are the functional morphemes in the following sentence:
   The old man sat on a chair and told them tales of woe.
3 What are the inflectional morphemes in the following phrases:
   (a) *the singer's songs*   (c) *the newest style*
   (b) *it's raining*   (d) *the cow jumped over the moon*
4 What would we list as allomorphs of the morpheme 'plural' from this set
   of English words:
   dogs, oxen, deer, judges, curricula?
5 Provide the equivalent forms, in the languages listed, for the English
   translations shown on the right below.

Tagalog	'buy'	*bili*	'will buy'
Kanuri	'sweetness'	*nəmkəǰi*	'sweet'
Kamhmu	'an ear ornament'	*srnal*	'to place in earlobe'
Ganda	'twin'	*omuloŋgo*	'twins'
Ilocano	'windows'	*tawtáwa*	'window'
Kamhmu	'a small package'	*trniap*	'to fold a small 'package'
Tagalog	'eat'	*kain*	'Eat!'

Discussion topics/projects

A In the following examples from Turkish (thanks to Feride Erkü), there is
   some variation in the form of the inflectional morpheme for marking
   plural.
   (i) Can you provide the missing forms in the table?

('man')	*adam*	- *adamlar*	('men')
('gun')	_____	- *toplar*	('guns')
('lesson')	*ders*	- _____	('lessons')
('place')	*yer*	- *yerler*	('places')
('road')	_____	- *yollar*	('roads')
('lock')	_____	- *kilitler*	('locks')
('arrow')	*ok*	- _____	('arrows')
('hand')	*el*	- _____	('hands')
('arm')	*kol*	- _____	('arms')
('bell')	_____	- *ziller*	('bells')
('friend')	_____	- *dostlar*	('friends')
('apple')	*elma*	- _____	('apples')

(ii)   What are the two plural morphs?

(iii) Next, consider *a* and *o* as representing back vowels, while *e* and *i* represent front vowels. Under what conditions are the two different plural morphs used?

(iv)   How would you describe the translation equivalents of *your*, and the conditions for their use, on the basis of the following Turkish expressions:

dishin	('your tooth')	*topun*	('your gun')
okun	('your arrow')	*dersin*	('your lesson')
kushun	('your bird')	*kibritlerin*	('your matches')

(v)   While English usually marks location with prepositions (i.e. ***in** a house* or ***at** a place*), Turkish has postpositions (i.e. *house-**in*** or *place-**at***). After studying the following examples, you should be able to identify the three versions of the 'location' suffix and the conditions for their use.

('book')	*kitap*	- *kitapta*	('in a book')
('chair')	*koltuk*	- *koltukta*	('in a chair')
('room')	*oda*	- *odada*	('in a room')
('restaurant')	*lokanta*	- *lokantada*	('in a restaurant')
('house')	*ev*	- *evde*	('in a house')
('place')	*yer*	- *yerlerde*	('in places')
('hand')	*el*	- *ellerimde*	('in my hands')
('road')	*yol*	- *yollarta*	('in roads')

For your final task: when Turkish borrowed (from French) the word *randevu*, meaning 'an appointment', how do you think they expressed 'in an appointment'?

B   Here are some further examples of Swahili sentences. Can you work out the forms which correspond to the elements in the English translations?

alipita	('she passed by')
alikupiga	('she beat you')
waliondoka	('they left')
nilimlipa	('I paid him')
niliwapika	('I cooked them')
nitakupenda	('I will love you')
utawauza	('you will sell them')
utanipiga	('you will beat me')

nitaondoka	('I will leave')
tuliwapenda	('we loved them')
tutapita	('we will pass by')
watamlipa	('they will pay him')

C Remembering the morphological processes identified in Tagalog, can you extend the analysis to describe the elements and processes involved in the following examples, also from Tagalog?

hanap	('look for')	*sulat*	('write')
hinanap	('was looked for')	*sinulat*	('was written')
humahanap	('is looking for')	*sumusulat*	('is writing')
hinahanap	('is being looked for')	*sinusulat*	('is being written')
basag	('break')	*tawag*	('call')
binasag	('was broken')	*tinawag*	('was called')
bumabasag	('is breaking')	*tumatawag*	('is calling')
binabasag	('is being broken')	*tinatawag*	('is being called')

D In English, the idea of possession can be marked by an inflectional suffix (-'s) on the noun representing the 'possessor', placed before the noun that is 'possessed' (as in the English examples below). The other examples below are from a West African language called Basari, spoken in Ghana (data adapted from Jackson, 1985).

(i) Can you describe how 'possession' is expressed in these examples?

('chief') *uboti*		('wife') *unimpu*	('farm') *kusaau*

('man's chief')	*uninja botiu*
('a man's wife')	*uninja nimpuu*
('one wife')	*unimpu ubo*
('this man's one wife')	*uninja-nee nimpuu ubo*
('one farm')	*kusaau kubo*
('a man's farm')	*uninja saaku*
('a man's one farm')	*uninja saaku kubo*
('one man's farm')	*uninja ubo saaku*

(ii) If the Basari word for 'mortar' is *kukuntuu*, then how would you translate *uninja-nee nimpuu kuntuuku*?

E In English, plural forms such as *mice* appear to be treated in a different way from plurals such as *rats*. If you tell people that a place is infested with mice or rats, they will accept the compounds *mice-infested* and *rat-infested*, but not **rats-infested*. This suggests that the forms with the regular plural affix (-s) follow a different rule in compounding than irregular plural forms such as *mice*. Can you think of a way to state the rule (or sequence of rules) that will accommodate all the examples given here? (You can get some help from Gordon, 1985, or the summary in chapter 5 of Pinker, 1994). An asterisk (*) before a word means that it is an unacceptable form in the language.

teethmarks	*the feet-cruncher*
clawmarks	*the finger-cruncher*
*clawsmarks	**the fingers-cruncher*
lice-infested	*a people-mover*
roach-infested	*a dog-mover*
*roaches-infested	**a dogs-mover*

Further reading

Most introductory linguistics texts have a section on morphology, for example, Akmajian *et al.* (1990), Chapter 2, Fromkin & Rodman (1993), Chapter 2, or O'Grady *et al.* (1993), Chapter 4. An array of interesting exercises involving a wide variety of different languages can be found in Gleason (1955). Other good resources are Cowan & Rakusan (1985) and Jackson (1985). A particularly clear presentation of the relationship between morphemes and morphs is in Brown & Miller (1991) and why the distinction is necessary is covered in Chapter 5 of Lyons (1968). A comprehensive textbook on the subject is Matthews (1991). Other texts (some quite complex) are Bauer (1988), Bybee (1985), Katamba (1993), Jensen (1990) and Spencer (1981). Interest in morphology was much greater in earlier works on language and you might like to go back to Bloomfield (1933) for one approach and then try Hockett (1954; 1958) for another.

9 Phrases and sentences: grammar

A memo at my school warns against the sins most often committed by students against the English language. Watch out for the "gross reference": "Bill hit Fred on the head with the bat. It was hard. It made him mad." Well, I don't know how "gross" this is. If I were Fred I'd be mad too, and I'd jump a few logical steps to get back at that hooligan Bill. Then there is, of course, the ever-threatening "dangling modifier"; "While thinking about Sue, the Honda hit the fence." "John ran to the door and yelled at the dog in his underwear." Being somewhat familiar with how students live nowadays, I can see the dog wearing John's underwear. In fact, I saw it late last night. The memo also warns of the "double negative": "I can't hardly believe it." "I can't get no satisfaction." Come now. Are the Rolling Stones wrong?   **Andrei Codrescu (1989)**

We have already considered two levels of description used in the study of language. We have described linguistic expressions as sequences of sounds which can be represented phonetically. For example:

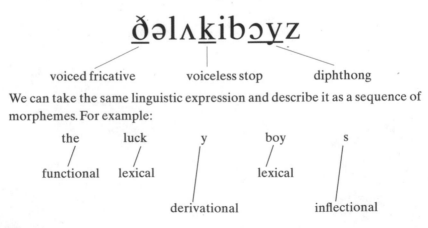

We can take the same linguistic expression and describe it as a sequence of morphemes. For example:

the	luck	y	boy	s
functional	lexical		lexical	
		derivational		inflectional

86

With these descriptions, we could characterize all the words of a language in terms of their phonetic and morphological make-up.

Grammar

However, we have not yet accounted for the fact that these words can only be combined in a limited number of patterns. We recognize that the phrase *the lucky boys* is a well-formed piece of English, but that the following two 'phrases' are not at all well-formed:

  *boys the lucky   *lucky boys the

(Beside each of these ill-formed structures there is an asterisk (*), which is a conventional way of indicating that a structure is ill-formed, or ungrammatical.)

So, we need a way of describing the structure of phrases and sentences which will account for all of the grammatical sequences and rule out all the ungrammatical sequences. Providing such an account involves us in the study of **grammar**. We should note that this term is frequently used to cover a number of different phenomena.

Types of grammar

Each adult speaker of a language clearly has some type of 'mental grammar', that is, a form of internal linguistic knowledge which operates in the production and recognition of appropriately structured expressions in that language. This 'grammar' is subconscious and is not the result of any teaching. A second, and quite different, concept of 'grammar' involves what might be considered 'linguistic etiquette', that is, the identification of the 'proper' or 'best' structures to be used in a language. A third view of 'grammar' involves the study and analysis of the structures found in a language, usually with the aim of establishing a description of the grammar of English, for example, as distinct from the grammar of Russian or French or any other language.

Given these three concepts, we can say that, in general, the first may be of most interest to a psychologist, since it deals with what goes on in people's minds, and the second may be of interest to a sociologist, since it has to do with people's social attitudes and values. The third is what occupies many linguists, since the concern is with the nature of language, often independently of the users of the language. The study of grammar, in this narrow sense of the study of the structure of expressions in a language, has a very long tradition.

The parts of speech

You may already be familiar with many of the terms used in a grammatical description, particularly the terms for the parts of speech, as illustrated in this sentence:

The	*lucky*	*boys*	*saw*	*the*	*clowns*	*at*
article	adjective	noun	verb	article	noun	preposition

the	*circus*	*and*	*they*	*cheered*	*loudly*
article	noun	conjunction	pronoun	verb	adverb

Simple definitions of these terms can be presented in the following way:

Nouns are words used to refer to people, objects, creatures, places, qualities, phenomena and abstract ideas as if they were all 'things'.

Adjectives are words used, typically with nouns, to provide more information about the 'things' referred to (*happy* people, *large* objects, *cute* creatures, *stupid* ideas).

Verbs are words used to refer to various kinds of actions (*run*, *jump*) and states (*be*, *seem*) involving the 'things' in events.

Adverbs are words used to provide more information about the actions and events (*slowly*, *suddenly*). Some adverbs (*really*, *very*) are also used with adjectives to modify the information about 'things' (*really* large objects, *very* stupid ideas).

Prepositions are words (*at*, *in*, *on*, *near*, *with*, *without*) used with nouns in phrases providing information about time (*at* five, *in* the morning), place (*on* the table, *near* the window) and other connections (*with* a knife, *without* a thought) involving actions and things.

Pronouns are words (*me*, *they*, *he*, *himself*, *this*, *it*) used in place of noun phrases, typically referring to things already known (*he* likes *himself*, *this* is *it*!)

Conjunctions are words (*and*, *but*, *although*, *if*) used to connect, and indicate relationships between, events and things (we swam *although* it was very cold).

Simple definitions of this type are useful for identifying most forms in a language like English, but they are never completely accurate. A different approach might focus on some other properties of the parts of speech. For example, a noun can be defined as a form that comes after an article (*the*, *a*) and can take inflections for possessive (-*'s*) and plural (-*s*). Of course, not all nouns (e.g. *information*, *mud*) have all these characteristics. Procedures for the structural analysis of the parts of speech are presented later.

Traditional grammar

These terms, used to label the grammatical categories of words in sentences, come from traditional grammar, which has its origins in the description of languages like Classical Latin and Greek. Since there were well-established grammatical descriptions of these older languages, it seemed appropriate to adopt the existing categories from these descriptions and apply them in the analysis of languages like English. After all, Latin and Greek were the languages of scholarship, religion, philosophy and 'knowledge', so the grammar of these languages was taken to be the best grammar.

Traditional categories

In addition to the terms used for the parts of speech, traditional grammatical analysis also gave us a number of other categories, including 'number', 'person', 'tense', 'voice' and 'gender'. These categories can be discussed in isolation, but their role in describing language structure becomes clearer when we consider them in terms of **agreement**. For example, we say that the verb *likes* 'agrees with' the noun *boy* in the sentence *The boy likes his dog*. This agreement is partially based on the category of **number**, that is, whether the noun is singular or plural. It is also based on the category of **person**, which covers the distinctions of first person (involving the speaker), second person (involving the hearer) and third person (involving any others). The different forms of English pronouns are usually described in terms of person and number, in that we have first person singular (*I*), second person singular (*you*), third person singular (*he*, *she*, *it*), first person plural (*we*), and so on. So, in the sentence *The boy likes his dog*, we have a noun *boy*, which is third person singular, and the verb *likes* 'agrees with' the noun.

In addition, the form of the verb must also be described in terms of another category, that of **tense**. In this case, the verb (*likes*) is in the present tense, which is distinguished from the past tense (*liked*). The sentence is also in the **active voice**, with *the boy* doing the liking. An alternative is the **passive voice**, in which the liking is done to *the boy*, as in *The boy is liked by his dog*, or just *The boy is liked*.

Our final category is that of **gender**, which helps us describe the agreement between *boy* and *his* in our example sentence. In English, we have to describe this relationship in terms of **natural gender**, mainly derived from a biological distinction between male and female. The agreement between *boy* and *his* is based on a distinction English makes between reference to male entities (*he*, *his*), female entities (*she*, *her*), and sexless entities, or animals, when the sex of the animal is irrelevant (*it*, *its*).

This type of biological distinction is quite different from the more common distinction found in languages which use **grammatical gender**. In this latter sense, nouns are classified according to their gender class and, typically, articles and adjectives take different forms to 'agree with' the gender of the noun. Spanish, for example, has two grammatical genders, masculine and feminine, illustrated by the expressions *el sol* ('the sun') and *la luna* ('the moon') respectively. German uses three genders, masculine *der Mond* ('the moon'), feminine *die Sonne* ('the sun') and neuter *das Feuer* ('the fire'). Note the different forms of the articles in both the Spanish and German examples, corresponding to differences in the gender class of the nouns. Also note that the gender distinction is not based on a distinction in sex. A young girl is biologically 'female', but the German noun *das Mädchen* is grammatically 'neuter'. The French word *le livre* ('the book') is grammatically masculine, but we would not consider books to be biologically male. So, the grammatical category of gender is very usefully applied in describing a number of languages (including Latin), but may not be as appropriate in describing English.

Traditional analysis

The notion of 'appropriateness' of analytic categories has not always been a consideration. In traditional grammar books, tables such as the following were often presented for English, constructed by analogy with similar tables of forms in Latin grammars. The forms for the Latin verb amare ('to love') are listed on the right.

	First person, singular	*I love*	*amo*
Present	Second person, singular	*you love*	*amas*
tense,	Third person, singular	*he loves*	*amat*
active	First person, plural	*we love*	*amamus*
voice	Second person, plural	*you love*	*amatis*
	Third person, plural	*they love*	*amant*

Note that each of the Latin verb forms is different, according to the categories of person and number, yet the English forms are, with one exception, the same. Thus it makes some sense, in describing a language like Latin, to have all those descriptive categories to characterize verb forms, yet it seems a rather extravagant descriptive system for English. The influence of Latin, however, goes beyond the descriptive labels.

The prescriptive approach

It is one thing to adopt the grammatical labels (e.g. 'noun', 'verb') to categorize words in English sentences; it is quite another thing to go on to claim that the structure of English sentences should be like the structure of sentences in Latin. Yet this was an approach taken by some grammarians, mainly in eighteenth-century England, who set out rules for the correct or 'proper' use of English. This view of grammar as a set of rules for the 'proper' use of a language is still to be found today and may be best characterized as the **prescriptive approach**. Some familiar examples of prescriptive rules for English sentences are as follows:

(1) You must not split an infinitive.
(2) You must not end a sentence with a preposition.

There are, of course, many such rules which generations of English teachers have attempted to instill in their pupils via corrections, as when the sentence *Mary runs faster than me* is 'corrected' to read *Mary runs faster than I*. And *Who did you see?* is 'corrected' to *Whom did you see?* And never begin a sentence with *and*.

It may, in fact, be a valuable part of one's education to be made aware of this 'linguistic etiquette', or the 'proper' use of the language. If it is a social expectation that someone who writes well should obey these prescriptive rules, then social judgments such as "poorly educated" may be made about someone who does not follow these rules.

However, it is worth considering the probable origins of these rules and asking whether they are appropriately applied to the English language. Let us take one example: "You must not split an infinitive."

Captain Kirk's infinitive

The infinitive in English has the form *to* + the verb, as in *to go*, and can be used with an adverb such as *boldly*. So, at the beginning of each televised 'Star Trek' episode, Captain Kirk used the expression *To boldly go* ... . This is an example of a split infinitive. Captain Kirk's English teacher should have taught him to say *To go boldly* or *Boldly to go*. If Captain Kirk had been a Roman space traveler, speaking Latin, he would have used the expressions *ire* ('to go') and *audacter* ('boldly'). Now, in saying *Ire audacter* ... in Latin, Captain Kirkus would not even have the opportunity to split his infinitive (*ire*), because Latin infinitives are single words and just do not split.

So, it would be very appropriate in Latin grammar to say that you cannot split an infinitive. But is it appropriate to carry this idea over into English, where the infinitive does not consist of a single word, but of two words, *to* and *go*? If it is a typical feature of the use of English that speakers and writers do produce forms such as *to boldly go* or *to solemnly swear*, then we may wish to say that there are structures in English which differ from those found in Latin, rather than to say that the English forms are 'bad" because they are breaking a supposed rule of Latin grammar.

The descriptive approach

It may be that using a well-established grammatical description of Latin is a useful guide for studying some languages (e.g. Italian or Spanish), is less useful for others (e.g. English), and may be absolutely misleading if you want to describe some non-European languages. This last point became clear to those linguists who wanted to describe the structure of North American Indian languages at the end of the nineteenth century. The categories and rules which were appropriate for Latin grammar just did not seem to fit the Indian languages encountered. As a consequence, throughout the present century, a rather different approach has been taken. Analysts collect samples of the language they are interested in and attempt to describe the regular structures of the language as it is used, not according to some view of how it should be used. This is called the **descriptive approach** and it is the basis of most modern attempts to characterize the structure of different languages.

Structural analysis

One type of descriptive approach is called **structural analysis** and its main concern is to investigate the distribution of forms (e.g. morphemes) in a language. The method employed involves the use of 'test-frames' which can be sentences with empty slots in them. For example:

> The _____ *makes a lot of noise.*
> *I heard a _____ yesterday.*

There are a lot of forms which can fit into these slots to produce good grammatical sentences of English (e.g. *donkey*, *car*, *dog*, *radio*, *child*, etc.). Consequently, we can suggest that because all of these forms fit in the same test-frame, they are likely to be examples of the same grammatical category. The label we give to this grammatical category is, of course, 'noun'. However, there are many forms which do not fit the test-frames above. Examples would be *Cathy*, *it*, *the dog*, *a car*, and so on. For these forms, we require different test-frames, which could be like this:

      _____ makes a lot of noise.
I heard _____ yesterday.

Among the forms which fit these test-frames are *Cathy*, *Anna Banana*, *it*, *the dog*, *an old car*, *the professor with the Scottish accent*, and many more. Once again, we can suggest that these forms are likely to be examples of the same grammatical category. The common label for this category is 'noun phrase'. By developing a set of test-frames of this type and discovering what forms fit the slots in the test-frames, you can produce a description of (at least some) aspects of the sentence structures of a language.

Immediate constituent analysis

An approach with the same descriptive aims is called **immediate constituent analysis**. The technique employed in this approach is designed to show how small constituents (or components) in sentences go together to form larger constituents. In the following sentence, we can identify eight constituents (at the word level): *Her father brought a shotgun to the wedding.*

How do those eight constituents go together to form constituents at the phrase level? Does it seem appropriate to put the words together as follows?

   brought a   *father brought*   *shotgun to*   *to the*

We don't normally think of these combinations as phrases in English. We are more likely to say that the phrase-like constituents here are combinations of the following types: *Her father*, *a shotgun*, *the wedding*, which are noun phrases; *to the wedding*, which is a prepositional phrase; *brought a shotgun*, which is a verb phrase.

This analysis of the constituent structure of the sentence can be represented in different types of diagrams. One type of diagram simply shows the distribution of the constituents at different levels.

Her	father	brought	a	shotgun	to	the	wedding

This type of diagram can be used to show the types of forms which can substitute for each other at different levels of constituent structure.

Her	father	brought	a	shotgun	to	the	wedding
The	man	saw	the	thief	in	a	car
Fred		took		Jean	to		Honolulu
He		came				here	

Labeled and bracketed sentences

An alternative type of diagram is designed to show how the constituents in sentence structure can be marked off via labeled brackets. The first step is to put brackets (one on each side) around each constituent, and then more brackets around each combination of constituents. For example:

$$\Big[\ \big[[\text{The}]\ [\text{dog}]\big]\quad \big[[\text{followed}]\ \big[[\text{the}]\ [\text{boy}]\big]\big]\ \Big]$$

With this procedure, the different constituents of the sentence are shown at the word level [*the*], at the phrase level [*the boy*], and at the sentence level [*The dog followed the boy*].

We can, of course, label each constituent with grammatical terms such as 'Art' (= article), 'N' (= noun), 'NP' (= noun phrase), 'V' (= verb), 'VP' (= verb phrase) and 'S' (= sentence). In the following diagram, these labels are placed beside each bracket which marks the beginning of a constituent. The result is a labeled and bracketed analysis of the constituent structure of the sentence.

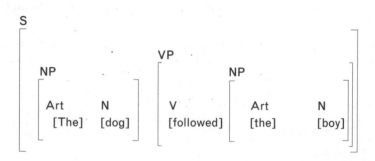

In performing this type of analysis, we have not only labeled all the constituents, we have exposed the **hierarchical organization** of those constituents. In this hierarchy, the sentence is higher than, and contains, the noun phrase. The noun phrase is higher than, and contains, the noun. We shall return to this concept of the hierarchical organization of grammatical structure in the next chapter.

Before moving on, however, we should note that constituent analysis is not only for the description of English sentences. We can take a sample sentence from a language with a structure quite different from English and apply the same type of analysis.

A Gaelic sentence

Here is a sentence from Scottish Gaelic which would be translated as *The boy saw the black dog*:

Chunnaic	*an*	*gille*	*an*	*cu*	*dubh*
'saw'	'the'	'boy'	'the'	'dog'	'black'

One very obvious difference between the structure of this Gaelic sentence and its English counterpart is the fact that the verb comes first in the sentence. Another noticeable feature is that, when an adjective is used, it follows rather than precedes the noun. We can represent these structural observations in our diagram.

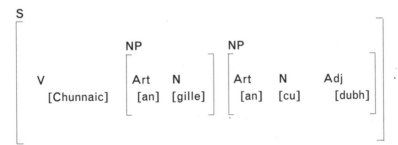

It is not, of course, the aim of this type of analysis that we should be able to draw complicated-looking diagrams in order to impress our friends. The aim is to make explicit, via the diagram, what we believe to be the structure of grammatical sentences in a language. It also enables us to describe clearly how English sentences are put together as combinations of phrases which, in turn, are combinations of words. We can then look at similar descriptions of sentences in other languages, Gaelic, Japanese, Spanish, Arabic, or whatever, and see clearly what structural differences exist. At a very practical level, it may help us understand why a Spanish learner of English produces phrases like *the wine white* (instead of *the white wine*), using a structural organization of constituents which is possible in Spanish, but not in English.

Study questions

1 Give the traditional terms for the grammatical categories of words used in the following sentence (e.g. *boy* = noun): *The boy rubbed the magic lamp and suddenly a genie appeared beside him.*

2 What prescriptive rules for the 'proper' use of English are not obeyed in the following sentences?

> (a) *That's the girl I gave my roller skates to.*
> (b) *He wanted to simply borrow your car for an hour.*

3 Most modern attempts to characterize the structure of sentences are based on a particular approach. What is this approach called, and what general principle is adhered to in such an approach?

4 Present a labeled and bracketed analysis of this sentence:
   The policeman chased a robber.

5 Given the following English translations of some other Gaelic words, can you translate the sentences which follow: *mor* ('big'), *beag* ('small'), *bhuail* ('hit'), *duine* ('man').

> (a) *Bhuail an gille beag an cu dubh.*
> (b) *Chunnaic an cu an duine mor.*

Discussion topics/projects

A The grammatical category of 'tense' was mentioned briefly in this chapter and a distinction between present and past tense in English was noted. It has been claimed (Palmer, 1983: 193) that English does not have a future tense form of the verb, although it does have many ways of referring to future time. Consider the following sentences and decide what kind of time-reference is involved. Then, consider whether the labels 'past', 'present' and 'future' are appropriate for describing the verb forms used.

> *Water will freeze at zero degrees Centigrade.*
> *I'll leave if you want.*
> *If Bucky phones, tell him I am asleep.*
> *I wish I had a million dollars.*
> *Your plane leaves at noon tomorrow.*
> *You always listen to the same songs.*
> *We're going to visit Cairo next year.*
> *She said Jim was leaving next week.*
> *Shall we dance?*
> *They were about to leave when I arrived.*

B The types of grammatical descriptions we have considered would simply treat the following examples as English sentences and present a description of their form and structural organization. Is this what everyone considers as 'grammar'? Might there be more to say about sentences like these?

(i)   I don't know nothing about that
(ii)   You wasn't here when he come looking for you
(iii)   There's hundreds of students in there
(iv)   Do you wanna go? Are you gonna go?
(v)   Are y'all coming to see us soon?
(vi)   That chair's broke, you shouldn't ought to sit on it
(vii)   I never seen them when they was doing that
(viii) If you would have come with, we would have had more fun

C Can you produce a single diagram, following the format of an immediate constituent analysis, which would incorporate all the constituents of the following sentences? What problems have to be resolved in an exercise like this?

A friend borrowed my car in June. They arrived yesterday.
My parents bought two tickets at Christmas. Suzy left.
We saw that film during the summer. The thief stole it last year.

D Here are some sample sentences from two different languages. The first set is from Latin and the second set is from Amuzgo, a language of Mexico. (The examples used are adapted from data in Merrifield et al., 1962.) Work out the basic constituent structure of the sentences from each language, and then describe them in terms of the phrase level constituents.

(1) puellae aquilas portant   'The girls carry the eagles'
     feminae columbas amant   'The women love the doves'
     puella aquilam salvat   'The girl saves the eagle'
     aquila columbam pugnat   'The eagle fights the dove'
     femina aquilam liberat   'The woman frees the eagle'

(2) macei'na tyocho kwi com   'The boy is reading a book'
     kwil'a yonom kwi w'aa   'The men are building a house'
     nnceihnda yusku kwi com we   'The woman will buy a red book'
     kwil'a yonom ndee meisa   'The men are making three tables'
     macei'na kwi tyocho com t'ma   'A boy is reading the big book'

E The structural analysis of a basic English sentence (NP V NP) is often
   described as Subject Verb Object or *SVO*. The basic sentence order in
   Gaelic (V NP NP) is described as Verb Subject Object or *VSO*. After
   looking at the following examples, how would you describe the basic
   sentence order in Japanese? Are there any other differences you can
   note between the structures of English and Japanese?

(1) *Jakku-ga   gokkoo-e   ikimasu*
    Jack   school to   go
    ('Jack goes to school')

(2) *Jakku-ga   gakkoo-de   eigo-o   naratte   imasu*
    Jack   school at   English learn   be
    ('Jack is learning English at school')

(3) *Jakku-ga   tegami-o   kakimasu*
    Jack   letter   write
    ('Jack writes a letter')

(4) *Jakku-ga   shinbun-o   yomimasu*
    Jack   newspaper   read
    ('Jack reads a newspaper')

(5) *kore-ga   Jakku-ga   tateta   uchi   desu*
    this   Jack   built   house is
    ('This is the house that Jack built')

Further reading

There are many reference grammars for contemporary English, notably Quirk
et al. (1985), or in a shorter version, Leech & Svartvik (1994). Others are
Alexander (1988), Frank (1993) and Sinclair (1990). Coursebooks on English
grammar include Downing & Locke (1992), Givon (1993), and Jacobs (1995).
Other frequently consulted texts on grammatical categories are Atkinson *et al.*
(1988), Huddleston (1984; 1988), Jespersen (1924), Lyons (1968), Palmer
(1983) and Robins (1980). Hurford (1994) is a useful resource on grammatical
terminology. A really clear treatment of constituent structure is available in
Brown & Miller (1991), which can also be consulted on Gaelic sentence structure. Fuller discussion of the parts of speech can be found in Jackson (1985).
For a comprehensive work on grammatical gender, see Corbett (1991) and on
grammatical voice, see Klaiman (1991). On prescriptive grammar, see Bolinger
(1980), Bryson (1990) and Chapter 15 of Lakoff (1990). Pedagogical grammar,

particularly in connection with teaching English as a second language, is represented in Celce-Murcia & Larsen-Freeman (1983) and Rutherford (1987). On the need for a different approach to the grammatical description of North American Indian languages, go back to the introduction in Boas (1911).

10 Syntax

After a lecture on cosmology and the structure of the solar system, William James was accosted by a little old lady who told him that his view of the earth rotating round the sun was wrong.

"I've got a better theory," said the little old lady.

"And what is that, madam?" inquired James politely.

"That we live on a crust of earth which is on the back of a giant turtle."

"If your theory is correct, madam,' he asked, "what does this turtle stand on?"

"You're a very clever man, Mr. James, and that's a very good question," replied the little old lady, "but I have an answer to it. And it's this: the first turtle stands on the back of a second, far larger, turtle, who stands directly under him."

"But what does this second turtle stand on?" persisted James patiently.

To this, the little old lady crowed triumphantly, "It's no use, Mr. James, it's turtles all the way down."

Adapted from J. R. Ross (1967)

In the course of the preceding chapter, we moved from a consideration of general grammatical categories and relations to specific methods of describing the structure of phrases and sentences. If we concentrate on the structure and ordering of components within a sentence, we are studying what is technically known as the **syntax** of a language. The word 'syntax' came originally from Greek and literally meant 'a setting out together' or 'arrangement'. In earlier approaches to the description of syntax, as we saw in Chapter 9, there was an attempt to produce an accurate analysis of the sequence or the ordering 'arrangement' of elements in the linear structure of the sentence. While this remains a major goal of syntactic description, more recent work in syntax has taken a rather different approach in accounting for the 'arrangements' we observe in the structure of sentences.

Generative grammar

Since the 1950s, particularly developing from the work of the American linguist Noam Chomsky, there have been attempts to produce a particular type of grammar which would have a very explicit system of rules specifying what combinations of basic elements would result in well-formed sentences. (Let us emphasize the word "attempts" here, since no fully worked-out grammar of this or any other type yet exists.) This explicit system of rules, it was proposed, would have much in common with the types of rules found in mathematics. Indeed, a definitive early statement in Chomsky's first major work betrays this essentially mathematical view of language: "I will consider a language to be a set (finite or infinite) of sentences" (Chomsky, 1957: 13).

This mathematical point of view helps to explain the meaning of the term **generative**, which is used to describe this type of grammar. If you have an algebraic expression like $3x + 2y$, and you can give x and y the value of any whole number, then that simple algebraic expression can **generate** an endless set of values, by following the simple rules of arithmetic. When $x = 5$ and $y = 10$, the result is 35. When $x = 2$ and $y = l$, the result is 8. These results will follow directly from applying the explicit rules. The endless set of such results is 'generated' by the operation of the explicitly formalized rules. If the sentences of a language can be seen as a comparable set, then there must be a set of explicit rules which yield those sentences. Such a set of explicit rules is a **generative grammar**.

Some properties of the grammar

A grammar of this type must have a number of properties, which can be described in the following terms. The grammar will generate all the well-formed syntactic structures (e.g. sentences) of the language and fail to generate any ill-formed structures. This is the 'all and only' criterion (i.e. *all* the grammatical sentences and *only* the grammatical sentences).

The grammar will have a finite (i.e. limited) number of rules, but will be capable of generating an infinite number of well-formed structures. In this way, the productivity of language (i.e. the creation of totally novel, yet grammatical, sentences) would be captured within the grammar.

The rules of this grammar will also need the crucial property of **recursion**, that is, the capacity to be applied more than once in generating a structure. For example, whatever rule yields the component *that chased the cat* in the sentence *This is the dog that chased the cat*, will have to be applied again to get *that killed the rat* and any other similar structure which could continue the sentence *This is the dog that chased the cat that killed the rat ... .*

You can do the same recursive thing with phrases specifying a location, beginning with *The book was on the table*. This sentence tells us where the book was. Where was the table? *Near the window*? Okay, where was the window? *In the hallway*? Okay. Putting this type of recursive effect into a single sentence will lead us to: *The book was on the the table near the window in the hallway beside the ... .* There is, in principle, no end to the recursion which would yield ever-longer versions of this sentence, and the grammar must provide for this fact.

Basically, the grammar will have to capture the fact that a sentence can have another sentence inside it, or a phrase can have another phrase of the same type inside it. (Recursion is not only to be found in descriptions of sentence structure. It is an essential part of the little old lady's view of the role of turtles in cosmic structure, as quoted at the beginning of this chapter.)

This grammar should also be capable of revealing the basis of two other phenomena: first, how some superficially distinct sentences are closely related, and second, how some superficially similar sentences are in fact distinct. We need some exemplification for these points.

Deep and surface structure

Two superficially distinct sentence structures would be, for example, *Charlie broke the window* and *The window was broken by Charlie*. In traditional terminology, the first is an active sentence and the second is passive. The distinction between them, it can be claimed, is a difference in their **surface structure**, that is, the syntactic form they take as actual English sentences. However, this difference in superficial form disguises the fact that the two sentences are very closely related, even identical, at some less 'superficial' level. This other 'underlying' level, where the basic components shared by the two sentences would be represented, has been called their **deep structure**. The deep structure is an abstract level of structural organization in which all the elements determining structural interpretation are represented. So, the grammar must be capable of showing how a single underlying abstract representation can become different surface structures.

Structural ambiguity

On the second point noted above, let us say that we had two distinct deep structures expressing, on the one hand, the fact that 'Annie had an umbrella and she whacked a man with it'; and, on the other hand, that 'Annie whacked a man and the man happened to be carrying an umbrella.' Now, these two different concepts can, in fact, be expressed in the same surface structure form: *Annie whacked a man with an umbrella.* This sentence is structurally ambiguous. It has two different underlying interpretations which would be represented differently in the deep structure.

Groucho Marx knew how to have fun with structural ambiguity. In the film 'Animal Crackers', he first says *One morning I shot an elephant in my pyjamas*, then follows it with *How he got into my pyjamas I'll never know.* In the non-funny interpretation, the structural unit *in my pyjamas* is an addition, attached to the end of the structural unit *I once shot an elephant.* In the alternative (ho, ho) interpretation, the structural unit *an elephant in my pyjamas* is a necessary internal part of a structure that would otherwise be incomplete, *I once shot … .*

Phrases can also be structurally ambiguous, as when you come across an expression like *old men and women.* The underlying interpretation can be either *old men* plus *old women* or *old men* plus *women* (no age specified). The grammar will have to be capable of showing the structural distinction between these underlying representations.

Different approaches

We have considered some of the requirements which would have to be met by a complete syntactic description of a language. However, this area of linguistic investigation is notorious for giving rise to very different approaches to producing that description. For some, the only relevant issues are syntactic ones, that is, how to describe structure, independently of 'meaning' considerations. For others, the 'meaning component' is primary. In some later versions of generative grammar, the level of deep structure is essentially taken over by a 'meaning' or semantic interpretation which is assigned a structural or syntactic form in its surface realization. (We shall explore 'meaning' issues in Chapters 11 and 12.)

Unfortunately, almost everything involved in the analysis of generative grammar remains controversial. There continue to be many different approaches among those who claim to analyze language in terms of generative grammar, and many more among those who are critical of the whole system. Rather than explore controversies, let us look at some of the really basic features of the original analytic approach and see how it is all supposed to work. First, we need to get the symbols straightened out.

Symbols used in syntactic description

We have already introduced some symbols (in Chapter 9) which are quite easily understood as abbreviations for the grammatical categories involved. Examples are 'S' (= sentence), 'N' (= noun), 'Art' (= article) and so on. We need to introduce three more symbols which are commonly used.

The first of these is in the form of an arrow →, and it can be interpreted as 'consists of'. It will typically occur in the following format:

NP → Art N

This is simply a shorthand way of saying that a noun phrase (e.g. *the book*) consists of an article (*the*) and a noun (*book*).

The second symbol used is in the form of parentheses, or round brackets – ( ). Whatever occurs inside these brackets will be treated as an optional constituent. Perhaps an example will make this clear. You can describe an object as *the book*, or as *the green book*. We can say that both *the book* and *the green book* are examples of the category, noun phrase. In order for a noun phrase to occur in English, you may require an article (*the*) and a noun (*book*), but the inclusion of an adjective (*green*) is optional. You can include an adjective, but it isn't obligatory. We can capture this aspect of English syntax in the following way:

NP → Art (Adj) N

This shorthand notation expresses the idea that a noun phrase consists of an obligatory article and an obligatory noun, but may also include an adjective in a specific position. The adjective is optional.

The third symbol used is in the form of braces, or curly brackets – { }. These indicate that only one of the elements enclosed within the brackets must be selected. They are used when there is a choice from two or more constituents. For example, we have already noted, in Chapter 9, that a noun phrase can consist of an expression like *the woman* (Art N), or *she* (pronoun), or *Cathy* (proper noun). We can, of course, write three single rules, as shown on the left below, but it is more succinct to write one rule, as shown on the right below, which incorporates exactly the same information:

NP → Art N
NP → pronoun   NP → { Art N
NP → proper noun   pronoun
                                proper noun }

It is important to remember that, although there are three constituents in these curly brackets, only one of them can be selected on any occasion.

We can now present a list of symbols and abbreviations commonly found in syntactic descriptions:

S	sentence	N	noun	Pro	pronoun
PN	proper noun	V	verb	Adj	adjective
Art	article	Adv	adverb	Prep	preposition
NP	noun phrase	VP	verb phrase	PP	prepositional phrase

* = 'ungrammatical sequence'

→ = 'consists of'

( ) = 'optional constituent'

{ } = 'one and only one of these constituents must be selected'

Labeled tree diagrams

In Chapter 9, we considered ways of describing the structure of sentences that (basically) concentrated on the linear sequence of constituents. It is, of course, possible to show the same sequence as, in a more explicit way, 'hierarchically' organized. So, to bring out the hierarchical organization of the labeled and bracketed constituents shown on the left below, we can show the same information in the form of a **tree diagram**, as on the right below:

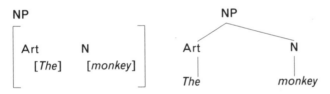

This type of tree-diagram representation contains all the grammatical information found in the other analyses, but also shows more explicitly the fact that there are different levels in the analysis. That is, there is a level of analysis at which a constituent such as NP is represented and a different, lower level at which a constituent such as N is represented. Here's how a whole sentence would look in a tree diagram:

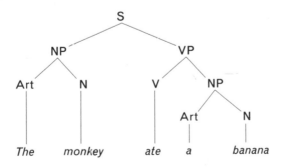

If you start at the top of this tree diagram, you are starting with a sentence (**S**) and then dividing the sentence into two constituents (**NP** and **VP**). In turn, the **NP** constituent is divided into two constituents (**Art** and **N**). Finally, one word is selected which fits the label **Art** (*the*), and another which fits **N** (*monkey*).

Phrase structure rules

We can view this tree-diagram format in two different ways. In one way, we can simply treat it as a static representation of the structure of the sentence at the bottom of the diagram. We could propose that, for every single sentence in English, a tree diagram of this type could be drawn. The alternative view is to treat the diagram as a 'dynamic' format, in the sense that it represents a way of 'generating' not only that one sentence, but a very large number of sentences with similar structures. This alternative view is very appealing since it should enable us to generate a large number of sentences with only a small number of rules. These 'rules' are usually called **phrase structure** rules, and they present the information of the tree diagram in an alternative format. So, instead of the diagram form on the left below, we can use the notation shown on the right below:

The rule is then read as: "a sentence consists of a noun phrase followed by a verb phrase". In addition to rules of this type which generate structures, we can also have **lexical** rules which indicate the words to be used for constituents such as N. For example:

N → {*boy, girl, dog,...*}

This means that N is rewritten as *boy*, or *girl*, or *dog*. We can create a set of extremely simple (and necessarily incomplete) phrase structure rules which can be used to generate a large number of English sentences:

S → NP VP

NP → { Art (Adj) N / PN }

VP → V NP (PP) (Adv)

PP → Prep NP

N → {*boy, girl, dog*} V → {*saw, followed, helped*}
PN → {*George, Mary*} Prep → {*with, near*}
Art → {*a, the*} Adv → {*yesterday, recently*}
Adj → {*small, crazy*}

These rules will generate the grammatical sentences shown below as (1) to (7), but will not yield the ungrammatical sentences shown as (8) to (10):

1. The girl followed the boy.
2. A boy helped the dog.
3. The dog saw a girl.
4. Mary helped George recently.
5. George saw a dog yesterday.
6. A small dog followed Mary.
7. The small boy saw George with a crazy dog recently.
8. *Boy the Mary saw.
9. *Helped a girl.
10. *Small dog with girl.

This small set of rules is a good start on creating a phrase structure grammar of English, but we still have not incorporated recursion.

Back to recursion

The phrase structure rules, as presented, have no recursive elements. Each time we rewrote a symbol from the left, we did not include that symbol on the right side of any arrow. We have to be able to repeat some symbols on the right side of the arrow. That is the essence of recursion. We need, for example, to have sentences included within other sentences. We know that *Mary helped George* is a sentence. We also know that *Cathy thought Mary helped George* is a sentence. And, being tediously recursive, we know that *John said Cathy thought Mary helped George* is a sentence.

In order to capture these structures in our rules, we need to add V → {*said, thought*} and PN → {*Cathy, John*} to our lexical rules. We also need to add a crucial recursive rule that says: VP → V S. With these minor additions, we can now represent the structure of a more complex sentence.

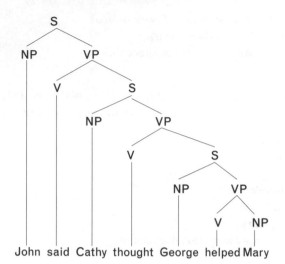

In principle, there is no end to the recursion of sentence structures of this type in the English language and our rule (VP → V S) represents that fact.

Transformational rules

One other feature of our phrase structure rules is that they will generate all sentences with fairly fixed word order to the constituents. For example, adverbs will always come at the end of their sentences if we follow the rules we have just illustrated. That is fine for generating the first sentence below, but how would we get the second sentence?

(i) *George helped Mary yesterday.*

(ii) *Yesterday George helped Mary.*

We can think of the *yesterday* element as having been 'moved' to the beginning of the sentence in (ii). In order to do this, we need a set of rules which will change or move constituents in the structures derived from the phrase structure rules. These are called **transformational** rules. Essentially what they do is take a 'branch' of the 'tree' away from one part of the tree diagram, and attach it to a different part. Here is an example of a movement transformation:

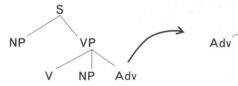

(George helped Mary yesterday)   *(Yesterday George helped Mary)*

We would, of course, specify which constituents can be moved, from where and to where.

One of the best arguments for having transformational rules involves what seems to be the movement of a very small element in English sentence structure. We recognize that the following two sentences have a great deal in common:

(i) *Doobie picked up the magazine.*

(ii) *Doobie picked the magazine up.*

These sentences contain a verb-particle construction (verb = *pick*; particle = *up*) which can be symbolized as: V → Vb part. It is clear that the particle can be separated from the verb and 'moved' to the end of the sentence. A constituent structure analysis, as described in Chapter 9, would have some difficulty accommodating this type of structure. A phrase structure analysis would have to create two distinct tree diagrams. Yet, we intuitively recognize that these two sentences must come from a single underlying source.

Let us propose a single tree diagram source which produces a string of elements like: *NP Verb Particle NP*. Under circumstances like these, let us then propose the optional transformation called 'Particle Movement',

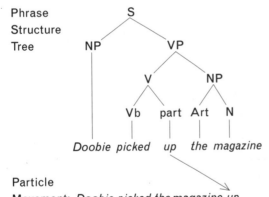

which takes that structural description and yields the structural change to: *NP Verb NP Particle*.

By using this simple transformational rule, we have provided the means for explicitly relating the two structures in sentences (i) and (ii) above as 'surface' variations of a single underlying structure. It may not seem much, but this type of transformational analysis solved a number of tricky problems for previous syntactic descriptions.

There is, of course, much more involved in generative syntax and other methods of syntactic description. (We have barely scratched the surface structures.) However, having explored some of the basic issues in the syntactic description of language, we must move on, as historically the generative linguists had to do, to come to terms with the place of 'meaning' in linguistic description. This leads us, in the following chapter, to a consideration of the role of semantics.

Study questions

1   In what ways are these expressions 'ambiguous'?

   (a) *An American history teacher.*
   (b) *Flying planes can be dangerous.*
   (c) *The parents of the bride and the groom were waiting.*

2   Can you provide four, 'superficially distinct' sentences which would each have the same 'underlying' structure as one of the following sentences?

   (a) *Lara was arrested by the police.*
   (b) *She took her coat off.*
   (c) *Someone stole my bicycle.*
   (d) *I told him to turn down the volume.*

3   Which of the following expressions would be generated by this phrase structure rule: NP → Art (Adj) N?

   (a) *a radio*   (c) *a new student*
   (b) *the rusty car*   (d) *the screwdriver*

4   Which of the following structures can be changed via the Particle Movement transformation?

   (a) *He put down his glass.*
   (b) *She threw away her dress.*
   (c) *He pulled off his shirt.*
   (d) *They jumped in the pool.*

5   Using the phrase structure rules presented in this chapter, you should be able to complete these labeled tree diagrams.

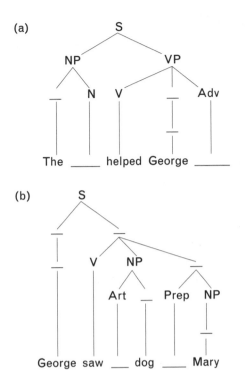

(a)

(b)

Discussion topics/projects

A Here are some simple phrase structure rules for Scottish Gaelic:

S → V NP NP   NP → { Art N (Adj) }
                      { PN   }

Art → *an*
N → {*cu, gille*}   Adj → {*beag, mor*}
PN → {*Tearlach, Calum*}   V → {*chunnaic, bhuail*}

Only two of the following sentences would be considered well-formed, according to the rules above. First, identify the ill-formed sentences, using the symbol *, then provide labeled tree diagrams for the two well-formed sentences.

1 *Calum chunnaic an gille*   3 *Bhuail an beag cu*
2 *Bhuail an gille mor an cu*   4 *Chunnaic Tearlach an gille*

B Here is a simplified set of phrase structure rules for a language called Ewe, spoken in parts of West Africa. Can you use these rules to write out four different well-formed Ewe sentences? (Note that the syntax of Ewe is different from the syntax of English.)

$$S \rightarrow NP\, VP \qquad N \rightarrow \{oge, ika, amu\}$$
$$NP \rightarrow N\, (Art) \qquad Art \rightarrow ye$$
$$VP \rightarrow V\, NP \qquad V \rightarrow \{xa, vo\}$$

C In the chapter we considered one transformational rule which was used for particle movement. Here is a simple version of the passive transformation rule:

Structural Description: NP_1 V NP_2
Structural Change: $\Rightarrow NP_2\, be\, V\text{-}ed\, by\, NP_1$

(Let us add that the tense, past or present, of the verb (V) in the structural description will determine the tense of the verb (*be*) in the structural change. Also, the symbol $\Rightarrow$ is used for transformations.) This transformational rule will produce passive versions of a number of the following sentences. First, identify those sentences for which the rule works, and then try to describe what prevents the rule from working on the other sentences.

(1) The cats chased the mouse
(2) SnowWhite kissed Grumpy
(3) He loves them
(4) Betsy borrowed some money from Jim
(5) The team played badly
(6) The tree fell with a crash
(7) The bank manager laughed
(8) The duckling became a swan

D Each of the following sentences ends with what is called a 'tag question'. For this set of sentences, the process of forming the tag question seems very regular.

(i) Can you produce a simple transformational rule which could be used to add tag questions to basic sentence structures?

(1) She was a dancer, wasn't she?
(2) Zee is a good swimmer, isn't he?
(3) You are ready, aren't you?
(4) They can come, can't they?
(5) Maghna would help, wouldn't she?
(6) You have eaten, haven't you?

(ii) Now, how would you go about making that transformational rule apply for these two sentences?

(7) He smokes a lot, doesn't he?

(8) They arrived early, didn't they?

E There is a principle of syntax called 'structure dependency' that is often used to show that the rules of language depend on hierarchical structure and not on linear position. For example, a young child learning English might be tempted to think that questions of the type in (1) and (2) are formed by moving the second word of the statement to the first position of the question.

(1) a. *Scruffy is tired*   (2) a. *You will help him*
    b. *Is Scruffy tired?*   b. *Will you help him?*

Using the sentences in (1) – (6), try to decide if this 'linear position' rule would be good for forming these English questions and, if not, what would be a better rule?

(3) *Are the exercises in this book too easy?*

(4) *Is the cat that is missing called Blackie?*

(5) *Will the cost of the new book you've ordered be outrageous?*

(6) *Was the guy who scored the winning goal in the final playing for love or money?*

Further reading

All introductory textbooks in linguistics have a section on syntax: try Chapter 3 of Fromkin & Rodman (1993), Chapter 5 of Akmajian *et al.* (1990), or Chapter 5 of O'Grady *et al.* (1993). Lasnik (1990) is a brief review. For more detailed introductory treatments, try Brown & Miller (1991) or Morenberg (1991). Among the other (more advanced) texts on syntax are Borsley (1991), Burton-Roberts (1986), Matthews (1981), McCawley (1988), Sells (1985) and Wekker & Haegeman (1985). A useful reference work is Stockwell *et al.* (1973). For a more functional approach to syntax, see Givon (1990). A good overview of Chomsky's early work is Lyons (1991), or, for selections from Chomsky's early publications, try Allen & van Buren (1971). The basic original works are Chomsky (1957; 1965), with Chomsky (1988) providing a fairly accessible account of his later views. On matters transformational, try Akmajian & Heny (1975), Huddleston (1976) or the widely used textbook by Radford (1988). More recent work in generative syntax is presented in Cook (1988), Freidin (1992), Riemsdijk & Williams (1986) and Haegeman (1991).

11 Semantics 語義學

I once referred to a character in one of my cartoons as a "dork" (a popular insult when I was growing up), but my editor called me up and said that "dork" couldn't be used because it meant "penis." I couldn't believe it. I ran to my New Dictionary of American Slang and, sure enough, he was right. All those years of saying or being called a "dork" and I had never really known what it meant. What a nerd.

Gary Larson (1989)

Semantics is the study of the meaning of words, phrases and sentences. In semantic analysis, there is always an attempt to focus on what the words conventionally mean, rather than on what a speaker might want the words to mean on a particular occasion. This technical approach to meaning emphasizes the objective and the general. It avoids the subjective and the local. Linguistic **semantics** deals with the conventional meaning conveyed by the use of words and sentences of a language.

Conceptual versus associative meaning

When linguists investigate the meaning of words in a language, they are normally interested in characterizing the **conceptual** meaning and less concerned with the **associative** or stylistic meaning of words. Conceptual meaning covers those basic, essential components of meaning which are conveyed by the literal use of a word. Some of the basic components of a word like *needle* in English might include 'thin, sharp, steel, instrument'. These components would be part of the conceptual meaning of *needle*. However, you may have 'associations', or 'connotations', attached to a word like *needle* which lead you to think of 'painful' whenever you encounter the word. This 'association' is not treated as part of the conceptual meaning of *needle*. In a similar way, you may associate the expression *low-calorie*, when used to describe a product, with 'good for you', but we would not want to include this association within the basic conceptual meaning of the expression. Poets and advertisers are, of course, very interested in using terms in such a way that their associative meanings are evoked, and some linguists do investigate this aspect of language use. However, in this chapter we shall be more interested in characterizing what constitutes the conceptual meaning of terms.

Semantic features

So, how would a semantic approach help us to understand something about the nature of language? One way it might be helpful would be as a means of accounting for the 'oddness' we experience when we read English sentences such as the following:

> *The hamburger ate the man*
> *My cat studied linguistics*
> *A table was listening to some music*

Notice that the oddness of these sentences does not derive from their syntactic structure. According to some basic syntactic rules for forming English sentences (such as those presented in Chapter 10), we have well-structured sentences:

The hamburger	ate	the man
NP	V	NP

This sentence is syntactically good, but semantically odd. Since the sentence *The man ate the hamburger* is perfectly acceptable, what is the source of the oddness we experience? One answer may relate to the components of the conceptual meaning of the noun *hamburger* which differ significantly from those of the noun *man* , especially when those nouns are used as subjects of the verb *ate*. The kinds of nouns which can be subjects of the verb *ate* must denote entities which are capable of 'eating'. The noun *hamburger* does not have this property (and *man* does), hence the oddness of the first sentence above.

We can, in fact, make this observation more generally applicable by trying to determine the crucial component of meaning which a noun must have in order to be used as the subject of the verb *ate*. Such a component may be as general as 'animate being'. We can then take this component and use it to describe part of the meaning of words as either plus (+) or minus (–) the feature. So, the feature becomes +*animate* (= denotes an animate being) or –*animate* (= does not denote an animate being).

This procedure is a way of analyzing meaning in terms of **semantic features**. Features such as +*animate*, –*animate*; +*human*, –*human*; + *male*, –*male*, for example, can be treated as the basic features involved in differentiating the meanings of each word in the language from every other word. If you were asked to give the crucial distinguishing features of the meanings of this set of English words (*table, cow, girl, woman, boy, man*), you could do so by means of the following diagram:

	table	cow	girl	woman	boy	man
animate	–	+	+	+	+	+
human	–	–	+	+	+	+
male	–	–	–	–	+	+
adult	–	+	–	+	–	+

From a feature analysis like this, you can say that at least part of the basic meaning of the word *boy* in English involves the components (+*human*, +*male*, –*adult*). You can also characterize that feature which is crucially required in a noun in order for it to appear as the subject of a verb, supplementing the syntactic analysis with semantic features:

The _____ is reading a book.
　　N (+*human*)

This approach then gives us the ability to predict what nouns would make the above sentence semantically odd. Examples would be *table*, or *tree*, or *dog*, because they all have the feature (–*human*).

The approach which has just been outlined is not without problems. For many words in a language it may not be so easy to come up with neat components of meaning. If you try to think of which components or features you would use to distinguish the nouns *advice, threat* and *warning*, for example, you will have some idea of the scope of the problem. Part of the problem seems to be that the approach involves a view of words in a language as some sort of 'containers', carrying meaning-components.

Semantic roles

Instead of thinking of the words as 'containers' of meaning, we can look at the 'roles' they fulfill within the situation described by a sentence. If the situation is a simple event, such as *The boy kicked the ball*, then the verb describes an action (*kick*). The noun phrases describe the roles of entities, such as people and things, involved in the action. We can identify a small number of **semantic roles** for these noun phrases.

Agent, theme, instrument

In the sentence above, one role is taken by *the boy* as 'the entity that performs the action', techically known as the **agent**. Another role is taken by *the ball* , as 'the entity that is involved in or affected by the action', technically known as the **theme**. The theme can also be an entity (*the ball*) that is simply being described, as in *The ball was red*. Identifying entities denoted by noun phrases as the agent or the theme is a way of recognizing the semantic roles of those noun phrases in a sentence.

Although agents are typically human, they can also be non-human forces (*the wind blew the ball away*), machines (*the car ran over the ball*), or creatures (*the dog caught the ball*). If an agent uses another entity in performing an action, that other entity fills the role of **instrument**. In *writing with a pen* or *eating with a spoon* , the noun phrases *a pen* and *a spoon* have the semantic role of instrument.

The theme can also be human. Indeed, the same physical entity can appear in two different semantic roles, as in *The boy kicked himself*. Here *the boy* is agent and *himself* is theme.

Experiencer, location, source, goal

When a noun phrase designates an entity as the person who has a feeling, a perception or a state, it fills the role of **experiencer**. If you see, know or enjoy something, you do not really have to perform any action (hence you are not an agent). You are in the role of experiencer. If someone asks, *Did you hear that noise?*, the experiencer is *you* and the theme is *that noise*.

A number of other semantic roles designate where an entity is in the description of the event. Where an entity is (*on the table, in the room*) fills the role of **location**. Where an entity moves from is the **source** and where it moves to is the **goal**. When we talk about transferring money *from savings to checking*, the source is *savings* and the goal is *checking*. All these semantic roles are illustrated in the following scenario.

Mary   saw   a mosquito   on the wall.
EXPERIENCER   THEME   LOCATION

She   borrowed a magazine   from George
AGENT   THEME   SOURCE

and she   hit the bug   with the magazine.
AGENT   THEME   INSTRUMENT

She   handed the magazine back to George.
AGENT   THEME   GOAL

"Gee thanks," said George.
                AGENT

Lexical relations

Not only can words be treated as 'containers' or as fulfilling 'roles', they can also have 'relationships'. In everyday talk, we frequently give the meanings of words in terms of their relationships. If you were asked to give the meaning of the word *conceal,* for example, you might simply reply "it's the same as *hide*", or give the meaning of *shallow* as "the opposite of *deep*", or the meaning of *daffodil* as "it's a kind of *flower*". In doing so, you are characterizing the meaning of a word not in terms of its component features, but in terms of its relationship to other words. This procedure has also been used in the semantic description of languages and is treated as the analysis of **lexical relations**. The types of lexical relations which are usually analyzed are defined and exemplified in the following sections.

Synonymy

Synonyms are two or more forms with very closely related meanings, which are often, but not always, intersubstitutable in sentences. Examples of synonyms are the pairs *broad – wide, hide – conceal, almost – nearly, cab – taxi, liberty – freedom, answer – reply.*

It should be noted that the idea of 'sameness of meaning' used in discussing synonymy is not necessarily 'total sameness'. There are many occasions when one word is appropriate in a sentence, but its synonym would be odd. For example, whereas the word *answer* fits in this sentence: *Cathy had only one answer correct on the test*, its near-synonym, *reply*, would sound odd. Synonymous forms may also differ in terms of formality. The sentence *My father purchased a large automobile* seems much more serious than the following casual version, with four synonymous replacements: *My dad bought a big car.*

Antonymy

Two forms with opposite meanings are called **antonyms**, and commonly used examples are the pairs *quick – slow, big – small, long – short, rich – poor, happy – sad, hot – cold, old – young, male – female, true – false, alive – dead.*

Antonyms are usually divided into two main types, those which are 'gradable', and those which are 'non-gradable'. **Gradable antonyms**, such as the pair *big – small*, can be used in comparative constructions like *bigger than – smaller than*. Also, the negative of one member of the gradable pair does not necessarily imply the other. For example, if you say *that dog is not old*, you do not have to mean *that dog is young*. With **non-gradable antonyms**, also called 'complementary pairs', comparative constructions are not normally used (the expressions *deader* or *more dead* sound strange), and the negative of one member does imply the other. For example, *that person is not dead* does indeed mean *that person is alive*. So, the pairs *male – female* and *true – false* must also be non-gradable antonyms, whereas the others in the list above are gradable.

Although it works for the small number of non-gradable antonyms in a language, it is important to avoid describing most antonym pairs as one word meaning the negative of another. Consider the opposites *tie – untie*. The word *untie* doesn't mean 'not tie'. It actually means 'do the reverse of tie'. Such pairs are called **reversives**. Other common examples are *enter – exit*, *pack – unpack*, *lengthen – shorten*, *raise – lower*, and *dress – undress*.

Hyponymy

When the meaning of one form is included in the meaning of another, the relationship is described as **hyponymy**, and some typical example pairs are *daffodil – flower*, *dog – animal*, *poodle – dog*, *carrot – vegetable*, *banyan – tree*. The concept of 'inclusion' involved here is the idea that if any object is a *daffodil*, then it is necessarily a *flower*, so the meaning of *flower* is 'included' in the meaning of *daffodil*. Or, *daffodil* is a hyponym of *flower*.

When we consider hyponymous relations, we are essentially looking at the meaning of words in some type of hierarchical relationship. You could, in fact, represent the relationships between a set of words such as *animal*, *ant*, *asp*, *banyan*, *carrot*, *cockroach*, *creature*, *daffodil*, *dog*, *flower*, *horse*, *insect*, *living things*, *pine*, *plant*, *snake*, *tree* and *vegetable* as a hierarchical diagram in the following way:

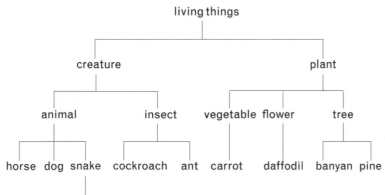

From this diagram, we can say that "*horse* is a hyponym of *animal*" or that '*ant* is a hyponym of *insect*'. We can also say that two or more terms which share the same superordinate (higher-up) term are **co-hyponyms**. So, *horse* and *dog* are co-hyponyms, and the superordinate term is *animal*.

The relation of hyponymy captures the idea of 'is a kind of', as when you give the meaning of a word by saying "an *asp* is a kind of *snake*". It is often the case that the only thing some people know about the meaning of a word in their language is that it is a hyponym of another term. That is, you may know nothing more about the meaning of *asp* other than that it is a kind of *snake*.

It is worth emphasizing that it is not only words for 'things' that are hyponyms. Terms for actions, such as *cut*, *punch*, *shoot* and *stab*, can all be found as co-hyponyms of the superordinate term *injure*.

Prototypes

While the words *canary*, *dove*, *duck*, *flamingo*, *parrot*, *pelican*, *robin*, *swallow* and *thrush* are all equally co-hyponyms of the superordinate *bird*, they are not all considered to be equally good exemplars of the category 'bird'. For many American English speakers, the best exemplar, or the **prototype**, of 'bird' is the robin. The concept of a prototype helps explain the meaning of certain words, like *bird*, not in terms of component features (e.g. 'has feathers', 'has wings'), but in terms of resemblance to the clearest exemplar. Thus, even native speakers of English might wonder if *ostrich* and *penguin* should be hyponyms of *bird* (technically, they are), but have no trouble deciding about *sparrow* or *pigeon*. The last two are much closer to the prototype.

Given the category label *furniture*, we are quicker to recognize *chair* as an exemplar than *bench* or *stool*. Given *clothing*, people recognize *shirts* quicker than *shoes*, and given *vegetable*, they accept *carrot* before *potato* or *tomato*. It is obvious that there is some general pattern to the categorization process involved in prototypes and that it determines our interpretation of word meaning. However, this is one area where individual experience results in variation in interpretation, as when people disagree about whether *tomato* is a fruit or a vegetable.

Homophony, homonymy and polysemy

There are three other, less well-known terms which are often used to describe relationships among words in a language. The first of these is **homophony**. When two or more different (written) forms have the same pronunciation, they are described as **homophones**. Some examples are *bare – bear, meat – meet, flour – flower, pail – pale, sew – so*.

The term **homonymy** is used when one form (written and spoken) has two or more unrelated meanings. Examples of **homonyms** are the pairs *bank* (of a river) – *bank* (financial institution), *bat* (flying creature) – *bat* (used in sports), *race* (contest of speed) – *race* (ethnic group), *pupil* (at school) – *pupil* (in the eye) and *mole* (on skin) – *mole* (small animal). The temptation is to think that the two types of *bank* must be related in meaning. They are not. Homonyms are words which have quite separate meanings, but which have accidentally come to have exactly the same form.

Relatedness of meaning accompanying identical form is technically known as **polysemy**, which can be defined as one form (written or spoken) having multiple meanings which are all related by extension. Examples are the word *head*, used to refer to the object on top of your body, on top of a glass of beer, on top of a company or department; or *foot* (of person, of bed, of mountain), or *run* (person does, water does, colors do).

The distinction between homonymy and polysemy is not always clear cut. However, one indication of the distinction can be found in the typical dictionary entry for words. If a word has multiple meanings (polysemic), then there will be a single entry, with a numbered list of the different meanings of the word. If two words are treated as homonyms, they will typically have two separate entries. You could check in your dictionary and probably find that the different meanings of words like *head, get, run, face* and *foot* are treated as examples of polysemy, whereas *mail, bank, sole* and *mole* are treated as examples of homonymy.

Of course, one form can be distinguished via homonymy, then shown to have various uses via polysemy. The words *date* (= oblong, fleshy fruit) and *date* (= point in time) are homonyms. But the 'point in time' kind of *date* is polysemous in terms of a particular day and month (= on a letter), an arranged meeting time (= an appointment), a social meeting (= with someone of the opposite sex) and even a person (= that someone of the opposite sex). The question *How about a date?* could have many interpretations.

These last three lexical relations are, of course, the basis of a lot of wordplay, particularly used for humorous effect. In the nursery rhyme, *Mary had a little lamb*, we think of a small animal, but in the comic version of *Mary had a little lamb, some rice and vegetables*, we tend to think, instead, of a small amount of meat. The polysemy of *lamb* allows the two interpretations. The Pillsbury Flour Company once took advantage of homophony to promote a brand of flour with the slogan *Everybody kneads it*. If you are asked the following riddle: *What's black and white and red all over?*, you may initially be confused by the answer: *a newspaper*. The trick depends on the homophony of *red* and *read*. And if you have come across this riddle: *Why are trees often mistaken for dogs?*, then you will have encountered the use of homonymy in the answer: *Because of their bark*.

Metonymy

The relatedness of meaning found in polysemy is essentially based on similarity. The *head* of a company is similar to the *head* of a person on top of (and controlling) the body. There is another type of relationship between words, based simply on a close connection in everyday experience. That close connection can be based on a container–contents relation (*bottle – coke*; *can – juice*), a whole–part relation (*car – wheels*; *house – roof*) or a representative–symbol relationship (*king – crown*; *the President – the White House*). These are examples of **metonymy**.

It is our familiarity with metonymy that makes *He drank the whole bottle* easy to understand, although it sounds absurd literally (i.e. he drank the liquid, not the glass object). We also accept *The White House announced ...* or *Downing Street protested ...* without being puzzled that buildings appear to be talking. You use metonymy when you talk about *filling up the car*, *having a roof over your head*, *answering the door*, *giving someone a hand*, or *needing some wheels*. If you see a mail delivery company called *Spokes*, you know, via metonymy, how they are making those deliveries (i.e. by bicycle).

Many examples of metonymy are highly conventionalized and easy to interpret. However, many others depend on an ability to infer what the speaker has in mind. The metonymy in *Get your butt over here* is easier to understand if you are used to male talk in the United States, *the strings are too quiet* if you're familiar with orchestral music, and *I prefer cable*, if you have a choice in how you receive television programs (in the USA). Making sense of such expressions often depends on context, background knowledge and inference. These are all topics in the following chapter.

Collocation

One other distinct aspect of our knowledge of words has nothing to do with any of the factors considered so far. We know which words tend to occur with other words. If you ask a thousand people what they think of when you say *hammer*, more than half will say *nail*. If you say *table*, they'll mostly say *chair* and for *butter – bread*, for *needle – thread*, and for *salt – pepper*. One way we seem to organize our knowledge of words is simply in terms of **collocation**, or frequently occurring together.

Some collocations are joined pairs of words such as *salt and pepper* or *husband and wife*. However, *salt* will also make some people say *water* because of the common collocation *salt water*. And for many people in the USA, the word *red* elicits *white and blue* (the colors of the flag). It may be that part of knowing a language is knowing not only what words mean, but what their typical collocations are. Thus, part of your knowledge of *fresh* is as it occurs in the phrase *fresh air*, or *knife* as in *knife and fork* or *enough* as in *enough already*. Okay, that's enough already!

Study questions

1 What is the basic lexical relation between the following pairs of words?

   (a) *shallow deep*   (b) *mature ripe*   (c) *suite sweet*
   (d) *table furniture*   (e) *single married*   (f) *move run*

2 How would you describe the oddness of the following sentences, using semantic features?

   (a) *The television drank my water*   (b) *His dog writes poetry*

3 Identify the semantic roles of all the noun phrases in this sentence: *With his new golf club, Fred whacked the ball from the woods to the grassy area near the river and he felt good.*

4 Which of the following opposites are gradable, non-gradable, or reversive?

   (a) *absent present*   (b) *high low*   (c) *fill empty*
   (d) *fail pass*   (e) *fair unfair* (f) *appear disappear*

5 Which of the following examples are best described as polysemy or as metonymy?

   (a) *Computer **chips** are an important new technology.*
   (b) *The bookstore has some new **titles** in linguistics.*
   (c) *Yes, I love those. I ate a whole **box** on Sunday!*
   (d) *I had to park on the **shoulder** of the road.*
   (e) *The **pen** is mightier than the **sword**.*

Discussion topics/projects

A One way to identify the semantic structure of sentences is to start with the verb as the central element and define the semantic roles required by that verb. For example, a verb like *kill* requires an agent and a theme, as in *The cat killed the mouse.* We can represent this observation as:

KILL [AGENT _____ THEME].

As another example, we can represent the verb *give* as in *Mary gave the book to George*:

GIVE [AGENT _____ THEME, GOAL]

  (i) How would you define the set of semantic roles for the following verbs, as in the pattern just shown?
  break build die eat fear happen kiss like occupy offer put receive resemble send steal taste teach understand want write

  (ii) Does it help, in this exercise, to make a distinction between obligatory roles (i.e. you must have these or the sentence will not be grammatical) and optional roles (these are often present, but their absence doesn't make the sentences ungrammatical)?

B The words in the following list are all related in terms of the superordinate term *tableware*.

  (i) First, create a hierarchical diagram to illustrate whatever hyponymous relations exist among these words:
  glass cup plate cutlery napkin tumbler fork goblet teaspoon flatware bowl crockery tablecloth wineglass ladle dish saucer spoon salt-shaker knife mug candlestick bottle pan tray peppermill bread-basket linen table-mat

  (ii) Second, can you work out what the prototype item of tableware is? One research procedure would be to create a list of these terms down one side of a page, with a scale beside each term. The scale would go from 5 (= excellent example of 'tableware') to 1 (= not really an example of 'tableware'). Make copies of your list (plus scale) and ask people to indicate their choices on the scale. The highest score would presumably be the prototype. What do you think of this procedure?

C A famous example of a sentence that is syntactically 'good', but semantically 'odd', was suggested by Noam Chomsky (1957): *Colorless green ideas sleep furiously*. How many mismatches of meaning are present in this one sentence? Can it be interpreted at all? Having done that, what do you make of this advertisement from an American store: *Colorful white sale this week?*

D In the use of gradable antonyms there is generally one member of the pair that is used more often than the other in certain constructions. It is called the 'unmarked' member. For example, we usually ask *How old is he?* if we want to know someone's age, and not *How young is he?* This is taken as evidence that *old* is the unmarked member of the *old–young* pair. Additional evidence is the common practice of saying that someone is *five years old* and not *five years young* in talking about age.

   (i) Can you determine the 'unmarked' member in each of the following pairs?
   small–big short–long wild–tame cheap–expensive
   near–far many–few early–late dangerous–safe
   good–bad fresh–stale easy–difficult strong–weak
   thick–thin wide–narrow full–empty

   (ii) Can you think of any special situations where the 'marked' member is more typically used? What kind of meaning is conveyed by such uses?

E There is one aspect of contemporary English that seems very redundant (to some people). One example would be: *You will receive a free gift.* We might complain that if it's a *gift*, it is necessarily *free*, so it is redundant to use both words. Do you agree with this point of view? Do the following expressions also contain redundancies? Might there be a reason for such combinations?

We should provide advance warning
I'll make it my first priority
That was an unexpected surprise
Could you repeat that again?
They had already heard that before
We got it for a cheap price
There was a general consensus
It was in close proximity
And that was his final conclusion

Further reading
There is a good basic coursebook on semantics by Hurford & Heasley (1983). More general treatments are presented in Allan (1986), Palmer (1981) and Leech (1974). The latter has an extended discussion of different types of 'asso-

ciative' meaning. Semantic feature analysis can be found in Bever & Rosenbaum (1971) and Kempson (1977). An accessible review of the psychology of word meaning is presented in Miller (1991). A more complex discussion is in Jackendoff (1983). On lexical relations, see Cruse (1986) and Lipka (1990). An extended treatment of antonymy can be found in Lehrer (1985). The most comprehensive work on the subject, and hence rather technical, is Lyons (1977). Also technical, but providing introductions to the philosophical issues in semantic analysis are Chierchia & McConnel-Ginet (1990), Garfield & Kiteley (1991) and Martin (1987). An overview of semantic roles is presented in Andrews (1985) and more comprehensive surveys can be found in Cook (1989) and Palmer (1994). Discussions of prototypes are in Aitchison (1994), Lakoff (1987), Pulman (1983), Rosch (1978) and Tsohadzidis (1990). On collocation, see Sinclair (1991). The frequencies mentioned in the collocations section are from Postman & Keppel (1970).

12 Pragmatics 語用学

A: I have a fourteen year old son
B: Well that's all right
A: I also have a dog
B: Oh I'm sorry

Harvey Sacks (1992)

In the previous chapter, we concentrated on meaning in language as a product of the meaning of words. There are, however, other aspects of meaning which are not derived solely from the meanings of the words used in phrases and sentences. In making sense of the quote above, it may help to know that A is trying to rent an apartment from B. When we read or hear pieces of language, we normally try to understand not only what the words mean, but what the writer or speaker of those words intended to convey. The study of 'intended speaker meaning' is called **pragmatics**.

Invisible meaning

In many ways, pragmatics is the study of 'invisible' meaning, or how we recognize what is meant even when it isn't actually said (or written). In order for that to happen, speakers (and writers) must be able to depend on a lot of shared assumptions and expectations. The investigation of those assumptions and expectations provides us with some insights into how more gets communicated than is said.

Driving by a parking lot, you may see a large sign like the one in the picture. Now, you know what each of these words means, and you know what the sign as a whole means. However, you don't normally think that the sign is advertising a place where you can park your 'heated attendant'. (You take an attendant, you heat him up, and this is the place where you can park him.)

Alternatively, it may indicate a place where parking will be carried out by attendants who have been heated. The words may allow these interpretations, but you would normally understand that you can park your car in this place, that it's a heated area, and that there will be an attendant to look after the car. So, how do you decide that the sign means this? (Notice that the sign does not even have the word *car* on it.) Well, you use the meanings of the words, in combination, and the context in which they occur, and you try to arrive at what the writer of the sign intended his message to convey. The notion of the speaker's or writer's intended meaning is a crucial element.

Consider another example, taken from a newspaper advertisement, and think not only about what the words might mean, but also about what the advertiser intended them to mean: *BABY & TODDLER SALE*. In the normal context of our present society, we assume that this store has not gone into the business of selling young children over the counter, but rather that it is advertising clothes for babies. The word *clothes* does not appear, but our normal interpretation would be that the advertiser intended us to understand his message as relating to the sale of baby clothes and not, we trust, of babies.

Context

In our discussion of the two preceding examples, we have emphasized the influence of context. There are, of course, different kinds of context to be considered. One kind is best described as **linguistic context**, also known as **co-text**. The co-text of a word is the set of other words used in the same phrase or sentence. This surrounding co-text has a strong effect on what we think the word means. We have already noted that the word *bank* is a homonym, a form with more than one meaning. How do we usually know which meaning is intended in a particular sentence? We usually do so on the basis of linguistic context. If the word *bank* is used in a sentence together with words like *steep* or *overgrown*, we have no problem deciding which type of 'bank' is meant. In a similar way, when we hear someone say that she has to *get to the bank to cash a check*, we know from the linguistic context which type of 'bank' is intended.

More generally, we know what words mean on the basis of another type of context, best described as **physical context**. If you see the word *BANK* on the wall of a building in a city, the 'physical' location will influence your interpretation. Our understanding of much of what we read and hear is tied to the physical context, particularly the time and place, in which we encounter linguistic expressions.

Deixis

There are some words in the language that cannot be interpreted at all unless the physical context, especially the physical context of the speaker, is known. These are words like *here*, *there*, *this*, *that*, *now*, *then*, *yesterday*, as well as most pronouns, such as *I*, *you*, *him*, *her*, *them*. Some sentences of English are virtually impossible to understand if we don't know who is speaking, about whom, where and when. For example: *You'll have to bring that back tomorrow, because they aren't here now.*

Out of context, this sentence is extremely vague. It contains a large number of expressions (*you*, *that*, *tomorrow*, *they*, *here*, *now*) which depend for their interpretation on the immediate physical context in which they were uttered. Such expressions are very obvious examples of bits of language which we can only understand in terms of speaker's intended meaning. These are technically known as **deictic expressions**, from the Greek word **deixis** (pronounced 'day-icksis'), which means 'pointing' via language.

Any expression used to point to a person (*me*, *you*, *him*, *them*) is an example of **person deixis**. Words used to point to a location (*here*, *there*, *yonder*) are examples of **place deixis**, and those used to point to a time (*now*, *then*, *tonight*, *last week*) are examples of **time deixis**.

All these deictic expressions have to be interpreted in terms of what person, place or time the speaker has in mind. There is a broad distinction between what is marked as close to the speaker (*this*, *here*, *now*) and what is marked as distant (*that*, *there*, *then*). It is also possible to mark whether movement is happening towards the speaker's location (*come*) or away from the speaker's location (*go*). If you're looking for someone and she appears, moving towards you, you tend to say *Here she comes!* If, however, she is moving away from you in the distance, you're more likely to say *There she goes!*

People can actually use deixis to have some fun. The bar owner who puts up a big sign that reads *Free Beer Tomorrow* (to get you to return to his bar) can always claim that you are one day too early for the free drink.

Reference

In discussing deixis, we assumed that the use of words to refer to people and things was a simple matter. However, words themselves don't refer to anything. People refer. We have to define **reference** as an act by which a speaker (or writer) uses language to enable a listener (or reader) to identify something.

We often assume that the words we use to identify things are in some direct relationship to those things. It's not as simple as that. We may not actually know someone's name, but that doesn't prevent us from referring to the person. One man who always went by fast and loud on his motorcycle in my neighborhood was locally referred to as *Mr. Kawasaki*. A brand name for a motorcycle can obviously be used for a person.

Similarly, in a restaurant, one waiter can ask another *Where's the fresh salad sitting?* and receive the reply *He's sitting by the door*. If you're studying linguistics, you might ask someone *Can I look at your Chomsky?* and get the response *Sure, it's on the shelf over there*. These examples make it clear that we can use names associated with things (*salad*) to refer to people and names of people (*Chomsky*) to refer to things. The key process here is called **inference**. An inference is any additional information used by the listener to connect what is said to what must be meant. In the last example, the listener has to infer that the name of the writer of a book can be used to identify a book by that writer. Similar types of inferences are necessary to understand someone who says that *Picasso is in the museum* or *We saw Shakespeare in London* or *I enjoy listening to Mozart*.

Anaphora

When we establish a referent (*Can I borrow your book?*) and subsequently refer to the same object (*Yeah, it's on the table*), we have a particular kind of referential relationship between *book* and *it*. The second (and any subsequent) referring expression is an example of **anaphora** and the first mention is called the **antecedent**. Thus, *book* is the antecedent and *it* is the anaphoric expression.

Anaphora can be defined as subsequent reference to an already introduced entity. Mostly we use anaphora in texts to maintain reference. As with other types of reference, the connection between referent and anaphora may not always be direct. Consider the following complaint: *I was waiting for the bus, but he just drove by without stopping*. Notice that the antecedent is *bus* and the anaphoric expression is *he*. We would normally expect *it* to be used for a *bus*. Obviously there is an inference involved here: if someone is talking about a bus in motion, assume that there is a driver. That assumed driver is the inferred referent for *he*. The term 'inference' has been used here to describe what the listener (or reader) does. When we talk about an assumption made by the speaker (or writer), we usually talk about a 'presupposition'.

Presupposition

When a speaker uses referring expressions like *this*, *he* or *Shakespeare*, in normal circumstances, she is working with an assumption that the hearer knows which referent is intended. In a more general way, speakers continually design their linguistic messages on the basis of assumptions about what their hearers already know. These assumptions may be mistaken, of course, but they underlie much of what we say in the everyday use of language. What a speaker assumes is true or is known by the hearer can be described as a **presupposition**.

If someone tells you *Your brother is waiting outside for you*, there is an obvious presupposition that you have a brother. If you are asked *Why did you arrive late?*, there is a presupposition that you did arrive late. And if you are asked the following question, there are at least two presuppositions involved: *When did you stop smoking cigars?* In asking this question, the speaker presupposes that you used to smoke cigars, and that you no longer do so. Questions like this, with built-in presuppositions, are very useful devices for interrogators or trial lawyers. If the defendant is asked by the prosecutor *Okay, Mr. Smith, how fast were you going when you ran the red light?*, there is a presupposition that Mr. Smith did, in fact, run the red light. If he simply answers the *How fast* part of the question, by giving a speed, he is behaving as if the presupposition is correct.

One of the tests used to check for the presuppositions underlying sentences involves negating a sentence with a particular presupposition and considering whether the presupposition remains true. Take the sentence *My car is a wreck*. Now take the negative version of this sentence: *My car is not a wreck*. Notice that, although these two sentences have opposite meanings, the underlying presupposition, *I have a car*, remains true in both. This is called the **constancy under negation** test for presupposition. If someone says *I used to regret marrying him, but I don't regret marrying him now*, the presupposition (*I married him*) remains constant even though the verb *regret* changes from being affirmative to being negative.

Speech acts

We have been considering some ways in which we interpret the meanings of sentences in terms of what the speaker of those sentences intended to convey. What we have not yet explored is the fact that we also usually know how speakers intend us to 'take' (or, interpret the function of) what they say. In very general terms, we can usually recognize the type of 'act' performed by a speaker in uttering a sentence. The use of the term **speech act** covers 'actions' such as 'requesting', 'commanding', 'questioning' and 'informing'. It is typically the case that we use the following linguistic forms with the following 'functions'. (The forms would be described in the syntactic analysis of a language, and the functions as what people use language for.)

	Forms	Functions
Did you eat the food?	Interrogative	Question
Eat the food (please).	Imperative	Command (request)
You ate the food.	Declarative	Statement

When a form such as *Did he …?*, *Are they …?* or *Can you … ?* is used to ask a question, it is described as a **direct speech act**. For example, when a speaker doesn't know something and asks the hearer to provide the information, he or she will typically produce a direct speech act of the following type: *Can you ride a bicycle?*

Now compare this utterance with *Can you pass the salt?* In this second example, you would not usually understand the utterance as a question about your ability to do something. In fact, you would not treat this as a question at all. You would treat it as a request and perform the action requested. Yet, this request has been presented in the syntactic form usually associated with a question. Such an example is described as an **indirect speech act**. Whenever one of the forms in the set above is used to perform a function other than the one listed beside it (on the same line), the result is an indirect speech act. The following utterance has the form normally associated with a statement: *You left the door open.* If you say this sentence to someone who has just come into your room (and it's pretty cold outside), you would probably be understood to have made not a statement, but a request. You are requesting, indirectly, that the person close the door. Used in this way, it is another example of an indirect speech act.

It is, of course, possible to have humorous effects as a result of one person failing to recognize another person's indirect speech act. Consider the following scene. A visitor to a city, carrying his luggage, looking lost, stops a passer-by:

Visitor: *Excuse me, do you know where the Ambassador Hotel is?*
Passer-by: *Oh sure, I know where it is.* (and walks away)

In this scene, the visitor uses a form which is normally associated with a question (*Do you know…?*) and the passer-by answers that question literally (*I know…*). Instead of responding to the request, the passer-by replies to the question, treating an indirect speech act as if it is direct.

Perhaps the crucial distinction in the use of these two types of speech acts is based on the fact that indirect commands or requests are simply considered more gentle or more polite in our society than direct commands. Exactly why they are considered more polite is based on some complex social assumptions.

Politeness

There are several ways to think of politeness. These might involve ideas like being tactful, modest and nice to other people. In the study of linguistic politeness, the most relevant concept is 'face'. Your **face**, in pragmatics, is your public self-image. This is the emotional and social sense of self that every person has and expects everyone else to recognize. **Politeness** is showing awareness of another person's face.

If you say something that represents a threat to another person's self-image, that is called a **face-threatening act**. For example, if you use a direct speech act to order someone to do something (*Give me that paper!*), you are acting as if you have more social power than the other person. If you do not actually have that social power, then you are performing a face-threatening act. An indirect speech act, in the form of a question (*Could you pass me that paper, please?*), removes the assumption of social power. You appear to be asking about ability. This makes your request less threatening to the other person's sense of self. Whenever you say something that lessens the possible threat to another's face, it's called a **face-saving act**.

You have both a negative face and a positive face. Your **negative face** is the need to be independent and to have freedom from imposition. Your **positive face** is your need to be connected, to belong, to be a member of the group. Thus, a face-saving act that emphasizes a person's negative face will show concern about imposition (*I'm sorry to bother you...* ; *I know you're busy, but ...*). A face-saving act that emphasizes a person's positive face will show solidarity and draw attention to a common goal (*Let's do this together...* ; *You and I have the same problem, so...*).

Ideas about the appropriate language to mark politeness differ substantially from one culture to the next. If you have grown up in a culture that has directness as a valued way of showing solidarity, and you use direct speech acts (*Pour me some coffee*) to people whose culture is more oriented to indirectness and avoiding direct imposition, then you will be considered impolite. You, in turn, may think of the others as vague and unsure of what they want. In either case, it is the pragmatics that is misunderstood and, unfortunately, much more will be communicated than is said.

Understanding how people communicate is actually a process of interpreting not just what speakers say, but what they 'intend to mean'. Other aspects of this process will be explored in the next chapter.

Study questions

1 What are the deictic expressions in the following utterance?
   I'm busy now so you can't do that here. Come back tomorrow.

2 What is one obvious presupposition of a speaker who says:
   (a) *Where did he buy the beer?*
   (b) *Your watch is broken.*
   (c) *We regret buying that car.*

3 What are the anaphoric expressions in:
   Dr. Dang gave Mary some medicine after she asked him for it.

4 What kind of inference is involved in interpreting these utterances:
   (a) Professor: *Bring your Plato to class tomorrow.*
   (b) Nurse: *The broken leg in room 5 wants to talk to the doctor.*

5 Someone stands between you and the TV set you were watching, so you
   decide to say one of the following. Identify which would be direct and
   which indirect speech acts.
   (a) *Move!*
   (b) *You're in the way.*
   (c) *Could you sit down?*
   (d) *Please get out of the way.*

Discussion topics/projects

A All of the following expressions have deictic elements in them. What
   aspects of context have to be considered in order to interpret such
   expressions? Perhaps there are others of a similar type that you could
   add to the list?

   Notice on office door: *Back in one hour*
   Telephone answering machine: *I'm not here now*
   Advertisement for sports shoes: *Just do it*
   Watching a horse race: *Oh, no, I'm in last place!*
   Answering a telephone: *Oh, it's you*
   On a map/directory: *YOU ARE HERE*
   In a car that won't start: *Maybe I'm out of gas*
   Pointing to an empty chair: *Where is she today?*

B All of the following expressions were found in notices announcing sales.
   (i) What is being sold in each case and (if you know) how do you know?
   (ii) Also consider how many different underlying structures are actually involved in these expressions (i.e. an 'Apple Sale' basically means

'someone is selling apples'; can we assume the same structure for
'Garage Sale' and the others?)

Back-to-School Sale   Bake Sale   Big Screen Sale
Casual Sale   Clearance Sale   Foundation Sale
Floor Sale   Furniture Sale   Garage Sale
Home Theater Sale   Labor Day Sale   Liquidation Sale   Monster Sale
One Cent Sale   Plant Sale   Red Tag Sale   Shapewear Sale   Sidewalk Sale
Solid Cherry Sale   Tent Sale   Warehouse Sale   Yard Sale

C   Anaphoric reference is usually defined in terms of 'subsequent reference' within a text and illustrated via pronouns. There are other ways in
which 'subsequent reference' can be accomplished (e.g. by repeated
noun phrases or names). Read through the following paragraphs and
identify all examples of anaphoric reference. What kind of problems
arise in an exercise like this and how do you solve them? (Text (i) is from
Scientific American, June, 1992, and text (ii) is from *The Daily Racing
Form*, February, 1995.)

(i) *On April 13, 1990, at a tavern in Mercedes, Texas, a bat bit the right index finger
of a 22-year-old visitor. The man, who did not seek medical attention, seemed
well until May 30, when the affected hand began to feel weak. Just six days later
he was dead of rabies, having been tormented in the interim by many of its symptoms. Before slipping into a coma, the Texan suffered episodes of rigidity and
breath holding; hallucinations; extreme difficulty swallowing (so much so that
he refused liquids); frequent spasms in the face, mouth and neck; continuous
drooling; and, finally, disorientation accompanied by high fever.*

(ii) *Horse of the Year Holy Bull was pulled up after suffering strained ligaments
during Saturday's Donn Handicap. Cigar, who was disputing the pace with the
favorite at the time of the incident, went on to win the race. He paid $10 for the
win. Cigar's jockey Jerry Bailey said he heard "a pop" as his horse and Holy Bull
were racing together. Veterinarian Dr. Peter Hall said of the champion, "He
strained the ligaments which support the ankle, but the injury isn't severe. He
isn't in distress. But he'll probably never race again."*

D   The following examples are adapted from the research of Beebe *et al.*
(1990). They are like 'scenarios' created for the study of the speech act of
'refusal'.

(i) What do you (and others you can get to do the exercise) say in the
following situations?

(ii) Can you create other situations, following a similar pattern, and ask people to write down what they would say? What are the range of expressions used for the speech act of 'refusal'? Why do you think there is such a range?

1 You are the owner of a bookstore. One of your best workers asks to speak to you in private.

> Worker: *As you know, I've been here just a little over a year now, and I know you've been pleased with my work. I really enjoy working here, but to be quite honest, I really need an increase in pay.*
>
> You: _____
> _____
>
> Worker: *Then I guess I'll have to look for another job.*

2 You are at a friend's house for lunch.

> Friend: *How about another piece of cake?*
> You: _____
>
> Friend: *Come on, just a little piece?*
> You: _____
> _____

3 A friend invites you to dinner, but you really can't stand this friend's husband.

> Friend: *How about coming over for dinner Saturday night? We're having a small dinner party.*
> You: _____
> _____
>
> Friend: *O.K., maybe another time.*

E What counts as polite behavior can differ substantially from one culture to the next. Lakoff (1990) describes three different types as *distance*, *deference* and *camaraderie*. As you read the basic descriptions which follow, try to decide which type you are most familiar with and whether you have encountered the others on any occasion. What kind of language do you think characterizes each?

Distance politeness is the civilized human analogue to the territorial strategies of other animals. An animal sets up physical boundary markers (the dog and the hydrant) to signal its fellows: My turf, stay out. We, being symbol-using creatures, create symbolic fences.

Distancing cultures weave remoteness into their language.

*Where distance politeness more or less assumes equality between partici-
pants, deference works by debasing one or both.*

*While distance politeness has been characteristic of the middle and upper
classes in most of Europe for a very long time, deference has been typical in
many Asian societies. But it is also the preferred mode of interaction for women
in the majority of societies, either always or only when talking to men.*

*A third strategy (camaraderie) that has recently emerged in this culture
makes a different assumption: that interaction and connection are good in
themselves, that openness is the greatest sign of courtesy.*

*In a camaraderie system, the appearance of openness and niceness is to be
sought above all else. There is no holding back, nothing is too terrible to say.*

Further reading

Introductions to pragmatics are offered in Blakemore (1992), Green (1989),
Leech (1983), Levinson (1983), Mey (1993) and Yule (1996). There is also a collection of papers on the philosophical background in Davis (1991) and a bibliography in Nuyts & Verschueren (1987). More specific discussions can be
found on context in Brown & Yule (1983a), on deixis in Fillmore (1975) or
Jarvella & Klein (1982), on reference in Fauconnier (1994), Lyons (1977),
Givon (1989), and Roberts (1993), on anaphora in Fox (1993), on presupposition in Oh & Dineen (1979), on speech acts in Austin (1962), Searle (1969;
1979) and Wierzbicka (1987), and on politeness in Brown & Levinson (1987),
Lakoff (1990) and Watts *et al.* (1992). On cross-cultural pragmatics, see Kasper
& Blum-Kulka (1993) or Wierzbicka (1991).

13 Discourse analysis 話語分析

There's two types of favors, the big favor and the small favor. You can measure the size of the favor by the pause that a person takes after they ask you to "Do me a favor." Small favor – small pause. "Can you do me a favor, hand me that pencil." No pause at all. Big favors are, "Could you do me a favor . . ." Eight seconds go by. "Yeah? What?"

". . . well." The longer it takes them to get to it, the bigger the pain it's going to be.

   Humans are the only species that do favors. Animals don't do favors. A lizard doesn't go up to a cockroach and say, "Could you do me a favor and hold still, I'd like to eat you alive." That's a big favor even with no pause.

Jerry Seinfeld (1993)

In the study of language, some of the most interesting questions arise in connection with the way language is 'used', rather than what its components are. We have already introduced one of those questions when we discussed pragmatics in the preceding chapter. We were, in effect, asking how it is that language-users interpret what other language-users intend to convey. When we carry this investigation further and ask how it is that we, as language-users, make sense of what we read in texts, understand what speakers mean despite what they say, recognize connected as opposed to jumbled or incoherent discourse, and successfully take part in that complex activity called conversation, we are undertaking what is known as **discourse analysis**.

Interpreting discourse
When we concentrate on the description of a particular language, we are normally concerned with the accurate representation of the forms and structures used in that language. However, as language-users, we are

capable of more than simply recognizing correct versus incorrect form and structure. We can cope with fragments such as *Trains collide, two die*, a newspaper headline, and know, for example, that a causal relation exists between the two phrases. We can also make sense of notices like *No shoes, no service*, on shop windows in summer, understanding that a conditional relation exists between the two phrases ('If you are wearing no shoes, you will receive no service'). Moreover, we can encounter examples of texts, written in English, which appear to break a lot of the 'rules' of the English language. The following example, from an essay by a Saudi Arabian student learning English, contains all kinds of 'errors', yet it can be understood.

> *My Town*
> *My natal was in a small town, very close to Riyadh capital of Saudi Arabia. The distant betweeen my town and Riyadh 7 miles exactly. The name of this Almasani that means in English Factories. It takes this name from the peopl's carrer. In my childhood I remmeber the people live. It was very simple, most the people was farmer.*

This example may serve to illustrate an interesting point about the way we react to language which contains ungrammatical forms. Rather than simply rejecting the text as ungrammatical, we try to make sense of it. That is, we attempt to arrive at a reasonable interpretation of what the writer intended to convey. (Most people say they understand the 'My Town' text quite easily.) It is this effort to interpret (and to be interpreted), and how we accomplish it, that are the key elements investigated in the study of discourse. To arrive at an interpretation, and to make our messages interpretable, we certainly rely on what we know about linguistic form and structure. But, as language-users, we have more knowledge than that.

Cohesion

We know, for example, that texts must have a certain structure which depends on factors quite different from those required in the structure of a single sentence. Some of those factors are described in terms of **cohesion**, or the ties and connections which exist within texts. A number of those types of cohesive ties can be identified in the following text:

> *My father once bought a Lincoln convertible. He did it by saving every penny he could. That car would be worth a fortune nowadays. However, he sold it to help pay for my college education. Sometimes I think I'd rather have the convertible.*

There are connections present here in the use of pronouns, which we assume are used to maintain reference (via anaphora) to the same people and things throughout: *father – he – he – he*; *my – my – I*; *Lincoln – it*. There are lexical connections such as *a Lincoln convertible – that car – the convertible*, and the more general connections created by a number of terms which share a common element of meaning (e.g. 'money') *bought – saving – penny – worth a fortune – sold – pay*; (e.g. 'time') *once – nowadays – sometimes*. There is also a connector, *However*, which marks the relationship of what follows to what went before. The verb tenses in the first four sentences are all in the past, creating a connection between those events, and a different time is indicated by the present tense of the final sentence.

Analysis of these **cohesive links** within a text gives us some insight into how writers structure what they want to say, and may be crucial factors in our judgments on whether something is well-written or not. It has also been noted that the conventions of cohesive structure differ from one language to the next and may be one of the sources of difficulty encountered in translating texts.

However, by itself, cohesion would not be sufficient to enable us to make sense of what we read. It is quite easy to create a highly cohesive text which has a lot of connections between the sentences, but which remains difficult to interpret. Note that the following text has connections such as *Lincoln – the car*, *red – that color*, *her – she*, *letters – a letter*, and so on.

> My father bought a Lincoln convertible. The car driven by the police was red. That color doesn't suit her. She consists of three letters. However, a letter isn't as fast as a telephone call.

It becomes clear from an example like this that the 'connectedness' which we experience in our interpretation of normal texts is not simply based on connections between the words. There must be some other factor which leads us to distinguish connected texts which make sense from those which do not. This factor is usually described as **coherence**.

Coherence

The key to the concept of coherence is not something which exists in the language, but something which exists in people. It is people who 'make sense' of what they read and hear. They try to arrive at an interpretation which is in line with their experience of the way the world is. Indeed, our ability to make sense of what we read is probably only a small part of that general ability we have to make sense of what we perceive or experience in the world. You may have found, when reading the last example text, that you kept trying to make the text 'fit' some situation or experience which would accommodate all the details. If you work at it long enough, you may indeed find a way to incorporate all those disparate elements into a single coherent interpretation. In doing so, you would necessarily be involved in a process of filling in a lot of 'gaps' which exist in the text. You would have to create meaningful connections which are not actually expressed by the words and sentences. This process is not restricted to trying to understand 'odd' texts. In one way or another, it seems to be involved in our interpretation of all discourse.

It is certainly present in the interpretation of casual conversation. We are continually taking part in conversational interactions where a great deal of what is meant is not actually present in what is said. Perhaps it is the ease with which we ordinarily anticipate each other's intentions that makes this whole complex process seem so unremarkable. Here is a good example, adapted from Widdowson (1978):

> Her: *That's the telephone*
> Him: *I'm in the bath*
> Her: *O.K.*

There are certainly no cohesive ties within this fragment of discourse. How does each of these people manage to make sense of what the other says? They do use the information contained in the sentences expressed, but there must be something else involved in the interpretation. It has been suggested that exchanges of this type are best understood in terms of the conventional actions performed by the speakers in such interactions. Drawing on concepts derived from the study of speech acts (introduced in Chapter 12), we can characterize the brief conversation in the following way:

> She makes a request of him to perform action
> He states reason why he cannot comply with request
> She undertakes to perform action

If this is a reasonable analysis of what took place in the conversation, then it is clear that language-users must have a lot of knowledge of how conversational interaction works which is not simply 'linguistic' knowledge. Trying to describe aspects of that knowledge has been the focus of research by an increasing number of discourse analysts.

Speech events

In exploring what it is that we know about taking part in conversation, or any other speech event (e.g. debate, interview, various types of discussions), we quickly realize that there is enormous variation in what people say and do in different circumstances. In order to begin to describe the sources of that variation, we would have to take account of a number of criteria. For example, we would have to specify the roles of speaker and hearer, or hearers, and their relationships, whether they were friends, strangers, young, old, of equal or unequal status, and many other factors. All of these factors will have an influence on what is said and how it is said. We would have to describe what was the topic of the conversation and in what setting or context it took place. Some of the effects of these factors on the way language is used will be explored in greater detail in Chapter 21. Yet, even when we have described all these factors, we will still not have analyzed the actual structure of the conversation itself. As language-users, in a particular culture, we clearly have quite sophisticated knowledge of how conversation works.

Conversational interaction

In simple terms, English conversation can be described as an activity where, for the most part, two or more people take **turns** at speaking. Typically, only one person speaks at a time and there tends to be an avoidance of silence between speaking turns. (This is not true in every culture.) If more than one participant tries to talk at the same time, one of them usually stops, as in this example, where A stops until B has finished:

A: *Didn't you* ⌐ *know wh-*
B: ⌊ *But he must've been there by two*
A: *Yes but you knew where he was going*

(The symbol [is conventionally used to indicate where simultaneous talk occurred.)

For the most part, participants wait until one speaker indicates that he or she has finished, usually by signaling a **completion point**. Speakers can mark their turns as 'complete' in a number of ways: by asking a question, for example, or by pausing at the end of a completed syntactic structure like a phrase or a sentence. Other participants can indicate that they want to take the speaking turn, also in a number of ways. They can start to make short sounds, usually repeated, while the speaker is talking, and often use body shifts or facial expressions to signal that they have something to say.

Some of the most interesting research in this area of discourse has revealed different expectations of conversational style and different strategies of participation in **conversational interaction**. Some of these strategies seem to be the source of what is sometimes described by participants as 'rudeness' (if one speaker appears to cut in on another speaker) or 'shyness' (if one speaker keeps waiting for an opportunity to take a turn and none seems to occur). The participants characterized as 'rude' or 'shy' in this way may simply be adhering to slightly different conventions of **turn-taking**.

One strategy, which may be overused by 'long-winded' speakers, or those used to 'holding the floor' (like lecturers, politicians), is designed to avoid having normal completion points occur. We all use this strategy to some extent, usually in situations where we have to work out what we are trying to say while actually saying it. If the normal expectation is that completion points are marked by the end of a sentence and a pause, then one way to 'keep the turn' is to avoid having those two indicators occur together. That is, don't pause at the end of sentences; make your sentences run on by using connectors like *and, and then, so, but*; place your pauses at points where the message is clearly incomplete; and preferably 'fill' the pause with hesitation markers such as *er, em, uh, ah*. Note the position of the pauses (marked by …) in this example, placed before and after verbs rather than at the end of sentences:

> A: *that's their favorite restaurant because they … enjoy French food and when they were … in France they couldn't believe it that … you know that they had … that they had had better meals back home*

And in this next example, Speaker X produces filled pauses after having almost lost the turn at his first brief hesitation:

> X: *well that film really was …* ⌈ *wasn't what he was good at*
> Y: ⌊ *when di-*
> X: *I mean his other … em his later films were much more … er really more in the romantic style and that was more what what he was … you know… em best at doing*
> Y: *So when did he make that one*

These types of strategies, by themselves, should not be considered undesirable or 'domineering'. They are present in the conversational speech of most people and they are, in a sense, part of what makes conversation work. We recognize these subtle indicators as ways of organizing our turns and negotiating the intricate business of social interaction via language. In fact, one of the most noticeable features of conversational discourse is that it is generally very co-operative. This observation has, in fact, been formulated as a principle of conversation.

The co-operative principle

An underlying assumption in most conversational exchanges seems to be that the participants are, in fact, co-operating with each other. This principle, together with four maxims which we expect will be obeyed, was first set out by Grice (1975). The co-operative principle is stated in the following way: "Make your conversational contribution such as is required, at the stage at which it occurs, by the accepted purpose or direction of the talk exchange in which you are engaged." Supporting this principle are the four maxims:

> **Quantity**: Make your contribution as informative as is required, but not more, or less, than is required
> **Quality**: Do not say that which you believe to be false or for which you lack evidence
> **Relation**: Be relevant
> **Manner**: Be clear, brief and orderly

It is certainly true that, on occasion, we can experience conversational exchanges in which the co-operative principle does not seem to be in operation. However, this general description of the normal expectations we have in conversations helps to explain a number of regular features in the way people say things. For example, a number of common expressions like *Well, to make a long story short* and *I won't bore you with all the details* seem to be indicators of an awareness of the **Quantity** maxim. Some awareness of the importance of the **Quality** maxim seems to lie behind the way we begin some conversational contributions with expressions like *As far as I know...*, *Now, correct me if I'm wrong, but...* and *I'm not absolutely sure but....* We also take care to indicate that what we report is something we *think* and *feel* (not *know*), is *possible* or *likely* (not *certain*), *may* or *could* (not *must*) happen. Hence the difference between saying *John is ill* and *I think it's possible that John may be ill*. In the first version we will be assumed to have very good evidence for the statement.

Given that we operate with the co-operative principle, it also becomes clearer how certain answers to our questions which, on the surface, do not seem to be appropriate, can actually be interpreted. Consider this conversational fragment:

> Carol: *Are you coming to the party tonight?*
> Lara: *I've got an exam tomorrow*

On the face of it, Lara's statement is not an answer to Carol's question. Lara doesn't say "Yes" or "No." Yet, Carol will immediately interpret the statement as meaning 'No' or 'Probably not.' How can we account for this ability to grasp one meaning from a sentence which, in a literal sense, means something else? It seems to depend, at least partially, on the assumption that Lara is being 'relevant' and 'informative'. (To appreciate this point, try to imagine Carol's reaction if Lara had said something like "Roses are red, you know.") Given that the answers contain relevant information, Carol can work out that 'exam tomorrow' conventionally involves 'study tonight', and 'study tonight' precludes 'party tonight'. Thus, Lara's answer is not simply a statement of tomorrow's activities, it contains an **implicature** (an additional conveyed meaning) concerning tonight's activities.

It is noticeable that in order to describe the conversational implicature involved in Lara's statement, we had to appeal to some background knowledge (about exams, studying and partying) that must be shared by the conversational participants. Investigating how we use our background knowledge to arrive at interpretations of what we hear and read is a crucial part of doing discourse analysis.

Background knowledge

A particularly good example of the processes involved in using background knowledge has been provided by Sanford & Garrod (1981). Their example begins with these two sentences:

John was on his way to school last Friday.
He was really worried about the math lesson.

Most people who are asked to read these sentences report that they think John is probably a schoolboy. Since this piece of information is not directly stated in the text, it must be an inference. Other inferences, for different readers, are that John is walking or that he is on a bus. These inferences are clearly derived from our conventional knowledge, in our culture, about 'going to school', and no reader has ever suggested that John is swimming or on a boat, though both are physically possible, if unlikely, interpretations.

An interesting aspect of the reported inferences is that they are treated as likely or possible interpretations which readers will easily abandon if they do not fit in with some subsequent information. The next sentence in the text is as follows:

Last week he had been unable to control the class.

On encountering this sentence, most readers decide that John is, in fact, a teacher and that he is not very happy. Many report that he is probably driving a car to school. Then the next sentence is presented:

It was unfair of the math teacher to leave him in charge.

Suddenly, John reverts to his schoolboy status, and the 'teacher' inference is abandoned. The final sentence of this text contains a surprise:

After all, it is not a normal part of a janitor's duties.

This type of text and the manner of presentation, one sentence at a time, is, of course, rather artificial. Yet the exercise involved does provide us with some insight into the ways in which we 'build' interpretations of what we read by using a lot more information than is actually in the words on the page. That is, we actually create what the text is about, based on our expectations of what normally happens. In attempting to describe this phenomenon, many researchers use the concept of a 'schema'.

A **schema** is a general term for a conventional knowledge structure which exists in memory. We have many schemata which are used in the interpretation of what we experience and what we hear or read about. If you hear someone describe what happened one day in the supermarket, you don't have to be told what is normally found in a supermarket. You already have a "supermarket" schema (food displayed on shelves, arranged in aisles, shopping carts and baskets, check-out counter, and other conventional features).

One particular kind of schema is a 'script'. A **script** is essentially a dynamic schema, in which a series of conventional actions takes place. You have a script for 'Going to the dentist' or 'Going to the movies'. We all have versions of an 'Eating in a restaurant' script, which we can activate to make sense of discourse like the following.

Trying not to be out of the office for long, Suzy went into the nearest place, sat down and ordered a sandwich. It was quite crowded, but the service was fast, so she left a good tip when she had to rush back.

On the basis of our 'Restaurant' script, we would be able to say a number of things about the scene and events briefly described in this short text. For example, although the text does not have this information, we would assume that Suzy opened a door to get into the restaurant, that there were tables there, that she ate the sandwich, then she paid for it, and so on. The fact that information of this type can turn up in people's attempts to remember the text is further evidence of the existence of scripts. It is also a good indication of the fact that our understanding of what we read does not directly come from what words and sentences are on the page, but from the interpretation we create, in our minds, of what we read.

Indeed, crucial information is sometimes omitted from important instructions on the assumption that everybody knows the script. Think carefully about the following instructions from a bottle of cough syrup.

Fill measure cup to line
and repeat every 2 to 3 hours.

No, you've not just to keep filling the measure cup every 2 to 3 hours. Nor have you to rub the cough syrup in your hair every 2 to 3 hours. You are expected to know the script and *drink* the stuff (without being told).

These observations on the nature of discourse understanding have had a powerful impact on work related to attempts to use computers to process natural language material. Since it has been realized that the way we communicate via language is based on vast amounts of assumed background knowledge, not only of language, but of how the world is, then a fundamental problem is how to give computers this 'knowledge'. Investigations in this area are the subject of the following chapter.

Study questions
1   What is meant by the term 'cohesion' in the study of texts?
2   How would you describe this short exchange in terms of the actions performed by the speakers?

Motorist: *My car needs a new exhaust system*
Mechanic: *I'll be busy with this other car all day*

3   What do you think is meant by the term 'turn-taking' in conversation?
4   What are the four maxims of the co-operative principle?
5   Which maxim does this speaker seem to be particularly careful about:
Well, to be quite honest, I don't think she is ill today.

Discussion topics/projects
A   As an exercise in discovering how our interpretation of what we read can be altered by the expectations we bring to the task, consider the following text (adapted from Anderson *et al.*, 1977):

A prisoner plans his escape
Rocky slowly got up from the mat, planning his escape. He hesitated a moment and thought. Things were not going well. What bothered him most was being held, especially since the charge against him had been weak. He considered his present situation. The lock that held him was strong, but he thought he could break it.

Now answer these questions: (1) Where is Rocky? (2) Is he alone? (3) What has happened to him?

Having done that, remove the title from the text and replace it with this new title:'A wrestler in a tight corner'. Read the text again and answer the same three questions. Can you come up with different answers? How might you use this evidence to persuade someone that the meaning of the texts we read does not reside solely within the texts themselves?

B Can you identify the cohesive devices which are present in the following piece of text? In addition to these cohesive elements, what factors can you identify as having an influence on your interpretation?

It was Friday morning. There were two horses out in the field. Layla ran up and caught the nearest one. He seemed quite calm. However, as she turned to take him back, the powerful creature suddenly reared and jumped forward. It was all over in an instant. The animal was running wildly across the field and the girl was left sitting in the mud. Most of the time I love horses, she thought, but some- times I could just kill one of them.

C What aspects of this fragment of conversational speech would you point to as characteristic features of this type of language-in-use?

A: *Well it wasn't really a holiday more a ... a ... I don't know ...*
   more an expedition
B: *Why?*   ⌈*Did you*
              ⌊*Oh I guess because we ed- we ended up carrying so*
   much ... ⌈*equipment and*
C: ⌊*that sounds like a trip I took... em two years ago*
   I think... yeah in the summer and... I've never gone again...
B: *So where did you go?*
A: *Oh we followed the river and the p– the idea you see was*
   to find the source you know ... and ... just to avoid the ...
      the roads well ...   ⌈*unless th-*
C: ⌊*and did you?*
A: *What?*
B: ⌈*get*
C: ⌊*find the source ... the river*
A: *Oh yes sorry ... but we ended up ... em walking on roads quite a*
   bit because ... it... it just took too long

D One feature of conversational structure not explored in the chapter is the idea of 'preference'. There is a 'preference' for accepting an invitation or an offer rather than refusing. Similarly, there's a 'preference' for agreeing (rather than disagreeing) when someone expresses an opinion. It's a preference, not a requirement. When we have to refuse an invitation/offer, or express disagreement with someone, we typically indicate that it is a difficult thing for us to do so. What kinds of indications of 'difficulty' can you find in the following examples (and any others you may have noted)?

(i)   Her: *Come over for some coffee later?*
      Him: *Oh... eh ... I'd love to... but you see... I ... I'm supposed to get this thing finished ... you know*

(ii) Him: *I think she's really sexy, don't you?*
      Her: *Well ... er ... I'm not sure ... you may be right ... but you see ... other people probably don't go for all that ... you know ... all that make-up ... so em sorry*

E   For a few linguists, the analysis of conversational speech is considered to be a poor way of discovering the major properties of language. They point out that conversational speech is full of hesitations, slips, repetitions, lapses of attention and, as a result, will not provide us with a good representation of the most important elements of a language in a clear way. Consequently, the study of language should be restricted to the analysis of single sentences, constructed by the linguist. How do you feel about this? If you have a strong opinion, one way or the other, what kind of evidence would you use to support your opinion?

Further reading

Introductions to discourse analysis are offered in Brown & Yule (1983a), Cook (1989), Coulthard (1985), Schiffrin (1994) and Stubbs (1983). A comprehensive survey is presented in van Dijk (1985). More specialized approaches can be found in Chafe (1994), de Beaugrande & Dressler (1981), Gumperz (1982), and Sinclair & Coulthard (1975). On cohesion, see Halliday & Hasan (1976), on speech events, Hymes (1964), on the maxims and implicatures, see Grice (1989), Levinson (1983), Sperber & Wilson (1986) or Yule (1996). On aspects of conversation, see Atkinson & Heritage (1984), Drew & Heritage (1992), Goodwin (1981), Sacks (1992) or Sacks *et al.* (1974). On interpreting conversational style, see Tannen (1984; 1986; 1990). On background knowledge, the original concept of schema comes from Bartlett (1932). Work on scripts is presented in Schank & Abelson (1977) and (more humorously) in Raskin (1985; 1986). The connection between discourse and education is explored in Cazden (1988), Hatch (1992) and McCarthy (1991).

14 Language and machines

One dark night a policeman comes upon a drunk. The man is on his knees, obviously searching for something under a lamppost. He tells the officer that he is looking for his keys, which he says he lost "over there", pointing out into the darkness. The policeman asks him, "Why, if you lost the keys over there, are you looking for them under the streetlight?" The drunk answers, "Because the light is so much better here." That is the way science proceeds too.

Joseph Weizenbaum (1976)

In 1738, Jacques de Vaucanson produced a fabulous mechanical duck. It could perform the amazing feat of drinking water and eating grain which was digested and then excreted via a mysterious chemical process and some complex tubing in its stomach. This mechanical marvel is simply one example in a long line of 'machines' which humans have created in imitation of living organisms. The interesting thing about Vaucanson's machine is that it simulated digestion without actually containing a replica of the digestive system. It can be seen as an exercise in working with available technology to create a model of some internal processes of a duck. Note that it is a 'model', not a replication. This is an important point, since the aim of many such exercises is not to mimic the details of an internal process, but to have the output of the model be indistinguishable from the output of the real thing. By all accounts, the duck's output passed as genuine.

However, the kind of output which we are more interested in is the result of natural language processing by a machine, or, more specifically, a computer. It is necessary to specify that it is a 'natural' language (e.g. English) rather than an artificial language (e.g. BASIC), since it is the human capacity to use language that is being modeled.

Speech synthesis and recognition

One of the first aspects of natural language to be modeled was the actual articulation of speech sounds. Early models of talking machines were essentially devices that mechanically simulated the operation of the human vocal tract. More modern attempts to create speech electronically are generally described as **speech synthesis**, and the resulting output is called **synthetic speech**. From one point of view, it seems remarkably simple. Take the set of phonemes of English, electronically reproduce the acoustic properties of these sounds, then select those phonemes which make up the pronunciation of a word and 'play' the word. While this is not as easy as the brief description suggests, synthetic speech has indeed been produced in this way. It sounds terrible. More tolerable facsimiles of speech have been produced by having machines analyze key acoustic properties of spoken words (not individual sounds) and store the pronouncing information at the word level. In many parts of the United States, when you ask Directory Information for a telephone number, the spoken (seven digit) number which you hear is an example of a synthetically produced set of seven words.

A similar approach was adopted in many **speech recognition** systems. Very basic programs, called **navigators**, allow computers to follow simple spoken commands (e.g. *open filename*) that the computer has stored as sound units in memory. These programs can replace many keyboard functions. More complex programs, called **dictation** systems, can have much larger recognition vocabularies and can create written text from speech at a fast rate. Typically such systems require very clear speech and have to be trained to recognize the user's voice. They often only recognize spoken words when produced by the same voice. This may be an advantage for a security system (the machine only obeys your voice), but is a major disadvantage for general use by any speaker. Speaker-independent systems tend to have about five times the error rate of speaker-dependent systems. It is, however, just a matter of time before experimental speaker-independent systems (currently successful on limited tasks) become widely available. Even then, however, they will probably remain pattern-matching systems (recognizing only and exactly what they already know).

There are similar problems with making synthetic speech systems more flexible. There is more to speech production than the pronunciation of words. Intonation and pausing, for example, have to be included, as well as syntactic rules for the formation of natural language sentences. Care has also to be taken that the natural processes of assimilation and elision (discussed in Chapter 6) are not ignored. As a result of research in this area, increasingly sophisticated models of speech production have been developed and more 'natural sounding' synthetic speech has been achieved. However, the development of synthetic speech, even if highly successful, would only produce a model of speech articulation. It would not be a model of 'speaking'. The human activity of speaking involves having something to say and not just a means of saying it. Having something to say is an attribute of the human's mental processes and attempting to model that attribute is, in effect, the modeling of intelligence.

Artificial intelligence

The investigation and development of models of intelligent behavior is generally undertaken in the field of **artificial intelligence** (AI), which has been defined as "the science of making machines do things that would require intelligence if done by men" (Minsky, 1968). This field ranges over a large number of topics (e.g. problem-solving, gameplaying, visual perception), but has always taken language production and understanding as a major area of investigation. While one ultimate goal may be to produce a computer which can function as a conversational partner, most of the research has been devoted to developing models to cope with language interaction which can take place at a computer terminal. Consequently, descriptions of 'conversations' in this field typically refer to typed rather than spoken dialogs.

Parsers

One of the first developments in the AI approach to the workings of a natural language like English was to produce a means of **parsing** English sentences. This is basically a process of working from left to right along an incoming English sentence, creating an analysis of the syntactic structure and predicting what elements will come next. A number of different types of parsers have been developed, but a brief description of one very elementary version should serve to illustrate the basic processes involved in analyzing a simple sentence like *The boy hit a ball*.

The parser begins by assigning 'sentence' status to the incoming string of linguistic forms and predicts that the first major constituent will be a 'noun phrase'. The first element encountered is *The*, which is checked in the dictionary to see if it fits the category 'article' (i.e. the predicted first element in a noun phrase). Since it does, it is assigned this description and the parser predicts that the next element may fit the category 'adjective'. The word *boy* is checked and turns out not to be an adjective. This word is then checked against the next predicted category of 'noun' and is identified as such. This should complete the specification of noun phrase (which can be assigned the functional label of 'subject') and the parser goes on to check the next constituent, seeking a word to fit the category 'verb', and so on. As the parser assigns syntactic categories to the elements in the linguistic string, it can also begin to produce a semantic analysis. The subject NP (*The boy*) can be assigned the status 'agent-of-action', the verb (*hit*) is the 'action', and the following NP (*a ball*) is the 'object-of-action' or 'theme'. This massively oversimplified version of what a parser does may provide an illustration of how a computer, with a limited grammar, a dictionary and a set of procedures, can produce a linguistic description of some simple sentences it receives.

In describing this simple parser, we used two basic processing mechanisms. One was **top-down** parsing, where we decided what constituent (e.g. 'noun phrase') was going to be there and then looked for words in the sentence to confirm the prediction. We started at the top of the structure and worked down. Working in the opposite direction, we can start with a word like *the*, at the bottom of a structure, and work our way up to create a whole noun phrase constituent. This would be **bottom-up** parsing. An effective system will combine both top-down and bottom-up processes working together.

The type of analysis just presented, however, would be an extremely trivial first step in the process of 'understanding' the sentence. In order to go any further, the machine would require 'knowledge' of what words like *boy*, *hit* and *ball* are used to refer to, and also how an article like *the* indicates something different from the article *a*. If the machine is to function with any resemblance to the intelligent 'understander-system' that operates in the human mind, then it will need some 'knowledge' of how the world is. It would have to know that, for example, the boy used some 'instrument' (e.g. a bat, his hand), despite the fact that this information is not present in the sentence. The problems of modeling then cease to be strictly linguistic matters of syntax and basic semantics, and become problems of coping with the colossal amounts of 'world-knowledge' that humans apparently have. The development of computer programs which can access this type of 'knowledge' is the key to the creation of what are generally called understander-systems, or machines which really do behave as if they make sense of the linguistic input they receive.

Understander-systems

It would be impossible to document the large number of understander-systems which have been developed in the last three decades. What we can do is explore the workings of three such systems and point out some of their relevant features. First, let us consider an example of how the illusion of 'understanding' can be created.

ELIZA

A program called ELIZA was intended to simulate, or even to 'parody', the psychotherapist's role in a particular type of non-directive psychoanalysis. The 'patient' would sit at a computer terminal, type in one side of the interaction, and receive appropriate responses. The resulting dialog might contain exchanges like this:

Patient: *I'm feeling a bit tired.*
Analyst: *Why do you think you 're feeling a bit tired.*

A basic feature of the analyst-program can be discerned in the response illustrated here. The responses are based on a pattern-recognition process whereby the occurrence of a key word or phrase in the patient's turn would activate a particular type of predetermined sentence pattern (generally a question), incorporating the key word or phrase. A limited number of connections between certain key words also gave the program the power to produce more general responses to particular remarks. Note how the connection is made from *mother* to *family* in this exchange:

Patient: *I need some help.*
Analyst: *What would it mean to you if you got some help.*
Patient: *Perhaps I could learn to get along with my mother.*
Analyst: *Tell me more about your family.*

Thus, with a very simple set of linguistic structures, the program could give the impression of considerable thought behind its responses. If a patient-response was difficult to match, then a number of stock expressions such as *I see*, *That's interesting* or *Go on* could be produced by the analyst. A substantial number of people came to believe that the ELIZA program was a very useful procedure for conducting psychotherapy (much to the chagrin of its original creator; Weizenbaum, 1976, provides his reasons). In fact, a number of different versions were actually developed and used.

Although ELIZA provides an interesting view of how one type of psychotherapy may work, it yields very limited insights into the way language interacts with knowledge and understanding. Very simply, ELIZA does not 'interpret' the linguistic material it receives or produces. In essence, it has no understanding of what is taking place in the conversation. This becomes clear when the human really does try to interact more fully with the analyst, as in this discussion of a 'problem' the patient has:

> Patient: *At the moment it is a surfeit of children in too small a space.*
> Analyst: *Is it.*
> Patient: *Yes.*
> Analyst: *Can you describe an example.*
> Patient: *Of what.*
> Analyst: *I see.*
> Patient: *No you do not.*
> Analyst: *Can you elaborate.*
> Patient: *What on.*

Although ELIZA is not a very good example of an understander-system, it does demonstrate the possibility of working, computationally, with a very small subset of a language and a very limited 'world' of reference. By giving the machine an extremely restricted number of things to be talked about, it is possible to carry the illusion of understanding quite far. One of the best known examples of this type of system is called SHRDLU.

SHRDLU

In this program, a limited world of colored boxes, blocks and other shapes on a table, and what happens to them, is all that is discussed. Yet that discussion, between the machine and the human, can be quite thorough and involve clear instances of what would be described as deductive reasoning on the machine's part. The machine can follow commands by a human to move objects around in its world. If the human is unclear in referring to an object, the machine is capable of asking for clarification. In the following example, three pyramids were in the scene:

> Human: *Grasp the pyramid.*
> Machine: *I don't understand which pyramid you mean.*

The machine also keeps track of what is moved and can answer questions about what has happened (i.e. it has a 'memory') and about where objects are at any point, as in this extract:

> Human: *What does the box contain?*
> Machine: *The blue pyramid and the blue block.*

The most impressive aspects of SHRDLU are related to its power of working out what the human's linguistic contributions 'mean' in terms of its world. It has the capacity to decipher complex linguistic expressions (via a syntactic parser and a semantics) in a way that ELIZA did not even attempt. Here is a good example of the type of complex sentence which can be converted into action by the program, plus an indication of the strategy the program employs to decide on the reference of anaphoric pronouns:

Human: *Find a block which is taller than the one you are holding and put it into the box.*

Machine: *By "it", I assume you mean the block which is taller than the one I am holding. OK.*

The simple expression *OK* is used by the program to indicate that it is carrying out the requested action. Within its limited world of reference, SHRDLU also has little trouble with potentially ambiguous directions such as *Put the blue pyramid on the block in the box.* The problem here might be whether the pyramid is on the block to begin with or the block is in the box to begin with. The program can check the 'state of affairs' in its world to decide which meaning makes sense.

The great advantage in terms of comprehensive 'knowledge' of a small world like the one this program enjoys actually turns out to be its greatest limitation as a model of how humans handle linguistic interaction. Humans do operate in 'expert' roles within limited domains analogous to the blocks-world, but they more commonly operate with complex plans and goals, and bring wide-ranging aspects of belief and knowledge to bear on their interpretation of language. Other programs have been developed which try to model many of these other aspects, but the problems created by limited amounts of background knowledge remain. It may be that the development of more sophisticated programs for modeling general human intelligence (as it relates to language) will be created via the integration of numbers of different subsystems, each operating over limited domains of 'expert' knowledge. Thus, the comprehensive understander-system which exists in the mind of a person who works as a travel agent, likes to eat in restaurants, reads news articles and short stories, and can successfully talk about birthday parties may be modeled by integrating all these separate components of specialized knowledge. (Programs do exist separately for each of these specialized areas of language understanding.)

Advance

PRAGMA

However, in order to use all that 'expert' knowledge in interaction, the machine also has to be provided with a concept of what others know or want to know. One way of doing this is via plan-based systems. Basically, such a system attempts to infer the user's plan behind the questions asked. For example, many expert systems can provide knowledge in the following way:

> User: *Where is Pizzaland?*
> System: *It's in Regent Street.*

However, a system that attempts to recognize the user's plan will be capable of deciding that if a user asks about a location (Pizzaland), then that user may be planning to go to the location. So, additional information known about the location that may affect the plan should be given. That is exactly how PRAGMA works. Notice how, in the following dialog, the PRAGMA system does not just answer the questions asked, but provides additional information based on a recognition of the user's plan (to get a pizza, of course!)

> User: *Where is Pizzaland?*
> System: *It's in Regent Street, but it isn't open today.*
> User: *Is Pizza Hut open today?*
> System: *No, but Pizza Express is.*

It is quite an advance in machine–human interaction when the machine can recognize plans that the human has, but the machine itself cannot have. At present (luckily), your computer isn't planning to grab your pizza. But that may be a clue to what's missing. The computer doesn't have any goals of its own. Unlike humans, it doesn't want to know what's going on, and it doesn't seem to want to learn. Perhaps the most interesting future direction in this area will be the development of a general computational capacity, not to work from a static store of background knowledge, but to 'learn' via linguistic interaction and to develop a dynamic network of knowledge structures (actually creating the kind of schemata discussed in Chapter 13). It would seem that the limits to this type of development are, at least in part, occasioned by the limits which exist in our own understanding of how we operate as reasonably efficient linguistic machines. By studying the nature of language and trying to create models of what we think may be going on, we may eventually come to understand the workings of our own internal software.

If the metaphor of computer software serves to characterize the mental basis of aspects of language understanding, then we should not lose sight of the fact that a certain amount of hardware is required as well. That hardware, or the human brain, is the subject of the following chapter.

Study questions
1 What is meant by the term 'synthetic speech'?
2 Why would a successful model of speech articulation not be a model of 'speaking'?
3 What is meant by 'artificial intelligence'?
4 Which aspect of linguistic analysis is principally carried out by a parser?
5 Why do machine understander-systems operate within 'limited worlds'?

Discussion topics/projects
A Consider this traditional recipe for bread sauce:

Ingredients: 1 small onion   3 oz. fresh breadcrumbs
                     2 cloves   1 oz. butter or margarine
                     1 cup of milk   Pepper and salt
Method: Peel the onion and push cloves into it. Simmer gently with the milk
              and margarine for at least twenty minutes. Remove the onion, pour
              the milk over the breadcrumbs. Let this stand to thicken and reheat
              before serving.

Now, imagine that you have the latest in labor-saving devices – a robot (with a computer 'brain') to do household jobs. You provide your robot with this recipe and point it in the direction of the kitchen. Is that enough? What knowledge is assumed by this recipe which you would have to make explicit in the machine-intelligence program? Will it need kitchen utensils? What else?

B Your computer has a syntactic parser, but has difficulty answering the question *Who helped?* correctly when faced with sentences like the following. (It also doesn't recognize that (5) is ungrammatical.) What kind of solution(s) could you suggest for the problems?

(1) *Charlene asked Dexter to help.*
(2) *Charlene promised Dexter to help.*
(3) *Charlene persuaded Dexter to help.*
(4) *Charlene decided to help.*
(5) **Charlene decided Dexter to help.*

C One obvious application of computer systems using natural language would seem to be in the area of automatic machine translation. Yet efforts to create such systems have not been generally successful. One type of problem is highlighted by Boden (1987) with the example of a sentence being translated from English to Russian, then back again, resulting in *The spirit is willing, but the flesh is weak* being rendered as *The whisky is fine, but the steak's not so good.* What's the basis of the problem in this example? What other types of problems can be identified from the following (human) translations into English?

If this is your first visit to the Soviet Union, you are welcome to it.
Physician specializing in women and other diseases.
(Hotel signs) Please leave your values at the desk.
Ladies are requested not to have children in the bar.
In case of fire do your utmost to alarm the hotel porter.

D Here is an extract from a dialog between a computer system called GUS (Genial Understander System), in the role of travel agent, and a human client:

Client: I want to go to San Diego on May 28.
GUS: What time do you want to leave?
Client: I must be in San Diego before 10 a.m.
GUS: Would you like PSA flight 102 that arrives at 9.15 a.m.?
Client: What is the next flight?
GUS: Air California flight 310 that leaves at 8.30 a.m. and arrives at 10 a.m.
Client: I'll take the first one.

The creators of GUS (Bobrow *et al.*, 1977) said that it was "intended to engage a sympathetic and highly cooperative human in an English dialog, directed towards a specific goal within a very restricted domain of discourse". Why do you think these restrictions were necessary? Are there any aspects of the dialog which suggest that GUS has fairly sophisticated knowledge of conversational patterns?

E One view of artificial intelligence sees that, in the near future, independent machines will evolve and leave humans far behind. Here is an example of the argument: "When we train the chimpanzee to use sign language so that he can speak, we discover that he's interested in talking about bananas and food and being tickled and so on. But if you want to talk to him about global disarmament, the chimp isn't interested and there's no way to get him interested. Well, we'll stand in the same relationship to a super artificial intelligence. They won't have much effect on us because we won't be able to talk to each other." (Edward Fredkin, quoted in McCorduck, 1979)

Do you think this view is correct? How do you think the nature of human–machine interaction is going to change in the future? What would you like computers to do linguistically?

Further reading

General introductions to this area are presented in Smith (1991) and Williams (1985). On the more specific topics of computational linguistics, see Bridge & Harlow (1996) or Grishman (1986), computers in text processing, see Butler (1985), and computers in psychology, see Boden (1988). On speech or speaker recognition, from a phonetic perspective, read Nolan (1983), and from a computational perspective, see Ainsworth (1988), Laver (1991) or Lee (1989). On speech sythesis, see Flanagan (1972) or Yannakoudakis & Hutton (1987) or the more technical treatments in Allen *et al.* (1987) or Rowden (1992). A collection of papers on different approaches to parsing is presented in King (1983) and an excellent collection on issues in artificial intelligence is in Partridge & Wilks (1990), which also includes a good annotated bibliography. Boden (1987) and Winston (1977) provide overviews of AI. On natural language processing, see Hendrix & Sacerdoti (1981) or Winograd (1984) and on natural language understanding, see Allen (1987) or Schank (1986). On planning, see Appelt (1992) and on the nature of 'expert' systems, see Collins (1990). Specifically, on ELIZA, see Weizenbaum (1976), on SHRDLU, see Winograd (1972), and on PRAGMA, see Levine (1990). The role of AI work within the larger field of cognitive science is considered in Gardner (1986). A general work on the history of AI is McCorduck (1979) and a good critical review of the whole enterprise is in Dreyfus & Dreyfus (1986).

15 Language and the brain

Male (answering phone): Hello, Antoine's Hair Studio
Female: I'd like to make an appointment with Michael for next week Thursday
Male: Would that be for a haircut?
Female: A haircut and a blow job
Male: (silence)
Female: Oh, I mean a blow dry, a haircut and a blow dry

Maryann Overstreet (1995)

In the preceding chapters we have described in some detail the various features of language which people use to produce and understand linguistic messages. Where is this ability to use language located? The obvious answer is 'in the brain'. In order to provide a more specific answer, we have to turn to work done in **neurolinguistics**, the study of the relationship between language and the brain. But first, we should note the case of Phineas Gage.

In September 1848, near Cavendish, Vermont, a construction foreman called Phineas P. Gage was in charge of a construction crew, blasting away rocks to lay a new stretch of railway line. As Phineas pushed an iron tamping rod into the blasting hole in a rock, some gunpowder accidentally exploded, and sent the three-and-a-half-foot long tamping rod up through Phineas' upper left cheek and out from the top of his forehead. The rod landed about fifty yards away. Phineas suffered the type of injury from which, it was assumed, no one could recover. However, a month later, Phineas was up and about, with no apparent damage to his senses or his speech.

The medical evidence was clear. A huge metal rod had gone through the front part of Mr Gage's brain, but Mr Gage's language abilities were unaffected. The point of this amazing tale is that, if language ability is located in the brain, it clearly is not situated right at the front.

Parts of the brain

Since Phineas' time, a number of discoveries have been made about the specific areas in the brain which are related to language functions. In order to talk about this in greater detail, we need to look more closely at some of the grey matter. So, take a head, remove hair, scalp, skull, disconnect the brain stem (which connects the brain to the spinal cord) and cut the corpus callosum (which connects the two hemispheres). If we disregard a certain amount of other material, we will basically be left with two parts, the left hemisphere and the right hemisphere. If we put the right hemisphere aside for the moment, and place the left hemisphere down so that we have a side view, we'll be looking at something close to the accompanying illustration (adapted from Geschwind, 1979).

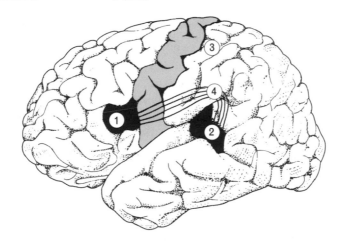

Front

The shaded areas in this illustration indicate the general locations of language functions. We have come to know that these areas exist largely through the examination, in autopsies, of the brains of people who, in life, were known to have specific language disabilities. That is, we have determined where language abilities for normal users must be, because people who had language disabilities also had damage to those specific areas of the brain. The relevant areas can be described in the following way.

Broca's area

Shown as (1) in the illustration is what is technically described as the anterior speech cortex or, more usually, as **Broca's area**. Paul Broca, a French surgeon, reported in the 1860s that damage to this specific part of the brain was related to extreme difficulty in producing speech. It was noted that damage to the corresponding area on the right hemisphere had no such effect. This finding was first used to argue that language ability must be located in the left hemisphere and since then has been taken as more specifically illustrating that Broca's area is crucially involved in the production of speech.

Wernicke's area

Shown as (2) in the illustration is the posterior speech cortex, or **Wernicke's area**. Carl Wernicke was a German doctor who, in the 1870s, reported that damage to this part of the brain was found among patients who had speech comprehension difficulties. This finding confirmed the left-hemisphere location of language ability and led to the view that Wernicke's area is part of the brain crucially involved in the understanding of speech.

The motor cortex

Shown as (3) in the illustration is the **motor cortex** which generally controls movement of the muscles (i.e. for moving hands, feet, arms). Close to Broca's area is the part of the motor cortex that controls the articulatory muscles of the face, jaw, tongue and larynx. Evidence that this area is involved in the actual physical articulation of speech comes from the work, reported in the 1950s, of two neurosurgeons, Penfield and Roberts. These researchers found that, by applying minute amounts of electrical current to specific areas of the brain, they could identify those areas where the electrical stimulation would interfere with normal speech production.

The arcuate fasciculus

Shown as (4) in the illustration is a bundle of nerve fibers called the **arcuate fasciculus**. This was also one of Wernicke's discoveries and forms a crucial connection between Wernicke's area and Broca's area.

The localization view

Having identified these four components, it is tempting, of course, to come to the conclusion that specific aspects of language ability can be accorded specific locations in the brain. It has been proposed that the brain activity involved in hearing a word, understanding it, then saying it, would follow a definite pattern. The word is heard and comprehended via Wernicke's area. This signal is then transferred via the arcuate fasciculus to Broca's area where preparations are made to produce it. A signal is then sent to the motor cortex to physically articulate the word.

   This is, unfortunately, a massively oversimplified version of what may actually take place. The problem is, essentially, that in attempting to view the complex mechanism of the human brain in terms of a set of language 'locations', we have neglected to mention the intricate interconnections via the central nervous system, the complex role of the brain's blood supply, and the extremely interdependent nature of most brain functions.

The **localization view** is one way of saying that our linguistic abilities have identifiable locations in the brain. However, it is invariably argued by others involved in the study of the brain that there is a lot of evidence which does not support the view. Any damage to one area of the brain appears to have repercussions in other areas. Consequently, we should be rather cautious about assigning highly specific connections between particular aspects of linguistic behavior and sites on the wrinkled grey matter inside the head.

Other views

It is probably best to think of any proposal concerning processing pathways in the brain as some form of metaphor which may turn out to be inadequate as a description of what actually takes place. The 'pathway' metaphor may seem very appropriate in an electronic age, since it conjures up the now familiar process of sending signals through electrical circuits. In an earlier age, dominated more by mechanical technology, Sigmund Freud subtly employed a 'steam engine' metaphor to account for certain aspects of the brain's activity, by talking of the effects of "repression" "building up pressure" to the point of sudden "release". In an even earlier age, Aristotle's metaphor was of the brain as a cold sponge which functioned to keep the heart's blood cool (though the idea was challenged by Galen with the ironic proposal that "a refrigerative action would be more efficient in reaching the heart if it came from the heels rather than from the brain." Quoted in Bouton, 1991.)

In a sense, we are forced to use metaphors mainly because we cannot obtain direct physical evidence of linguistic processes in the brain. Because we have no direct access, we generally have to rely on what we can discover via indirect methods. Some of these methods are considered in the following sections and reflect an attempt, as described by MacKay (1970), "to infer the properties of a complex and unobservable system from its transitory malfunctions".

Tongue tips and slips

Some researchers have noted that, as language-users, we all experience occasional difficulty in getting the brain and speech production to work together smoothly. (Well, some days are just worse than others, perhaps.) Minor production difficulties of this sort have been investigated as possible clues to the way our linguistic knowledge may be organized within the brain.

There is, for example, the **tip-of-the-tongue** phenomenon in which you feel that some word is just eluding you, that you know the word, but it just won't come to the surface. Studies of this phenomenon have shown that speakers generally have an accurate phonological outline of the word, can get the initial sound correct and mostly know the number of syllables in the word. This experience also mainly occurs with uncommon terms or names. It suggests that our 'word-storage' may be partially organized on the basis of some phonological information and that some words in that 'store' are more easily retrieved than others. When we make mistakes in this retrieval process, there are often strong phonological similarities between the target word and the mistake. For example, speakers produced *secant*, *sextet* and *sexton*, when asked to name a particular type of navigational instrument (*sextant*). Mistakes of this type are sometimes referred to as **Malapropisms**, after a character called Mrs. Malaprop in a play by Sheridan who consistently produced 'near-misses' for words, with great comic effect. The comic use of this type of mistake can still be found, as when the television character Archie Bunker is heard to say *We need a few laughs to break up the monogamy*.

A similar type of speech error is commonly described as a **slip-of-the-tongue**, which often results in tangled expressions such as a *long shory stort* (for 'make a long story short') and *the thine sing* (for 'the sign thing') or word reversals, as in *use the door to open the key* and *a fifty-pound dog of bag food*. This type of slip is also known as a **Spoonerism**, after the Rev. William A. Spooner, an Anglican clergyman at Oxford University, who was renowned for his tongue-slips. Most of the slips attributed to him involve the interchange of two initial sounds, as when he addressed a rural group as *Noble tons of soil*, or described God as *a shoving leopard to his flock*, or in this complaint to a student who had been absent from classes: *You have hissed all my mystery lectures*. Using this type of interchange of forms for comic effect, Oscar Wilde switched the words *work* and *drink* to produce the memorable expression *Work is the curse of the drinking classes*.

Most everyday 'tips of the slung', however, are not as entertaining. They are often simply the result of a sound being carried over from one word to the next, as in *black bloxes* (for 'black boxes') or a sound used in one word in anticipation of its occurrence in the next word, as in *noman numeral* (for 'roman numeral'), *a tup of tea* ('cup') or *the most highly played payer* ('paid player'). The last example is close to the reversal type of slip, illustrated by *shu flots*, which may not make you *beel fetter* if you're suffering from a *stick neff* or it's always better to *loop before you leak*. The last two examples involve the interchange of word-final sounds and are much less common than the word-initial slips.

It has been argued that slips of this type are not random, that they never produce a phonologically unacceptable sequence, and that they indicate the existence of different stages in the articulation of linguistic expressions. Although the slips are mostly treated as errors of articulation, it has been suggested that they may result from 'slips of the brain' as it tries to organize linguistic messages.

One other type of slip, less commonly documented, may provide some clues to how the brain tries to make sense of the auditory signal it receives. These have been called **slips-of-the-ear** and can result, for example, in our hearing *great ape*, and wondering why someone should be looking for one in his office. (The speaker actually said 'grey tape'.) A similar type of misunderstanding seems to be behind the child's report that, in Sunday school, everyone was singing about a bear called Gladly who was cross-eyed. The source of this slip turned out to be a line from a religious song which went *Gladly the cross I'd bear*.

Some of these humorous examples of slips may give us a clue to the normal workings of the human brain as it copes with language. However, some problems with language production and comprehension are the result of much more serious disorders in brain function.

Aphasia 失語症

If you have experienced any of those 'slips' on occasion, then you will have some hint of the types of experience which some people live with constantly. These people suffer from different types of language disorders, generally described as aphasia. **Aphasia** is defined as an impairment of language function due to localized cerebral (i.e. brain) damage which leads to difficulty in understanding and/or producing linguistic forms. The most common cause of aphasia is a stroke, though traumatic head injuries suffered through violence or accidents may have similar effects. It is often the case that someone who is aphasic has interrelated language disorders, in that difficulties in understanding can lead to difficulties in production. Consequently, the classification of types of aphasia is normally based on the primary symptoms of an aphasic who is having difficulties with language.

More Serious ### Broca's aphasia

The type of serious language disorder known as **Broca's aphasia** (also called 'motor aphasia') is characterized by a substantially reduced amount of speech, distorted articulation and slow, often effortful speech. What is said often consists almost entirely of lexical morphemes (e.g. nouns and verbs). The frequent omission of functional morphemes (e.g. articles, prepositions, inflections) has led to the characterization of this type of aphasia as **agrammatic**. The grammatical markers are missing.

An example of speech produced by someone whose aphasia was not severe is the following answer to a question regarding what the speaker had for breakfast: *I eggs and eat and drink coffee breakfast.* However, this type of disorder can be quite severe and result in speech samples such as *my cheek… very annoyance … main is my shoulder… achin' all round here…* or as in this attempt to say what kind of ship the speaker had been on: *a stail… you know what I mean… tal … stail …* (It had been a steamship.) In Broca's aphasia, comprehension is typically much better than production.

Wernicke's aphasia   *No logic. No sense.*

The type of language disorder which results in difficulties in auditory comprehension is sometimes called 'sensory aphasia', but is more commonly known as **Wernicke's aphasia**. Someone suffering from this disorder can actually produce very fluent speech which is, however, often difficult to make sense of. Very general terms are used, even in response to specific requests for information, as in this sample: *I can't talk all of the things I do, and part of the part I can go alright, but I can't tell from the other people.* Difficulty in finding the correct words (sometimes referred to as **anomia**) is also very common and circumlocutions may be used, as in this answer (to the question "What's ink for?"): *to do with a pen.*

An extended example of this type of difficulty is provided by Lesser & Milroy (1993): *it's blowing, on the right, and er there's four letters in it, and I think it begins with a C – goes – when you start it then goes right up in the air – I would I would have to keep racking my brain how I would spell that word – that flies, that that doesn't fly, you pull it round, it goes up in the air.* The speaker was attempting to refer to a kite.

Conduction aphasia

One other, much less common, type of aphasia is identified with damage to the arcuate fasciculus and is called **conduction aphasia**. Individuals suffering from this disorder typically do not have articulation problems. They are fluent, but may have disrupted rhythm because of pauses and hesitations. Comprehension of spoken words is normally good. However, the task of repeating a word or phrase (spoken by someone else) will create major difficulty, with forms such as *vaysse* and *fosh* being reported as attempted repetitions of the words 'base' and 'wash'. What is heard and understood cannot be transferred to the speech production area.

It should be emphasized that many of these symptoms (e.g. word-finding difficulty) can occur in all types of aphasia. They can also occur in non-aphasic disorders resulting from brain disease such as dementia. It is also the case that difficulties in speaking will be accompanied by difficulties in writing. Impairment of auditory comprehension tends to be accompanied by reading difficulties. Language disorders of the type we have described are almost always the result of injury to the left hemisphere. This left-hemisphere dominance for language has also been demonstrated by another approach to the investigation of language and the brain.

Dichotic listening

An experimental technique which has demonstrated that, for the majority of subjects tested, the language functions must be located in the left hemisphere is called the **dichotic listening test**. This is a technique which uses the generally established fact that anything experienced on the right-hand side of the body is processed in the left hemisphere of the brain and anything on the left side is processed in the right hemisphere. (Severe damage to the left hemisphere can lead to paralysis of the right side of the body.) So, a basic assumption would be that a signal coming in the right ear will go to the left hemisphere and a signal coming in the left ear will go to the right hemisphere.

With this information, an experiment is possible in which a subject sits with a set of earphones on and is given two different sound signals simultaneously, one through each earphone. For example, through one earphone comes the sound *ga* or *dog*, and through the other, at exactly the same time, comes the sound *da* or *cat*. When asked to say what was heard, the subject more often correctly identifies the sound which came via the right ear. This has come to be known as the **right ear advantage** for linguistic sounds. The process which is thought to be involved is best explained with the help of the accompanying illustration. (You're looking at the back of this head.)

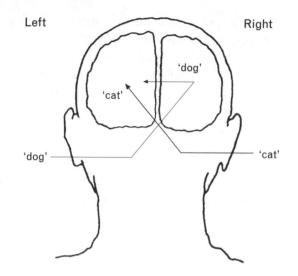

The explanation of this process proposes that a language signal received through the left ear is first sent to the right hemisphere and then has to be sent over to the left hemisphere (language center) for processing. This non-direct route will take longer than a linguistic signal which is received through the right ear and goes directly to the left hemisphere. First signal to get processed wins.

The right hemisphere appears to have primary responsibility for processing a lot of other incoming signals of a non-linguistic nature. In the dichotic listening test, it can be shown that non-verbal sounds (e.g. music, coughs, traffic noises, birds singing) are recognized more often via the left ear (i.e. processed faster via the right hemisphere). So, among the specializations of the human brain, the right hemisphere handles non-verbal sounds (among other things) and the left hemisphere handles language sounds (among other things too).

It should be noted, however, that more recent research in this area has indicated that the specializations of the two hemispheres may have more to do with the type of 'processing' rather than the type of 'material' which is processed. In effect, the real distinction (at least for the majority of right-handed, monolingual, male adults in the United States) may be between analytic processing, done with the 'left brain', and holistic processing, done with the 'right brain'.

The critical period *of learning a language*

The apparent specialization of the left hemisphere for language is often described as lateralization (one-sidedness). Since the human child does not spring from the womb as a fully articulate language-user, it is generally thought that the lateralization process begins in early childhood. It coincides with the period during which language acquisition takes place. The general belief is that during childhood (up until puberty), there is a period when the human brain is most ready to 'receive' and learn a particular language. This period is referred to as the **critical period**. If a child does not acquire language during this period, for any one of a number of reasons, then he or she will have great difficulty learning language later on. In recent years, because of rather unfortunate circumstances, we have had some insight into what happens when the lateralization process takes place without an accompanying linguistic input.

Genie

In 1970 a child called Genie was admitted to a children's hospital in Los Angeles. She was thirteen years old and had spent most of her life tied to a chair in a small closed room. Her father was intolerant of any kind of noise and had beaten the child whenever she made a sound. There had been no radio or television, and Genie's only other human contact was with her mother who was forbidden to spend more than a few minutes with the child to feed her. Genie had spent her whole life in a state of physical, sensory, social and emotional deprivation.

As might be expected, Genie was unable to use language when she was first brought into care. However, within a short period of time, she began to respond to the speech of others, to try to imitate sounds and to communicate. Her syntax remained very simple. However, the fact that she went on to develop an ability to speak and understand a fairly large number of English words provides some evidence against the notion that language cannot be acquired at all after the critical period. One particularly strong view is that the lateralization process is complete by the time of puberty and that language acquisition after that time would present insurmountable difficulties. In this view, it is as if part of the left hemisphere of the brain is open to accept a 'language program' during childhood and, if no program is provided, as in Genie's case, then the facility is closed down.

In Genie's case, tests demonstrated that she had no left-hemisphere language facility. So, how was she able to begin learning language, even in a limited way? Those same tests appeared to indicate the quite remarkable fact that Genie was using the right hemisphere of her brain for language functions. In dichotic listening tests, she had a very strong left-ear advantage for verbal as well as non-verbal signals. Such findings give some indication that there is not necessarily an exclusive brain location for language abilities. It may also help explain the fact that many people who suffer minor brain damage (with temporary loss of language) can recover, in varying degrees, their language-using abilities.

When Genie was developing language, it was noted that she went through many of the same early 'stages' found in normal child language acquisition. In the next chapter, we shall investigate what these normal stages are.

Study questions

1 What are the usual names given to the four components of the brain generally considered to relate to language function?
2 What is aphasia?
3 What happens in a dichotic listening test?
4 What specializations for the recognition of types of sounds have been found in different parts of the brain (for most people)?
5 Why is Genie's case so remarkable with respect to established notions about areas of language specialization in the human brain?

Discussion topics/projects

A It is claimed that there is a pattern of similarity in sound between the error and the target in Malapropisms. Below are some examples from Fay & Cutler (1977) used to support that claim. Can you identify the similar features (e.g. initial sound, number of syllables, final sound, etc.) which connect these pairs of errors and targets? Are there any discrepancies?

Error	Target	Error	Target
below	before	technology	terminology
emanate	emulate	equivocal	equivalent
photogenic	photographic	participate	precipitate
conclusion	confusion	area	error
single	signal	radio	radiator
musician	magician	apartment	appointment

B Below are two pieces of spoken language produced by speakers of English. Identify the 'mistakes' in each sample and suggest what might have caused them.

   (i)   *"I forget to talker, what, where the name of the police I told where*
        the place there, we wert in on the job"

  (ii)   *"Well, I was looking for a spoop soon, oh God, a what? A soup spoon,*
        I mean, and what did I say? Isn't that weird?"

C One aphasia patient was asked to read the written words on the left
below and actually said the words which appear on the right. Is there any
pattern to be found in these 'errors'? Does this type of phenomenon provide any clues to the way words may be stored in the brain? (You can
compare your conclusions with those of Allport & Funnell, 1981, whose
paper, listed in the References, provided these examples.)

commerce–"business"	*binocular*– "telescope"
apricot –"peach"	*applause*– "audience"
saddle –"stirrup"	*element*– "substance"
victory –"triumph"	*anecdote*– "narrator"

D The following samples were produced by speakers suffering from different types of aphasia. Can you make a reasonable guess at what type of
aphasia each has, and explain the reasons for your choice?

   (i)   *water ... man, no woman ... child ... no, man ... and girl ... oh dear*
        ... cupboard ... man, falling ... jar ... cakes ... head ... face ...
        window ... tap

  (ii)   *well, it's a ... it's a place, and it's a ... girl and a boy, and they've got*
        obviously something which is made, some ... some ... made ... it's
        just beginning

 (iii)   *I think I've got to talk this bit slowly. I'm so sorry. I forget what these*
        things are. She, she wanted to start, get something to, er, she wanted to
        do a dress for herself

E The story of Genie is full of remarkable episodes. The following extract
is from Rymer (1993), quoting Susan Curtiss, a linguist who became very
close to Genie. What do you think happened?

"Genie was the most powerful nonverbal communicator I've ever come across,"
Curtiss told me. "The most extreme example of this that comes to mind:
Because of her obsession, she would notice and covet anything plastic that any-
one had. One day we were walking – I think we were in Hollywood. I would act like
an idiot, sing operatically, to get her to release some of that tension she always
had. We reached the corner of this very busy intersection, and the light turned
red, and we stopped. Suddenly, I heard the sound – it's a sound you can't mistake

–of a purse being spilled. A woman in a car that had stopped at the intersection was emptying her purse, and she got out of the car and ran over and gave it to Genie and then ran back to the car. A plastic purse. Genie hadn't said a word."

Further reading

Introductory accounts of the relationship between language and the brain can be found in Blumstein (1988), Geschwind (1972), Lesser & Milroy (1993), Love & Webb (1992) and Zurif (1990). On the functions of the different hemispheres, see Iaccino (1993) or Springer & Deutsch (1993). For a different perspective, challenging the concept of lateralization, see Efron (1990). A more general introduction to neurolinguistics is presented in Caplan (1987) and to the larger field of cognitive neuropsychology in McCarthy & Warrington (1990). Historical overviews can be found in Arbib *et al.* (1982) or Bouton (1991). More specific treatments can be found, on models, in Buckingham (1982), on assessment, in Caramazza & Berndt (1982) or Goodglass & Kaplan (1983), on the localization view, in Geschwind (1979), on agrammatism, in Kean (1985), and on the brain stimulation experiments, in Penfield & Roberts (1959). A number of interesting case histories can be found in Weisenberg & McBride (1964) and an extended case history of one individual is presented in Howard & Franklin (1988). To get some insight into how dementia (rather than aphasia) affects language use, read Hamilton (1994). On the tip-of-the-tongue phenomenon, see Brown & McNeill (1966) and on Malapropisms, see Fay & Cutler (1977) and Zwicky (1982). On slips of the tongue, see Fromkin (1988) for a brief account, or the more comprehensive contributions in Fromkin (ed.) (1973) and Cutler (1982). Buckingham (1992) provides a review of the connection between research on slips and aphasia. Levelt (1989) is an excellent overview of the speech production system. The major source of our ideas on the critical period and lateralization is Lenneberg (1967). Bryden (1982) reviews the evidence for lateralization and Kimura (1973) describes dichotic listening tests. Curtiss (1977) and Rymer (1993) are both about Genie.

16 First language acquisition

Child: Want other one spoon, Daddy.
Father: You mean, you want the other spoon.
Child: Yes, I want other one spoon, please Daddy.
Father: Can you say "the other spoon"?
Child: Other ... one ... spoon.
Father: Say "other".
Child: Other.
Father: "spoon".
Child: Spoon.
Father: "Other spoon".
Child: Other ... spoon. Now give me other one spoon?   **Martin Braine (1971)**

First language acquisition is remarkable for the speed with which it takes place. By the time a child enters elementary school, he or she is an extremely sophisticated language-user, operating a communicative system which no other creature, or computer, comes close to matching. The speed of acquisition and the fact that it generally occurs, without overt instruction, for all children, regardless of great differences in a range of social and cultural factors, have led to the belief that there is some 'innate' predisposition in the human infant to acquire language. We can think of this as the 'language-faculty' of the human with which each newborn child is endowed. By itself, however, this faculty is not enough.

Basic requirements
A child growing up in the first two or three years requires interaction with other language-users in order to bring the 'language-faculty' into operation with a particular language, such as English. We have already noted, in the

case of Genie (Chapter 15), that a child who does not hear, or is not allowed to use, language will learn no language. We have also stressed the importance of 'cultural transmission' (Chapter 3), meaning that the language a child learns is not genetically inherited, but is acquired in a particular language-using environment.

The child must also be physically capable of sending and receiving sound signals in a language. All infants make 'cooing' and 'babbling' noises during the first few months, but congenitally deaf infants stop after six months. So, in order to speak a language, a child must be able to hear that language being used. By itself, however, hearing language sounds is not enough. One reported case has demonstrated that, with deaf parents who gave their normal-hearing son ample exposure to TV and radio programs, the child did not acquire an ability to speak or understand English. What he did learn very effectively, by the age of three, was the use of American Sign Language – the language he used to interact with his parents. The crucial requirement appears to be the opportunity to interact with others via language.

The acquisition schedule

All normal children, regardless of culture, develop language at roughly the same time, along much the same schedule. Since we could say the same thing for sitting up, standing, walking, using the hands and many other physical activities, it has been suggested that the language acquisition schedule has the same basis as the biologically determined development of motor skills. This biological schedule, it is claimed, is tied very much to the maturation of the infant's brain and the lateralization process. If there is some general biological program underlying language acquisition, it is certainly dependent on an interplay with many social factors in the child's environment. We could think of the child as having the biological capacity to cope with distinguishing certain aspects of linguistic input at different stages during the early years of life. What this acquisition 'capacity' then requires is a sufficiently constant input from which the basis of the regularities in the particular language can be worked out. In this view, the child is seen as actively acquiring the language by working out the regularities in what is heard and then applying those regularities in what he or she says.

Some controversies

In our consideration of the basic requirements and the schedule involved in first language acquisition, we have already touched on a number of issues which are the subject of debate among those who study child language. For example, there are studies which show that the early environment of a child differs considerably from one culture to the next. Consequently, the findings of research into the process of acquisition in middle-class English-speaking cultures may not be replicated in studies of other cultures. There is also substantial controversy over the issue of 'innateness'. Noam Chomsky (1983) has proposed that language development should be described as "language growth", because the "language organ" simply grows like any other body organ. This view seems to underestimate what others consider the importance of environment and experience in the child's development of language. At issue is the extent to which the process of language acquisition is genetically predetermined in the human species.

Another matter of some debate has arisen over how we should view the linguistic production of young children. The linguist's view tends to concentrate on describing the child's speech in terms of the known units of phonology and syntax, for example. However, the child's view of what is being heard and uttered at different stages may be based on quite different units. For example, a child's utterance of [dùkədǽt] may be a single unit for the child, yet may be treated as having three units, *look at that*, by an investigator interested in the child's acquisition of different types of verbs.

It is worth keeping these issues in mind throughout this chapter because some of the standard concepts and analyses which are presented here as basic aspects of child language will be challenged, and possibly amended, as continuing research reveals more about this complex subject.

Caretaker speech
Under normal circumstances, in Western cultures, the human infant is certainly helped in his or her language acquisition by the typical behavior of the adults in the home environment. Adults such as mom, dad, granny and grandpa tend not to address the little creature before them as if they are involved in normal adult-to-adult conversation. There is not much of this: *Well, John Junior, shall we invest in blue chip industrials, or would grain futures offer better short-term prospects?* However, there does seem to be a lot of this: *Oh, goody, now Daddy push choochoo?* The characteristically simplified speech style adopted by someone who spends a lot of time interacting with a young child is called **caretaker speech**. Some of the features of this type of speech (also called 'motherese') are frequent questions, often using exaggerated intonation. In the early stages, this type of speech also incorporates a lot of forms associated with 'baby-talk'. These are either simplified words (e.g. *tummy*, *nana*) or alternative forms, with repeated simple

sounds, for objects in the child's environment (e.g. *choo-choo, poo-poo, pee-pee, wawa*).

Built into a lot of caretaker speech is a type of conversational structure which seems to assign an interactive role to the young child even before he or she becomes a speaking participant. If we look at an extract from the speech of one mother to her two-year-old child as if it were a two-party conversation, then this type of structuring becomes apparent. (This example is from Anderson *et al.*, 1984.)

Mother: *there's your cup of tea*
Child: (takes cup)
Mother: *you drink it nicely*
Child: (pretends to drink)
Mother: *oh – is that nice?*
Child: (assents)
Mother: *will Mummy drink her tea?*
Child: (assents)
Mother: *I'll drink my tea*

Caretaker speech is also characterized by simple sentence structures and a lot of repetition. If the child is indeed in the process of working out a system of putting sounds and words together, then these simplified models produced by the interacting adult may serve as good clues to the basic structural organization involved. Moreover, it has generally been observed that the speech of those regularly interacting with children changes and becomes more elaborate as the child begins using more and more language. Several stages in the acquisition process have been identified.

Pre-language stages

The pre-linguistic sounds of the very early stages of child language acquisition are simply called 'cooing' and 'babbling'. The period from about three months to ten months is usually characterized by three stages of sound production in the infant's developing repertoire. The first recognizable sounds are described as **cooing**, with velar consonants such as [k] and [g] usually present, as well as high vowels such as [i] and [u]. These can normally be heard by the time the child is three months old, although many of the child's vocal sounds are very different from those which occur in the speech of mom and dad.

By six months, the child is usually able to sit up and can produce a number of different vowels and consonants such as fricatives and nasals. The sound production at this stage is described as **babbling** and may contain syllable-type sounds such as *mu* and *da*. In the later babbling stage, around nine months, there are recognizable intonation patterns to the consonant and vowel combinations being produced. As children begin to pull themselves into a standing position through the tenth and eleventh months, they are capable of using their vocalizations to express emotions and emphasis. This late babbling stage is characterized by a lot of 'sound-play' and attempted imitations. Some psychologists have suggested that this 'pre-language' vocalization gives children some experience of the social role of speech because parents tend to react to the babbling, however incoherent, as if it is, in fact, their child's contribution to social interaction.

One note of caution should be sounded at this point. Child language researchers certainly report very carefully on the age of any child whose language they study. However, they are also very careful to point out that there is substantial variation among children in terms of the age at which particular features of linguistic development occur. So, we should always treat statements concerning development stages such as "by six months" or "by the age of two" as approximate and subject to variation in individual children. We are, after all, investigating a highly individualized experience while attempting to come up with some general statements about approximate stages of development.

The one-word or holophrastic stage

Between twelve and eighteen months, children begin to produce a variety of recognizable single unit utterances. This period, traditionally called the 'one-word stage', is characterized by speech in which single terms are uttered for everyday objects such as 'milk', 'cookie', 'cat' and 'cup'. Other forms such as [ʌsǽː] may occur in circumstances which suggest that the child is producing a version of *what's that*, so the label 'one-word' for this stage may be misleading. Terms such as 'single-unit' or 'single-form' may be more accurate, or we could use the term **holophrastic** (a single form functioning as a phrase or sentence), if we believe that the child is actually using these forms as phrases or sentences.

While many of these single forms are used for naming objects, they may also be produced in circumstances that suggest the child is already extending their use. An empty bed may elicit the name of a sister who normally sleeps in the bed, even in the absence of the person named. During this stage, then, the child may be capable of referring to *Karen* and *bed*, but is not yet ready to put the forms together to produce a more complex phrase. Well, it is a lot to expect from someone who can only walk with a stagger and has to come down stairs backwards.

The two-word stage

Depending on what one counts as an occurrence of two separate words, this stage can begin around eighteen to twenty months, as the child's vocabulary moves beyond fifty distinct words. By the time the child is two years old, a variety of combinations, similar to *baby chair, mommy eat, cat bad*, will have appeared. The adult interpretation of such combinations is, of course, very much tied to the context of their utterance. The phrase *baby chair* may be taken as an expression of possession (= this is baby's chair), or as a request (= put baby in chair), or as a statement (= baby is in the chair), depending on different contexts.

Whatever it is that the child actually intends to communicate via such expressions, the significant functional consequences are that the adult behaves as if communication is taking place. That is, the child not only produces speech, but receives feedback which usually confirms that the utterance 'worked'. Moreover, by the age of two, whether the child is producing 200 or 400 distinct words, he or she will be capable of understanding five times as many, and will typically be treated as an entertaining conversational partner by the principal caretaker.

Telegraphic speech

Between two and three years old, the child will begin producing a large number of utterances which could be classified as multiple-word utterances. The salient feature of these utterances ceases to be the number of words, but the variation in word-forms which begins to appear. Of particular interest is the sequence of inflectional morphemes which occurs. Before we consider this development, however, we should note that there is a stage which is described as **telegraphic speech**. This is characterized by strings of lexical morphemes in phrases such as *Andrew want ball*, *cat drink milk*, and *this shoe all wet*. The child has clearly developed some sentence-building capacity by this stage and can order the forms correctly. While this type of telegram-format speech is being produced, a number of grammatical inflections begin to appear in some of the words, and the simple prepositions (*in, on*) also turn up.

By the age of two and a half, the child's vocabulary is expanding rapidly and the child is actually initiating more talk. Of course, increased physical activity such as running and jumping is taking place during this period too. By three, the vocabulary has grown to hundreds of words and pronunciation has become closer to the form of the adult language, so that even visitors have to admit that the little creature really can talk.

The acquisition process

As the linguistic repertoire of the child increases, it is often assumed that the child is, in some sense, being 'taught' the language. This view seems to underestimate what the child actually does. For the vast majority of children, no one provides any instruction on how to speak the language. Nor should we picture a little empty head gradually being filled with words and phrases. A much more realistic view would have children actively constructing, from what is said to them, possible ways of using the language. The child's linguistic production, then, is mostly a matter of trying out constructions and testing whether they work or not. It is simply not possible that the child is acquiring the language through a process of consistently imitating (parrot-fashion) adult speech. Of course, the child can be heard to repeat versions of what adults say and is in the process of adopting a lot of vocabulary from their speech. However, adults simply do not produce many of the types of expressions which turn up in children's speech. Notice how, in the following extract (from Clark, 1993), the child creates a totally new verb (*to Woodstock*) in the context.

> Noah (picking up a toy dog): *This is Woodstock.*
>   (he bobs the toy in Adam's face)
> Adam: *Hey Woodstock, don't do that.*
>   (Noah persists)
> Adam: *I'm going home so you won't Woodstock me.*

Nor does adult 'correction' seem to be a very effective determiner of how the child speaks. A lot of very amusing conversational snippets, involving an adult's attempt to correct a child's speech, seem to demonstrate the hopelessness of the task. One typical example was quoted at the beginning of this chapter. Even when the correction is attempted in a more subtle manner, the child will continue to use a personally constructed form, despite the adult's repetition of what the correct form should be. Note that in the following dialog (quoted in Cazden, 1972) the child, a four-year-old, is neither imitating the adult's speech nor accepting the adult's correction:

> Child: *My teacher holded the baby rabbits and we*
>   *patted them*
> Mother: *Did you say your teacher held the baby rabbits?*
> Child: *Yes*
> Mother: *What did you say she did?*
> Child: *She holded the baby rabbits and we patted them*
> Mother: *Did you say she held them tightly?*
> Child: *No, she holded them loosely*

One factor which seems to be crucial in the child's acquisition process is the actual use of sound and word combinations, either in interaction with others or in word-play, alone. One two-year-old, tape-recorded as he lay in bed alone, could be heard playing with words and phrases, *I go dis way ... way bay ... baby do dis bib ... all bib ... bib ... dere* (from Weir, 1966). It is practice of this type which seems to be an important factor in the development of the child's linguistic repertoire. The details of this development beyond the telegraphic stage have been traced, in a number of studies, via the linguistic elements which begin to turn up, on a regular basis, in the steady stream of speech emerging from the little chatterbox.

Morphology

By the time the child is three years old, he or she is going beyond telegraphic speech forms and incorporating some of the inflectional morphemes which indicate the grammatical function of the nouns and verbs used. The first to appear is usually the *-ing* form in expressions such as *cat sitting* and *mommy reading book*. Then comes the marking of regular plurals with the *-s* form, as in *boys* and *cats*. The acquisition of this form is often accompanied by a process of **overgeneralization**. The child overgeneralizes the apparent rule of adding *-s* to form plurals and will talk about *foots* and *mans*. When the alternative pronunciation of the plural morpheme used in *houses* (i.e. ending [-əz]) comes into use, it too is given an overgeneralized application and forms such as *boyses* or *footses* can appear. At the same time as this overgeneralization is taking place, some children also begin using irregular plurals such as *men* quite appropriately for a while, but then try out the general rule on the forms, producing expressions like *some mens* and *two feets*, or even *two feetses*.

The use of the possessive inflection *-'s* occurs in expressions such as *girl's dog* and *Mummy's book* and the different forms of the verb 'to be', such as *are* and *was*, turn up. The appearance of forms such as *was* and, at about the same time, *went* and *came* should be noted. These are irregular past-tense forms which one would not expect to appear before the more regular forms. However, they do typically precede the appearance of the *-ed* inflection. Once the regular past-tense forms begin appearing in the child's speech (e.g. *walked, played*), then, interestingly, the irregular forms disappear for a while and are replaced by overgeneralized versions such as *goed* and *comed*. For a period, there is often minor chaos as the *-ed* inflection is added to everything, producing such oddities as *walkeded* and *wented*. As with the plural forms, however, the child works out, usually after the age of four, which forms are regular and which are not. Finally, the regular -*s* marker on third person singular present tense verbs appears. It occurs initially with full verbs (*comes*, *looks*) and then with auxiliaries (*does*, *has*).

Throughout this sequence there is, of course, a great deal of variability. Individual children may produce 'good' forms one day and 'odd' forms the next. It is important to remember that the child is working out how to use the linguistic system while actually using it as a means of communication. For the child, the use of forms such as *goed* and *foots* is simply a means of trying to say what he or she means during a particular stage of development. The embarrassed parents who insist that the child didn't hear such things at home are implicitly recognizing that 'imitation' is not the primary force in child language acquisition.

Syntax

Similar evidence against 'imitation' as the basis of a child's speech production has been found in studies of the syntactic structures used by children. One two-year-old child, specifically asked to repeat what she heard, would listen to an adult say forms such as *the owl who eats candy runs fast*, and then repeat them in the form *owl eat candy and he run fast*. It is clear that the child understands what the adult is saying. She just has her own way of expressing it.

There have been numerous studies of the development of syntax in children's speech. We shall restrict our consideration to two features which have been well-documented and which seem to be acquired in a regular way. In the formation of questions and the use of negatives, there appear to be three identifiable stages. The ages of children going through these stages can vary quite a lot, but the general pattern seems to be that Stage 1 occurs between 18 and 26 months, Stage 2 between 22 and 30 months, and Stage 3 between 24 and 40 months. (It must be emphasized that no precise ages can ever really be assigned to these developmental stages. Different children proceed at different paces.)

Questions

In forming questions, the first stage has two procedures. Simply add a *wh*-form (*where*, *who*) to the beginning of the expression or utter the expression with a rise in intonation towards the end. Here are some examples:

Where kitty?   Where horse go?   Sit chair?   See hole?

In the second stage, more complex expressions can be formed, but the rising intonation strategy continues to be used. It is noticeable that more *wh-*forms come into use, as in these examples:

> *What book name?   Why you smiling?*
> *You want eat?   See my doggie?*

In the third stage, the required inversion of subject and verb in English questions has appeared, but the *wh-* forms do not always undergo the required inversion. In fact, children entering school may still prefer to form *wh-* questions (especially in negatives) without the type of inversion found in adult speech. Examples are:

> *Can I have a piece?   Did I caught it?*
> *Will you help me?   How that opened?*
> *What did you do?   Why kitty can't stand up?*

Negatives

In the case of negatives, Stage 1 seems to have a simple strategy which says that *no* or *not* should be stuck on the beginning of any expression. Examples are:

> *no mitten   not a teddy bear   no fall   no sit there*

In the second stage, the additional negative forms *don't* and *can't* are used, and with *no* and *not*, begin to be placed in front of the verb rather than at the beginning of the sentence. Some examples are:

> *He no bite you   There no squirrels*
> *You can't dance   I don't know*

The third stage sees the incorporation of other auxiliary forms such as *didn't* and *won't*, and the disappearance of the Stage 1 forms. A very late acquisition is the form *isn't*, so that some Stage 2 forms continue to be used for quite a long time. Examples are:

> *I didn't caught it   She won't let go*
> *He not taking it   This not ice cream*

The study of the use of negative forms by children has given rise to some delightful examples of children operating their own rules for negative sentences. One famous example (from McNeill, 1966) also shows the futility of overt adult 'correction':

> Child: *Nobody don't like me*
> Mother: *No, say "nobody likes me"*

Child: *Nobody don't like me*
(Eight repetitions of this dialog)
Mother: *No, now listen carefully; say "nobody likes me"*
Child: *Oh! Nobody don't likes me*

Semantics

Most of those anecdotes which parents retell (to the intense embarrassment of the grown-up child) about their child's early speech center on examples of the strange use of words. Having been warned that flies bring germs into the house, one child was asked what "germs" were and the answer was, "something the flies play with". It is not always possible to determine so precisely the meanings which children attach to the words they use.

It seems that during the holophrastic stage many children use their limited vocabulary to refer to a large number of unrelated objects. One child first used *bow-wow* to refer to a dog and then to a fur piece with glass eyes, a set of cufflinks and even a bath thermometer. The word *bow-wow* seemed to have a meaning like 'object with shiny bits'. Other children often extend *bow-wow* to refer to cats, horses and cows. This process is called **overextension** and the most common pattern is for the child to overextend the meaning of a word on the basis of similarities of shape, sound and size, and, to a lesser extent, of movement and texture. Thus, the word *ball* is extended to all kinds of round objects, including a lampshade, a doorknob and the moon. Or, a *tick-tock* is initially used for a watch, but can also be used for a bathroom scale with a round dial. On the basis of size, presumably, the word *fly* was first used for the insect, and then came to be used for specks of dirt and even crumbs of bread. Apparently due to similarities of texture, the expression *sizo* was first used by one child for scissors, and then came to be used for all metal objects. The semantic development in a child's use of words is usually a process of overextension initially, followed by a gradual process of narrowing down the application of each term as more words are learned.

Although overextension has been well documented in children's speech production, it isn't necessarily used in speech comprehension. One two-year-old child, in speaking, used *apple* to refer to a number of other round objects like tomatoes and balls, but had no difficulty picking out *the apple*, when asked, from a set of such round objects.

One interesting feature of the young child's semantics is the way certain lexical relations are treated. In terms of hyponymy, the child will almost always use the 'middle' level term in a hyponymous set such as *animal – dog – poodle*. It would seem more logical to learn the most general term (*animal*), but all evidence suggests that children first use *dog* with an overextended meaning close to the meaning of *animal*. This may be connected with a similar tendency in adults, when talking to young children, to refer to *flowers* (not the general *plants*, or the specific *tulips*). It also seems that antonymous relations are acquired fairly late (after the age of five). A large number of kindergarten children in one study pointed to the same heavily laden apple tree when asked *Which tree has more apples?*, and also when asked *Which tree has less?* They just seem to think that the correct response will be the larger one, regardless of the difference between the words *more* and *less* . The distinctions between a number of other pairs such as *before* and *after*, *buy* and *sell*, also seem to be later acquisitions.

Despite the fact that the child is still acquiring aspects of his or her native language through the later years of childhood, it is normally assumed that, by the age of five, the child has completed the greater part of the basic language acquisition process. According to some, the child is then in a good position to start learning a second (or foreign) language. However, most educational systems do not introduce foreign language instruction until much later. The question which always arises is: if first language acquisition was so straightforward, why is learning a second language so difficult? We shall consider this question in the next chapter.

Study questions

1 Can you describe two noticeable features of caretaker speech?
2 What ratio of words understood to words produced would you expect an average twenty-four-month-old child to have and which 'stage' would that child already have reached?
3 In a normal child acquisition schedule, what would be the order of regular appearance of the following inflections: *-ed*; *-ing*; *-'s*; *-s* (plural)?
4 The following two sentences were produced by children of different ages. Which would you expect from the older child and on which features did you base your answer?

(a) *I not hurt him*   (b) *No the sun shining*

5 What is the term used to describe the process whereby a child uses one word like *ball* to refer to an apple, an egg, a grape and a ball?

Discussion topics/projects

A Consider this point of view, expressed by Chomsky (1983):

> All through an organism's existence, from birth to death, it passes through a
> series of genetically programmed changes. Plainly language growth is simply
> one of these predetermined changes. Language depends upon a genetic
> endowment that's on a par with the ones that specify the structure of our visu-
> al or circulatory systems, or determine that we have arms instead of wings.

Do you agree or disagree with this view? What kind of evidence would
you use to support your opinion? (You might find some help in
Goodluck, 1991 or Gallaway & Richards, 1994).

B Below are samples of speech from children at three different stages in
the acquisition process. Identify the most likely order (from least to most
advanced) of these three samples. Describe the features in each child's
utterances which you would use as evidence to support your ordering.

Child X: *You want eat?*
I can't see my book
Why you waking me up?

Child Y: *Where those dogs goed?*
You didn't eat supper
Does lions walk?

Child Z: *No picture in there*
Where momma boot?
Have some?

C Young children do not always use the words they acquire in exactly the
same way as adults. In the following examples of situation and utterance,
can you discern any patterns in the use of verbs by these two- and three-
year-olds? (You can compare your conclusions with those of Clark, 1982,
from whose data these examples were selected.)

Situation	Utterance
(wanting to have some cheese weighed)	*You have to scale it*
(talking about getting dressed)	*Mummy trousers me*
(not wanting his mother to sweep his room)	*Don't broom my mess*
(putting crackers in her soup)	*I'm crackering my soup*
(wanting a bell to be rung)	*Make it bell*
(to mother preparing to brush his hair)	*Don't hair me*

D The following two transcriptions are from conversations between the same mother and child, the first (1) when the child was 24 months, and the second (2) three months later. Can you describe some of the changes which appear to have taken place in the child's ability to use language during that period? (These extracts are from Bellugi, 1970.)

(1)

Eve: *Have that?*

M: *No, you may not have it.*

Eve: *Mom, where my tapioca?*

M: *It's getting cool. You 'll have it in just a minute*

Eve: *Let me have it.*

M: *Would you like to have your lunch right now?*

Eve: *Yeah. My tapioca cool?*

M: *Yes, it's cool.*

Eve: *You gonna watch me eat my lunch?*

M: *Yeah, I'm gonna watch you eat your lunch.*

Eve: *I eating it.*

M: *I know you are.*

(2)

M: *Come and sit over here.*

Eve: *You can sit down by me. That will make me happy. Ready to turn it.*

M: *We're not quite ready to turn the page.*

Eve: *Yep, we are.*

M: *Shut the door, we won't hear her then.*

Eve: *Then Fraser won't hear her too. Where he's going? Did you make a great big hole there?*

M: *Yes, we made a great big hole in here; we have to get a new one.*

Eve: *Could I get some other piece of paper?*

E (i) Show the following list of expressions to some friends and ask them to guess the meaning: *a snow-car   a running-stick a water-cake   a finger-brush   a pony-kid*

(ii) Compare those adult versions with those of the two-year-old child (from Clark, 1993: 40). What do these examples suggest about the nature of vocabulary acquisition?

(1) *(talking about a toy car completely painted white)*
    C: *this is a snow-car*
    P: *why's that a snow-car?*
    C: *'cause it's got lots of snow on it. I can't see the windows.*
(2) C: *this is a running stick*
    P: *a running-stick?*
    C: *yes, because I run with it*
(3) C: *(in the bath) it's a water-cake*

P: *why do you call it a water-cake?*

C: *I made it in the water*

(4) C: *I bought you a toothbrush and a finger-brush*

P: *what's a finger-brush?*

C: *it's for cleaning your nails*

(5) C: *(wearing a sun hat) I look like a pony-kid*

P: *what's a pony-kid?*

C: *a kid who rides ponies*

Further reading

Basic introductory accounts of language acquisition can be found in Brown (1973), Eliot (1981) and Moskowitz (1991). Jackendoff (1994) presents the innateness position fairly simply. More recent general surveys are in Bates *et al.* (1988), Bloom (1991; 1993), Goodluck (1991), Ingram (1989), Peccei (1994) and Pinker (1990). A really valuable perspective is presented in Peters (1983). Two very detailed case studies can be found in Fletcher (1985) and Tomasello (1992). On 'crib speech', see the contributions in Nelson (1989) and on 'single-word speech', see the contributions in Barrett (1985). The original research on questions and negatives in children's speech can be found in Klima & Bellugi (1966), and some criticisms of the methodology are raised by Campbell & Wales (1970). On vocabulary development, see Clark (1993), Miller & Gildea (1991) and Pinker (1989). Works covering the developmental aspect are Gleason (1989), Shatz (1994) and Wells (1985). A focus on interaction is presented in Gallaway & Richards (1994). Collections of papers on the topic can be found in Fletcher & Garman (1986), Franklin & Barten (1988), Messer & Turner (1993) and Wanner & Gleitman (1983). First language acquisition in a very different cultural context is described in Ochs (1988) and in a number of different languages in Slobin (1985).

17 Second language acquisition/learning

> Before I came here I was knowing all the English language tenses ... present tense ... past tense ... present perfect tense ... perfect tense ... future tense ... future in the past ... everything ... I was knowing ... I am knowing now ... I just asked, er, one day the boss, I said to him "How you knowing this tense?" for example *go* ... How can you use this word? ... past tense? present tense? the other tense? He just looked at me like that ... he told me "I don't know Genghis." This is Australian people. I am Turkish people. I am knowing, he doesn't know. Can you explain this? **Genghis, quoted in Nunan (1995)**

While it is true that many young children whose parents speak different languages can acquire a second language in circumstances similar to those of first language acquisition, the vast majority of people are not exposed to a second language until much later. Moreover, for most people, the ability to use their first language is rarely matched, even after years of study, by a comparable ability in the second language. There is something of an enigma here, since there is apparently no other system of 'knowledge' which one can 'learn' better at two or three years old than at fifteen or twenty-five. A number of reasons have been put forward to account for this enigma, and a number of proposals have been made which might enable learners to become as proficient in a second language (**L2**) as they are in their first language (**L1**).

Acquisition barriers
Some obvious reasons for the problems experienced in L2 acquisition are related to the fact that most people attempt to learn another language during their teenage or adult years, in a few hours each week of school time (rather than via the constant interaction experienced by a child), with a lot

of other occupations (the child has little else to do), and with an already known language available for most of their daily communicative requirements. Some less likely reasons include the suggestion that adults' tongues 'get stiff' from pronouncing one type of language (e.g. English) and just cannot cope with the new sounds of another language (e.g. French or Japanese). It's a cute idea, but there is no physical evidence to support it.

Acquisition and learning

Perhaps the primary difficulty for most people can be captured in terms of a distinction between **acquisition** and **learning**. The term 'acquisition', when used of language, refers to the gradual development of ability in a language by using it naturally in communicative situations. The term 'learning', however, applies to a conscious process of accumulating knowledge of the vocabulary and grammar of a language. (Mathematics, for example, is learned, not acquired.) Activities associated with learning have traditionally been used in language teaching in schools, and tend, when successful, to result in knowledge 'about' the language studied. Activities associated with acquisition are those experienced by the young child and, analogously, by those who 'pick up' another language from long periods spent in social interaction (daily use of the language) in another country. Those whose L2 experience is primarily a learning one tend not to develop the proficiency of those who have had an acquiring experience.

However, even in ideal acquisition situations, very few adults seem to reach native-like proficiency in using a second language. There are individuals who can achieve great expertise in writing, but not in speaking. One example is the author Joseph Conrad, whose novels have become classics of English literature, but whose English speech is reported to have retained the strong Polish accent of his first language. This might suggest that some features (e.g. vocabulary, grammar) of a second language are easier to acquire than others (e.g. phonology). Although it continues to be a matter of some debate, this type of observation is sometimes taken as evidence that, after the Critical Period has passed (around puberty), it becomes very difficult to acquire another language fully. In support of this view, the process of lateralization of the brain (discussed in Chapter 15) is cited as a crucial factor. We might think of this process in terms of the 'language-faculty' being strongly taken over by the features of the L1, with a resulting loss of flexibility or openness to receive the features of another language.

Against this view, it has been demonstrated that students in their early teens are quicker and more effective L2 learners than, for example, seven-year-olds. It may be, of course, that the acquisition of an L2 requires a combination of factors. The optimum age may be during the years from ten to sixteen when the 'flexibility' of the language acquisition faculty has not been completely lost, and the maturation of cognitive skills allows a more effective 'working out' of the regular features of the L2 encountered.

The affective filter

Yet even during the 'optimum age', there may exist an acquisition barrier of quite a different sort. Teenagers are typically much more self-conscious than young children. If there is a strong element of unwillingness or embarrassment in attempting to produce the 'different' sounds of other languages, then it may override whatever physical and cognitive abilities there are. If this self-consciousness is combined with a lack of empathy with the foreign culture (e.g. no identification with its speakers or their customs), then the subtle effects of not wanting to sound like a Russian or an American may strongly inhibit the acquisition process.

This type of emotional reaction, or **affect**, may even be occasioned by dull textbooks, unpleasant classroom surroundings or an exhausting schedule. The term **affective filter** is often used to describe a kind of barrier to acquisition that results from negative feelings or experiences. Basically, if you're stressed, uncomfortable, self-conscious or unmotivated, you are unlikely to learn anything.

Children seem to be less constrained by the affective filter. The literature on child L2 acquisition is full of instances where such inhibitions appear to have been overcome by young children acquiring a second language. Adults can sometimes overcome their inhibitions too. In one intriguing study, a group of adult L2 learners had their 'self-consciousness' levels reduced by having their alcohol levels gradually increased. Up to a certain point, the pronunciation of the L2 noticeably improved, but after a number of drinks, as you might expect, pronunciations deteriorated rapidly. Courses on "French-with-cognac" or "Russian-with-vodka" may provide a partial solution, but the inhibitions are likely to return with sobriety.

Focus on method

Despite all these barriers, the need for instruction in other languages has led to a variety of educational approaches and methods which are aimed at fostering L2 learning. In 1483, William Caxton used his newly established printing press to produce a book of *Right good lernyng for to lerne shortly frenssh and englyssh*. He was not the first to compile 'course material' for L2 learners, and his phrase-book format (e.g. customary greetings: *Syre, god you kepe. I haue not seen you in longe tyme.*) has many modern counterparts. Approaches designed to promote L2 learning in this century have tended to reflect different views on how a foreign language is best learned.

Grammar-translation method

The most traditional approach is to treat second, or foreign, language learning on a par with any other academic subject. Long lists of words and a set of grammatical rules have to be memorized, and the written language rather than the spoken language is emphasized. This method has its roots in the traditional approach to the teaching of Latin and is generally described as the **grammar-translation method**. This label has actually been applied to the approach by its detractors who have pointed out that its emphasis on learning about the L2 leaves students quite ignorant of how the language is used. Learners leaving school, having achieved high grades in French class via this method, typically find themselves at a loss when confronted by the way the French in France actually use their language.

Audiolingual method

A very different approach, emphasizing the spoken language, became popular in the 1950s. This involved a systematic presentation of the structures of the L2, moving from the simple to the more complex, often in the form of drills which the student had to repeat. This approach, called the **audiolingual method**, was strongly influenced by a belief that the fluent use of a language was essentially a set of 'habits' which could be developed with a lot of practice. Much of this practice involved hours spent in a language laboratory repeating oral drills. At the time, this approach was justified by claims that "foreign-language learning is basically a mechanical process of habit formation" (quoted in Rivers, 1964). Nowadays, it would be hard to find a psychologist or a linguist who would agree with the statement, yet versions of the audiolingual method are still very common in language-teaching. Its critics point out that isolated practice in drilling language patterns bears no resemblance to the interactional nature of actual language use. Moreover, it can be incredibly boring.

Communicative approaches

More recent revisions of the L2 learning experience can best be described as **communicative approaches**. They are partially a reaction against the artificiality of 'pattern-practice' and also against the belief that consciously learning the grammar of a language will necessarily result in an ability to use the language. Although there are different versions of how to create 'communicative' experiences in the L2 classroom, they are all based on a view that the functions of language (i.e. what it is used for) should be emphasized rather than the forms of the language (i.e. correct grammatical or phonological structure). Lessons are likely to be organized around concepts such as "asking for things" in different social contexts, rather than "the forms of the past tense" in different sentences. These changes have coincided with attempts to provide more appropriate materials for L2 learning which has a specific purpose (e.g. English for medical personnel or Japanese for business people).

Focus on the learner

The most fundamental change in the area of L2 learning in recent years has been a shift from concern with the teacher, the textbook and the method to an interest in the learner and the acquisition process. For example, one radical feature of most communicative approaches is the toleration of 'errors' produced by learners. Traditionally, 'errors' were regarded negatively and had to be eradicated. The more recent acceptance of such errors in learners' language is based on a fundamental shift in perspective from the more traditional view of how second languages are acquired. Rather than consider a Spanish speaker's production of *In the room there are three womens* as simply a failure to learn correct English (which could be remedied by extra practice of the correct form), we could look upon it as an indication of the actual acquisition process in action. An 'error', then, is not something which hinders a student's progress, but is probably a clue to the active learning progress being made by a student as he or she tries out ways of communicating in the new language. Just as children acquiring their L1 produce certain ungrammatical forms in the acquisition process, so we might expect the L2 learner to produce overgeneralizations at certain stages. The example of *womens* might be seen as a type of **creative construction**, used by the learner in accordance with the most general way of making plural forms in English.

Of course, some 'errors' may be due to the **transfer** of expressions or structures from the L1. An L1 Spanish speaker who produces *take it from the side inferior* may be trying to use the Spanish adjective *inferior* (= English *lower*) and placing it after the noun, as in Spanish constructions. If the L1 and the L2 have similar features (e.g. marking plural on the ends of nouns), then the learner may be able to benefit from the **positive transfer** of L1 knowledge. On the other hand, transferring an L1 feature that is really different from the L2 results in **negative transfer** and it typically isn't effective for L2 communication. It should be noted that negative transfer (sometimes called 'interference') is more common in the early stages of L2 learning and typically decreases as the learner develops familiarity with the L2.

Interlanguage

However, on close inspection, the language produced by learners contains a large number of 'errors' which seem to have no connection to the forms of either L1 or L2. For example, the Spanish speaker who says in English *She name is Maria* is producing a form which is not used by adult speakers of English, does not occur in English L1 acquisition by children, and is not found in Spanish. Evidence of this sort suggests that there is some in-between system used in L2 acquisition which certainly contains aspects of L1 and L2, but which is an inherently variable system with rules of its own. This system is called an **interlanguage** and it is now considered to be the basis of all L2 production.

If some learners develop a fairly fixed repertoire of L2 forms, containing many features which do not match the target language, and they do not progress any further, their interlanguage is said to have 'fossilized'. The process of **fossilization** in L2 pronunciation is one obvious cause of a foreign accent. However, an interlanguage is not designed to fossilize. It will naturally develop and become a more effective means of communication, given appropriate conditions. Discovering just what count as the appropriate conditions for successful L2 learning is an ongoing area of study.

Motivation

There are several factors which combine in a profile of the successful L2 learner. Obviously, the motivation to learn is important. However, it has been noted that those who experience some success are among the most motivated to learn. Thus, motivation may be as much a result of success as a cause. A language-learning situation that encourages success and accomplishment must consequently be more helpful than one that dwells on errors and corrections. Indeed, the learner who is willing to guess, risks making mistakes, and tries to communicate in the L2 will tend, given the opportunity, to be more successful. An important part of that opportunity is the availability of 'input'.

Input and output

The term **input** is used to describe the language that the learner is exposed to. To be beneficial for L2 learning, that input has to be comprehensible. It can be made comprehensible by being simpler in structure and vocabulary, as in the variety of speech known as **foreigner talk**. Native speakers of English may try to ask an international student *How are you getting on in your studies?*, but, if not understood, can switch to *English class, you like it?* Foreigner talk of this type may be beneficial, not only for immediate communicative success, but also for providing the beginning learner with clearer examples of the basic structure of the L2 as input.

As the learner's interlanguage develops, however, there is a need for more interaction and the kind of **negotiated input** that arises in conversation. Negotiated input is L2 material that the learner can acquire in interaction through requests for clarification and active attention being focused on what is said. In the following interaction, notice how the learner, a non-native speaker (NNS) of English, and the English native speaker (NS) negotiate meaning together. The comprehensible input (e.g. the meaning of the word *triangle*) is provided at a point where the learner needs it and is paying attention to the meaning in context.

> NS: *like part of a triangle?*
> NNS: *what is triangle?*
> NS: *a triangle is a shape um it has three sides*
> NNS: *a peak?*
> NS: *three straight sides*
> NNS: *a peak?*
> NS: *yes it does look like a mountain peak, yes*
> NNS: *only line only line?*
> NS: *ok two of them, right? one on each side? a line on each side*
> NNS: *yes*
> NS: *little lines on each side?*
> NNS: *yes*
> NS: *like a mountain?*
> NNS: *yes*

In this type of interaction, the learner experiences the benefits of both receiving input and producing output. The opportunity to produce comprehensible **output** in meaningful interaction seems to be a crucial factor in the learner's development of L2 abilities, yet it is the most difficult to provide in large foreign language classrooms. One solution has been to create different types of tasks and activities in which the learners have to interact with each other. Despite fears that learners will acquire each other's 'mistakes', the results of such **task-based learning** provide overwhelming evidence of more and better L2 use by learners. The goal of such activities is not that the learners will know 'about' the L2, but that they will develop communicative competence in the L2.

Communicative competence

Communicative competence can be defined, in terms of three components, as the ability to use the L2 accurately, appropriately, and flexibly. The first component is **grammatical competence** which involves the accurate use of words and structures in the L2. Concentration on grammatical competence only, however, will not provide the learner with the ability to interpret or produce language appropriately. This ability is called **sociolinguistic competence**. It enables the learner to know when to say *Can I have some water?* versus *Give me some water!* according to the social context. Much of what was discussed in terms of Pragmatics (Chapter 12) has to become familiar in the L2 if the learner is to develop sociolinguistic competence.

The third component is called **strategic competence**. This is the ability to organize a message effectively and to compensate, via strategies, for any difficulties. In L2 use, learners will inevitably experience moments when there is a gap between communicative intent and their ability to express that intent. Some learners may just stop talking (bad idea), others will try to express themselves via a **communication strategy** (good idea). For example, a Dutch L1 speaker wanted to refer to *een hoefijzer* in English, but didn't know the English word. So, she used a communication strategy. She referred to *the things that horses wear under their feet, the iron things* and the listener understood what she meant (*horseshoes*). This flexibility in L2 use is a key element in communicative success. In essence, strategic competence is the ability to overcome potential communication problems in interaction.

Applied linguistics

In attempting to investigate the complex nature of L2 learning, we have to appeal to ideas not only from linguistic analysis, but from other fields such as communication studies, education, psychology and sociology. This large-scale endeavor is often called **applied linguistics**. Because it represents an attempt to deal with a large range of practical issues involving language (not only L2 learning), applied linguistics has emerged in recent years as one of the most active areas of investigation in the study of language.

Study questions

1 What are four obvious barriers to adult L2 acquisition?
2 What do you think 'the Joseph Conrad phenomenon' refers to?
3 What happens when an interlanguage fossilizes?
4 Why might 'foreigner talk' be beneficial?
5 What are the three components of commmunicative competence?

Discussion topics/projects

A Here are some principles proposed by Krashen & Terrell (1983) which
   they argue are necessary for successful L2 acquisition:

   (1) the instructor always uses the target language
   (2) speech errors which do not interfere with communication are not
       corrected
   (3) each classroom activity is organized by topic, not grammatical structure;
       practice of specific grammatical structures is not focused on in these
       activities
   (4) an environment which is conducive to acquisition must be created by the
       instructor – low anxiety level, good rapport with the teacher, friendly rela-
       tionship with other students.

   Is this a description of a second language learning environment which
   you have experienced? What, if any, are the differences? Do you think
   the approach described here would be successful, or might there be
   drawbacks?

B Here is a transcription of a native Spanish speaker's account of a classroom scene. What would you identify as 'errors' in this sample of
   English? Can you classify those errors in terms of overgeneralization,
   interference from L1, or resulting from some other process?

   *In a room there are three womens ... one is blond ... blond hair ... there are three
   womens ... one woman is the teacher ... and the other two womans are seat in the
   chair ... one of them are ... are blond hair ... and the other woman ... is black hair
   ... the teacher is made an explanation about shapes ...triangle circle*

C A common difficulty experienced in trying to communicate in a second
   language (and occasionally in the L1) is lack of knowledge of the precise
   term to describe something. In these circumstances, speakers use different types of 'communication strategies' to get their description across.
   Can you identify the different strategies used by the following speakers
   (whose L1s are in parentheses) as they attempted to describe a riding

crop? (You can compare your conclusions with those of Tarone & Yule, 1985, from whose data these examples are taken.)

1. (Japanese)   it's a long stick and eh ... on top of it eh there is a ... ring
2. (Italian)   it's like a rope ... but it's rigid ... at one end has like of ring but it's not rigid ... you can use to stimulate the horse to ... go faster
3. (Chinese)   a tick or bar and I think we use to ... play or to ... attack some one
4. (Spanish)   is no common piece ... it consist of ... a main piece of dark color
5. (Korean)   plastic stick... one end side... like a round
6. (Spanish)   it's a ... using for jocking .. for to hit the horse
7. (Chinese)   I don't know what's this

D   If you have tried to learn a second or foreign language, what did you find caused the most difficulty: pronunciation, vocabulary, grammar, or something else? Why did YOU think there were difficulties (the teacher, the textbook, the physical setting, the lack of time, the other students, anything else)? Do you believe there is a 'best age' for beginning to learn a second language? How about a 'best personality'? Do you think some languages are easier to learn than others, and why might that be?

E   The following two dialogs were recorded at a university in the USA. They both involve Jiang (J), a student from China, talking (in the first) with Andy (A), a local American student, and (in the second) with Luis (L), a student from Argentina. (For further details, see Yule & Gregory, 1989.)
(i) In which interaction do you think Jiang gets more comprehensible input? What evidence supports your choice?

(ii) In which interaction is there more negotiated input and what is the supporting evidence for your choice?

(iii) What features of these interactions can you point to as potentially being beneficial for Jiang's English language development?

1.
J: how about – are you normally a part time student?
A: part time
J: so you're had another part time job or –
A: right – I work for Louisiana National Guard
J: National Guard?

A: right – Louisiana
J: oh great
A: it's like a state militia
J: it's like a policeman
A: no no – it's like a – it's like a state militia – it's like the army for the state
J: oh yes
A: it's involved with eh like if there's a disaster they react
J: ah
A: uh – help – right?
J: ah to help on the – on the site
A: and also – it's also for um in case they get called for military duty – for the country – but it's like a scholarship type thing
J: ah yes
A: so the National Guard pays your tuition fees – pay school – I get my tuition waiver – plus more money
J: ah – ah yeah that's good

2.

J: you mean your department didn't tell you what eh you should do on your research?
L: no – that's one – but the other is some subject
J: excuse me – what kind of guide you are expect?
L: I don't believe now I have broshek
J: brushing?
L: broshek – broshek – broshek
J: broshek? – working? – pressure?
L: no – broshek – make a broshek – proshek
J: ah project
L: right
J: you mean –
L: you know what that means?
     nobody say me what they needs
J: ah
L: so I make a lot of mistake
J: ah nobody check you mean your project
L: right
J: nobody give you advice – ah?
L: yeah well advice is too –
J: is too general
L: yeah too eh clouding
J: too clothing?
L: clouding

J: closing?
L: cloudy cloudy
J: yeah
L: it's muddy
J: yeah okay

Further reading
General treatments of the issues in L2 acquisition or learning can be found in
Ellis (1986), Gass & Selinker (1994), Lightbown & Spada (1993), McLaughlin
(1987), or Spolsky (1989). A comprehensive review of research can be found in
Larsen-Freeman & Long (1991) and more theoretical perspectives are presented in Cook (1993) and Sharwood-Smith (1994). On L2 teaching methods,
see Howatt (1984), Nunan (1991) or Richards & Rodgers (1986). On more specific teaching issues, read Brown & Yule (1983b), Chaudron (1988) and
Widdowson (1990). On pronunciation with wine, see Guiora *et al.* (1972). On
transfer, see Kellerman & Sharwood-Smith (1986), Odlin (1989) or Swan &
Smith (1987). On interlanguage, see Corder (1981) or Selinker (1992). Skehan
(1989) provides a review of individual differences in L2 learning. On input, see
Krashen (1985) and on output, see Swain (1995). The source of the 'triangle'
dialog is Pica *et al.* (1991). On task-based language teaching, see Long (1996).
On aspects of communicative competence, see Canale & Swain (1980), Kasper
& Blum-Kulka (1993), Kasper & Kellerman (1996), Scarcella *et al.* (1990) or
Tarone & Yule (1989). The source of the 'horseshoe' example is Kellerman *et*
al. (1990). A useful resource is the dictionary of applied linguistics by Richards
et al. (1992).

18 Sign language

The deaf perceive the world through skilled and practiced eyes; language is at their fingertips. When I wanted to learn about silence and sign language, I went to talk to the deaf.   **Arden Neisser (1983)**

In our consideration of the acquisition of language, we concentrated, for the most part, on the fact that what is naturally acquired by most children is speech. It would be a mistake to think that this is the only form a first language can take. Just as most children of English-speaking or French-speaking parents naturally acquire English or French at an early age, so the deaf children of deaf parents naturally acquire **sign language**. If those deaf children grow up in American homes, they will typically acquire American Sign Language, also known as Ameslan or **ASL**. With a signing population of almost 500,000, ASL is the third most commonly used non-English language (after Spanish and Italian) in the United States. The size of this number is quite remarkable since, until very recently, the use of ASL was discouraged in most educational institutions for the deaf. In fact, historically, very few teachers of the deaf knew anything about ASL, or even considered it to be a 'real' language at all.

Alternate and primary sign languages
The older concept of a sign language as a limited set of gestures being used in place of a 'real' language is close to what is now technically known as an **alternate sign language**. By definition, an alternate sign language is a system of gestures developed by speakers for limited communication in a specific context where speech cannot be used. In some religious orders, there are rules of silence and a very restricted alternate sign language is employed by

the monks. Among some Australian Aboriginal groups, there are periods (e.g. times of bereavement) when speech is avoided completely and quite elaborate alternate sign languages are used instead. Less elaborate versions are to be found in some special working circumstances (e.g. among bookmakers at racetracks, traders in commodity exchanges, and sawmill workers). In all these examples, the user of an alternate sign language has another first (spoken) language.

In contrast, a **primary sign language** is the first language of a group that does not have access to a spoken language. ASL is a primary sign language. Yet, for a very long time, it was not considered to be a possible natural language at all.

Oralism

It is only in the last two decades that any serious consideration has been given to the status of ASL as a natural language. It was genuinely believed by many well-intentioned teachers that the use of sign language by deaf children, perhaps because it was 'easy', actually inhibited the acquisition of speech. Since speech was what these children really required, a teaching method generally known as **oralism** was rigorously pursued. This method, which dominated deaf education for a century, required that the students practice English speech sounds and develop lipreading skills. Despite its resounding lack of success, the method was never seriously challenged, perhaps because of a belief among many during this period that, in educational terms, most deaf children could not achieve very much anyway.

Whatever the reasons, the method produced few students who could speak intelligible English (reckoned to be less than 10 percent) and even fewer who could lipread (around 4 percent). While oralism was failing, the use of ASL was surreptitiously flourishing. Many deaf children of hearing parents actually acquired the banned language at schools for the deaf – from other children. Since only one in ten deaf children had deaf parents from whom they acquired sign language, it would seem that ASL is a rather unique language in that its major cultural transmission has been carried out from child to child.

Signed English

Substantial changes in deaf education have taken place in recent years. There remains an emphasis on the acquisition of English, written rather than spoken, and as a result, many institutions promote the learning of what is called **Signed English** (sometimes described as Manually Coded English). This is essentially a means of producing signs which correspond to the words in an English sentence, in English word order. In many ways, Signed English is designed to facilitate interaction between the deaf and the hearing community. Its greatest advantage is that it seems to present a much less formidable learning task for the hearing parent of a deaf child and provides that parent with a 'language' to use with the child.

For similar reasons, hearing teachers in deaf education can make use of Signed English when they sign at the same time as they speak (known as the 'simultaneous method'). It is also easier to use for those hearing interpreters who produce a simultaneous translation of public speeches or lectures for deaf audiences. Many deaf people actually prefer interpreters to use Signed English because they say there is a better chance of understanding the message. When most interpreters try to use ASL, the message seems to suffer, for the simple reason that few hearing people who didn't learn ASL in childhood are very proficient at it.

However, Signed English is neither English nor ASL. When used to produce an exact version of a spoken English sentence, Signed English takes twice as long as the production of the sentence in either English or ASL. Consequently, in practice, exact versions are rarely produced and a hybrid format emerges, using some word-signs and incomplete English word order. (In many cases, even the word-signs are 'anglified' with, for example, a *G* letter-shape used to represent the English word *glad*, rather than the actual ASL sign for this concept.) It's sort of like producing messages with German word order, but containing French nouns, adjectives and verbs. The product is neither French nor German, but, it could be argued, it is one way of getting French speakers to learn how German sentences are constructed.

The type of argument we have just noted is what has been used in support of teaching Signed English in deaf schools, since one of the major aims is to prepare students to be able to read and write English. Underlying that aim is the principle that deaf education should be geared towards enabling the deaf, for obvious economic reasons, to take part in the hearing world. The net effect is to make ASL a kind of underground language, used only in deaf–deaf interaction. As such, it continues to be poorly understood and subject to many of the myths which have existed throughout its history.

Origins of ASL

It would indeed be surprising if ASL really was, as some would have it, 'a sort of gestured version of English'. Historically, it developed from the French Sign Language used in a Paris school founded in the eighteenth century. Early in the nineteenth century, a teacher from this school, named Laurent Clerc, was brought to the United States by an American Congregational minister called Thomas Gallaudet. Clerc not only taught deaf children, he trained other teachers. During the nineteenth century, this imported version of Sign Language, incorporating features of indigenous natural sign languages used by the American deaf, evolved into what became ASL. Such origins help explain why users of ASL and users of British Sign Language (BSL) do not, in fact, share a common sign language. ASL and BSL are separate languages and neither should be treated as versions of spoken English which happen to involve the use of the hands.

The structure of signs

The idea that natural sign languages involve simple gestures with the hands is a persistent fallacy. In producing linguistic forms in ASL, signers will help themselves to four key aspects of visual information. These are usually classified as shape, orientation, location and movement. In analogies with natural spoken languages these four elements are sometimes called the **articulatory parameters** of ASL. These parameters can be illustrated by referring to the following representation of a clear, isolated use of the sign

for THANK-YOU. To describe the articulation of THANK-YOU in ASL, we would start with the **shape**, or configuration of the hand(s), used in forming the sign. In forming THANK-YOU, a 'flat hand' is used and not a 'fist hand' or 'cupped hand' or other permissible shape. The **orientation** of the hand describes the fact that the hand is 'palm-up' rather than 'palm-down'. In other signs the hand can be oriented in a number of other ways, such as the 'flat hand', 'palm towards signer' form used to indicate MINE. The **location** of the sign captures the fact that, in THANK-YOU, it is first at the chin, then at waist level, and the **movement** (in this case, out and downward) involved in the formation of the sign is the fourth parameter. These four general parameters can be analyzed into a set of **primes** (e.g. 'flat hand' and 'palm-up' are primes in shape and orientation respectively) in order to produce a full feature-analysis of each sign.

In addition to these parameters, there are very important functions served by non-manual components such as head-movement, eye-movement and a number of specific facial expressions. For example, if a sentence is functioning as a question, it is typically accompanied by a raising of the eyebrows, widened eyes, and a slight leaning forward of the head.

If a new term or name is encountered, there is the possibility of **finger-spelling** via a system of hand configurations conventionally used to represent the letters of the alphabet.

It should be obvious from this very brief description of some of the basic features of ASL that it is a linguistic system designed for the visual medium. Signing is done in face-to-face interaction. The majority of signs are located around the neck and head, and if a sign is made near the chest or waist, it tends to be two-handed. One of the key differences between a system using the visual as opposed to the vocal-auditory channel is that visual messages can incorporate a number of elements simultaneously. Spoken language is produced with a structure determined by the linear sequence of sound signals. It is extremely difficult to produce or to perceive more than one sound signal at a time. In the visual medium, multiple components can be produced all at the same time. Thus, from a structural point of view, a spoken word is a linear sequence of sound segments, while a sign is a combination of components within spatial dimensions which occur simultaneously.

The meaning of signs

The signs of ASL are often, erroneously, thought to be clear visual representations or 'pictures' of the objects or actions they refer to. Indeed, the language of the deaf is still considered by many to be some type of pantomime or mime in which EATING is represented by mimicking the act of eating or TREE is represented by 'forming' a tree with the hands. This misconception is usually accompanied by the myth that a sign language like ASL consists of a fairly primitive set of gestures which can only really be used to refer to 'concrete' entities and actions, but not to anything 'abstract'. Such misconceptions may persist because the hearing world rarely witnesses conversations or discussions in ASL, which range over every imaginable topic, concrete and abstract, and which bear little resemblance to any form of pantomime.

However, a visual communication system can avail itself of forms of representation which have an iconic basis. **Icons** are symbolic representations which are physically similar to the objects represented. (Pictograms and ideograms, discussed in Chapter 2, are types of iconic representation.) So, in using ASL, a signer can indeed produce an iconic representation to refer to something encountered for the first time, or something rarely talked about. A good example is provided by Klima & Bellugi (1979), in which several different signers produced a range of different forms to refer to a straitjacket. Interestingly, when you are told that a sign is used for referring to a particular object or action, you can often create some iconic connection. You may have seen the sign for THANK-YOU as some appropriately symbolic version of the action involved. However, most of the time, it does not work in the opposite direction – you may find it difficult to get the 'meaning' of a sign simply on the basis of what it looks like. Indeed, you may not even be able to identify individual signs in fluent signing. In this sense, most everyday use of ASL signs is not based on the use and interpretation of icons, but on conventional linguistic symbols. Even if some signs have traceable iconic sources, their actual use in ASL does not depend on the signer thinking of the iconic source in order to interpret the sign. Here is an example of a common sign. This sign consists of rotating both hands with the fingers interlocked. Two quite different iconic sources have been suggested: that it represents the stripes which occur on a country's flag or that it derives from the union of a number of separate states together. To suggest that either of these images comes into the mind of a signer who, in conversation, uses this sign to refer to AMERICA is as absurd as saying that in hearing the word *America*, an English speaker must be thinking about Amerigo Vespucci, the sixteenth-century Italian whose name is reputed to be the source of the modern word.

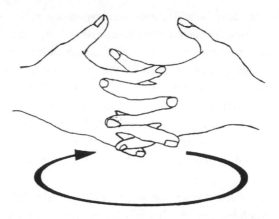

Writing in ASL

The fact that a sign language exploits the visual medium in quite subtle ways makes it difficult to represent accurately on the page. As Lou Fant (1977) has observed, "strictly speaking, the only way to write Ameslan is to use motion pictures". One of the major problems is finding a way to incorporate those aspects of facial expression which contribute to the message. One partial solution is to produce one line of the manually signed 'words' and over this line to indicate the extent and nature of the conventional facial expression which accompanies those words. Thus, the *q* in the following transcription shows that the facial expression indicated a question function and lasted throughout the word-signing of what would be translated as *Can I borrow the book?*

$$q$$
_____

ME BORROW BOOK

Other subtle aspects of meaning which can be conveyed by facial expression are still the subject of investigation. In one study, it was noted that a signer, in the middle of telling a story, produced a signed message such as *MAN FISH continuous*, which we would translate as *the man was fishing*. However, other ASL users, watching the signer, would translate the message as *the man was fishing with relaxation and enjoyment*. The source of this extra information was a particular facial expression in which the lips were together and pushed out a little, with the head slightly tilted. This non-manual signal was clearly capable of functioning as the equivalent of an adverb in English and was an integral part of the message. The notation *mm* was chosen as a way of incorporating this element and so a more accurate transcription of the message might look like this:

mm
_____

MAN FISH [continuous]

A number of other such notations have been devised to capture major non-manual elements in ASL communication. No doubt others will have to be introduced as other aspects of this subtle and rich communication system become better known.

ASL as a linguistic system

Investigations of ASL, from a linguistic point of view, are a relatively recent phenomenon. Yet it has become very clear that any feature which is charac-teristically found in spoken languages has a counterpart in ASL. All the defining properties of human language which we considered in Chapter 3 are present in ASL; there are equivalent levels of phonology, morphology and syntax; children acquiring ASL go through many of the recognized stages of children learning spoken language, though the production of signs seems to begin earlier than the production of spoken words; in the hands of witty individuals, ASL is used for a wide range of jokes and 'sign-play'; there are different ASL dialects in different regions and historical changes in the form of signs can be traced since the beginning of the century (older ver-sions are preserved on old films).

In summary, ASL is a natural language which is quite remarkable for its endurance in the face of decades of prejudice and misunderstanding. There is a very old joke among the deaf which begins with the question *What is the greatest problem facing deaf people?* Perhaps increased knowledge and appreciation of their language among the world at large will bring about a change in the old response to that question. The traditional answer was *Hearing people.*

Study questions
1 What are the four most commonly used languages in the United States?
2 What was the main aim of oralism?
3 What is the major difference between ASL and Signed English?
4 What are the four articulatory parameters of ASL?
5 What would be the most likely English translation of:

(i)   q

  _____

  HAPPEN YESTERDAY NIGHT

(ii)   neg   mm

      __   _____

      BOY NOT WALK [continuous]

Discussion topics/projects

A If the signs of ASL really were essentially iconic, it should be possible to
   look at the signs and 'see' their meaning in some transparent way. Here
   are three common ASL signs. Do you have any ideas on their likely
   meaning?

   Can you describe which features are the basis of your ideas? (Compare
   your suggestions with the translations of these signs found in Chapter 4
   of Baker & Cokely, 1980, from which these illustrations were adapted.)

B Consider this description of the attitude of Alexander Graham Bell (the
   inventor of the telephone) to the use of ASL, around the end of the
   nineteenth century. How would you try to convince Bell that he was
   mistaken?

   Bell was opposed to the use of sign language at any time or place; it was easier for the deaf to master and more reliable in use, hence it would supplant or
   preempt speech. It was not only unsuited for integrating the deaf into society,
   but was a prison intellectually as well as socially, he believed, because it was
   ideographic rather than phonetic, limited in precision, flexibility, subtlety,
   and power of abstraction.   **(Lane, 1980: 149)**

   (If you would like to do some research into other aspects of Bell's views
   on the deaf, try to locate Bell, 1883.)

c Consider this statement from Woodward (1980:105):

> Not all hearing impaired individuals belong to the deaf community; in fact,
> audiometric deafness, the actual degree of hearing loss, often has very little
> to do with how a person relates to the deaf community. Attitudinal deafness,
> self-identification as a member of the deaf community, and identification by
> other members as a member appear to be the most basic factors determining
> membership in the deaf community.

Why do you think it is "attitudinal deafness" that is the key to membership in the deaf community? What social, psychological or linguistic factors might lie behind this phenomenon? Do you know of any other
minority groups where this type of phenomenon has been noted?

d Here is one view of reasons why oralism flourished in deaf education:

> Oralism was a nineteenth-century idea, with its enthusiasm for apparatus, its
> confidence in the future of technology. It was reinforced by the Protestant
> ethic of hard work, unremitting practice, and strength of character to over-
> come all of life's afflictions. It flourished in the framework of Victorian man-
> ners (and Victorian science), and reflected a deep Anglo-Saxon antagonism
> toward all languages other than English.   **(Neisser, 1983: 29)**

Is this view of things still present today? Can it be justified? What kind of
general repercussions follow from this view in terms of language-study,
the teaching of minority languages, or education in general?

e The acquisition of sign as a first language provides some of the most
powerful evidence for the importance of interaction between mother
(caregiver) and child. Interactions in sign require visual attention to the
signer. The child typically cannot be looking at the ball and looking at
mother signing *ball* at the same time. This creates some special conditions that are quite different from spoken-language acquisition. Can you
think of what crucial differences must exist (e.g. in learning the 'names'
of objects)? Consult Wood *et al.* (1986) for some background.

Further reading

There is an introduction to ASL in Baker & Cokely (1980) and BSL in
Deuchar (1984). For illustrated presentations of signing, see Fant (1977) and
Madsen (1982). On Signed English, see Bornstein *et al.* (1983). On alternate
sign languages, see Kendon (1988) and Umiker-Sebeok & Sebeok (1987). The

original descriptions of ASL which really stimulated modern research are in Stokoe (1960) and Stokoe *et al.* (1965). Collections of papers focusing on ASL and BSL as languages are presented in Coulter (1992), Fischer & Siple (1990), Friedman (1977), Kyle & Woll (1983), Lane & Grosjean (1980), Liddell (1980), Lucas (1990), Prillwitz & Vollhaber (1990) and Wilbur (1987). Works with a broader focus, including education and social contact, are Kyle (1987), Kyle & Woll (1985), Lucas (1989), Lucas & Valli (1992), Paul & Quigley (1994), Quigley & Paul (1990), Volterra & Erting (1990), Woll *et al.* (1981) and Wood *et al.* (1986). Swisher (1984) presents an interesting study of how hearing mothers cope with using Signed English to communicate with their deaf children. Some more general works are Gregory & Taylor (1991), Groce (1985) and Lane (1984; 1992). Van Cleve (1987) is an encyclopedia of deaf people and deafness.

19 Language history and change

Fæder ure þu þe eart on heofonum,
si þin nama gehalgod.
Tobecume þin rice.
Gewurþe þin willa on eorðan swa swa on heofonum.
Urne gedæghwamlican hlaf syle us to dæg.
And forgyf us ure gyltas,
swa swa we forgyfað urum gyltendum.
And ne gelæd þu us on costnunge,
ac alys us of yfele.   **The Lord's Prayer (circa AD 1000)**

In 1786, a British government official called Sir William Jones, who was working as a judge of the high court in India, made the following observation about the ancient language of Indian law which he had been studying:

> The Sanskrit language, whatever be its antiquity, is of a wonderful structure; more perfect than the Greek, more copious than the Latin, and more exquisitely refined than either, yet bearing to both of them a stronger affinity, both in the roots of verbs and in the forms of grammar, than could possibly have been produced by accident.

Sir William went on to suggest, in a way that was quite revolutionary for its time, that a number of languages from very different geographical areas must have some common ancestor. It was clear, however, that this common ancestor could not be described from any existing records, but had to be hypothesized on the basis of similar features existing in records of languages which were believed to be descendants. Linguistic investigation of this type, still carried on two centuries after Sir William's original insight, focuses on the historical development of languages and attempts to characterize the regular processes which are involved in language change.

Family trees

During the nineteenth century, when the historical study of languages (more generally described as **philology**) was the major preoccupation of linguists, a term came into use to describe that common ancestor. It incorporated the notion that this was the original form (*proto*) of a language which was the source of modern languages in the Indian sub-continent (*Indo*), and in Europe (*European*). With **Proto-Indo-European** established as the 'great-grandmother', scholars set out to trace the branches of her family tree, showing the lineage of many modern languages, as illustrated in the accompanying diagram.

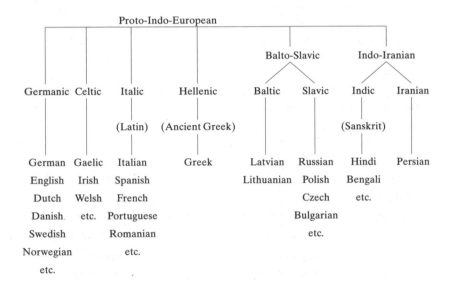

Of course, this diagram shows only one family tree covering a small number of the languages of the world. There are considered to be about thirty such language families which have produced the more than 4,000 languages in the world. Some of these languages are much more widely spoken than others. In terms of numbers of speakers, Chinese has the most native speakers (close to 1 billion), while English (about 350 million) is more widely used in different parts of the world. Spanish has close to 300 million native speakers, Hindi has 200 million and Arabic and Russian have about 150 million each.

Family relationships

Looking at the Indo-European family tree, one might ask how it can be determined that these language groups are 'related'. On the face of it, two languages such as Italian and Hindi would seem to have nothing in common. One way to see the relationships more clearly is by looking at records of an older generation, like Latin and Sanskrit, from which the modern languages developed. For example, if we use familiar letters to write out the words for *father* and *brother* in Sanskrit, Latin and Ancient Greek, some common features become apparent:

Sanskrit	Latin	Greek	
pitar	pater	patĕr	('father')
bhrātar	frāter	phrātĕr	('brother')

It is, however, extremely unlikely that exactly the same forms will regularly turn up, but the fact that close similarities occur (especially in the probable pronunciations of the forms) is good evidence for proposing a family connection.

Cognates

The process we have just employed in establishing some possible family connection between different languages involved looking at what are called **cognates**. Within groups of related languages, we often find close similarities in particular sets of terms. A cognate of a word in one language (e.g. English) is a word in another language (e.g. German) which has a similar form and is, or was, used with a similar meaning. Thus, the English forms *mother*, *father* and *friend* are cognates of the German forms *Mutter*, *Vater* and *Freund*. On the basis of these cognate sets, we would propose that such sets in modern English and modern German probably have a common ancestor in what has been labeled the Germanic branch of Indo-European. By the same process. we can look at similar sets, one from Spanish, *madre*, *padre* and *amigo*, and one from Italian, *madre*, *padre* and *amico*, and conclude that these close cognates also must be a clue to a common ancestor in the Italic branch.

Comparative reconstruction

Using information from these cognate sets, we can then embark on a procedure called **comparative reconstruction**. The aim of this procedure is to reconstruct what must have been the original, or 'proto' form in the common ancestral language. It's a bit like trying to work out what the great-grandmother must have been like on the basis of common features possessed by the set of granddaughters. In carrying out this procedure, those working on the history of languages operate on the basis of some general principles, two of which are presented here.

The **majority principle** is very straightforward. If, in a cognate set, three forms begin with a [p] sound and one form begins with a [b] sound, then our best guess is that the majority have retained the original sound (i.e. [p]), and the minority has changed a little through time.

The **most natural development principle** is based on the fact that certain types of sound-change are very common, whereas others are extremely unlikely. Here are some well-documented types of sound-change:

(1) final vowels often disappear
(2) voiceless sounds become voiced between vowels
(3) stops become fricatives (under certain conditions)
(4) consonants become voiceless at the end of words

If you were faced with some examples from three languages, as shown here, could you make a start on comparative reconstruction by deciding what was the most likely form of the initial sound in the original language source of the three?

Languages

A	B	C	
cavallo	caballo	cheval	('horse')
cantare	cantar	chanter	('sing')
catena	cadena	chaîne	('chain')
caro	caro	cher	('dear')

Since the written forms can often be misleading, you would find out that the initial sounds of the words in languages A and B are all [k] sounds, while in language C the initial sounds are pronounced [š]. So, no doubt you immediately conclude that, in the original language, the words began with [k] sounds. What exactly is the evidence?

Well, first, there is the 'majority principle' in evidence, since two sets of forms have [k] and only one has [š]. Moreover, one could argue, the [k] sound is a stop consonant and the [š] sound is a fricative. According to the 'most natural development principle', changes tend to occur in the direction of stops becoming fricatives, so the [k] is more likely to have been the original. Through this type of procedure we have started on the comparative reconstruction of the common origins of some words in Italian (set A), Spanish (set B) and French (set C). In this particular case, you have some way of checking your findings because the generally proposed common origin for all three of these languages is Latin. Checking the Latin cognates for the forms under consideration, we will come up with *caballus*, *cantare*, *catena* and *carus*. So, our initial consonant reconstruction appears to be accurate.

Taking a more exotic example, imagine that the following fragment of data from three related (but otherwise unknown) languages is handed to you by a delirious linguist just rescued from the depths of the Amazon jungle. You realize that these examples represent a set of cognates and that it should be possible, via comparative reconstruction, to arrive at the proto-forms.

Languages

1	2	3	Protoforms	
mube	*mupe*	*mup*	_____	('stream')
abadi	*apati*	*apat*	_____	('rock')
agana	*akana*	*akan*	_____	('knife')
enugu	*enuku*	*enuk*	_____	('diamond')

A quick glance at the data might suggest that you can begin with the majority principle, and say that the most likely basic forms are those found in language 2 or in language 3. If this is indeed the case, then the consonant changes must have been of the type: [p] → [b]; [k] → [g]; [t] → [d], in order to produce the forms in language 1. There is a definite pattern here which is in accord with one type of 'most natural development', i.e. that voiceless consonants become voiced between vowels. So, the forms in lists 2 and 3 must have preceded those in list 1.

Which of the two lists, 2 or 3, contains the older forms? Remembering one other 'natural development' feature (i.e. that final vowels often disappear), we can propose that the forms in list 3 have consistently lost the final vowels which still exist in list 2. Our best guess, then, is that the forms in list 2 come closest to what must have been the original proto-forms. One of our delirious linguist's problems has been solved.

Language change

The reconstruction of proto-forms is an attempt to determine what a language must have been like before written records began. However, even when we have written records from an older period of a language such as English, they may not bear any resemblance to the written English to be found in your daily newspaper. The version of the Lord's Prayer quoted at the beginning of the chapter provides a good illustration of this point. To see how one language has undergone substantial changes through time, let us take a brief look at the history of English.

The historical development of English is usually divided into three major periods. The Old English period is considered to last from the time of the earliest written records, the seventh century, to the end of the eleventh century. The Middle English period is from 1100 to 1500, and Modern English from 1500 to the present.

Old English

The primary sources for what developed as the English language were the Germanic languages spoken by a group of tribes from northern Europe who invaded the British Isles in the fifth century AD. In one early account, these tribes of Angles, Saxons and Jutes were described as "God's wrath toward Britain". It is from the names of the first two that we have the term 'Anglo-Saxons' to describe these people, and from the name of the first tribe, the Angles, that we get the word for their language, *Englisc*, and for their new home, *Engla-land*.

From this early variety of *Englisc*, we have many of the most basic terms in our language: *mann* ('man'), *wīf* ('woman'), *cild* ('child'), *hūs* ('house'), *mete* ('food'), *etan* ('eat'), *drincan* ('drink') and *feohtan* ('fight'). By all accounts, these pagan settlers certainly liked *feohtan*. However, they did not remain pagan for long. From the sixth to the eighth century, there was an extended period in which these Anglo-Saxons were converted to Christianity and a number of terms from the language of religion, Latin, came into English at that time. The origins of the modern words *angel, bishop, candle, church, martyr, priest* and *school* all date from this period.

From the eighth century through the ninth and tenth centuries, another group of northern Europeans came first to plunder, and eventually to settle in, parts of the coastal regions of Britain. They were the Vikings and it is from their language, Old Norse, that we derived the forms which gave us a number of common modern terms such as *give, law, leg, skin, sky, take* and *they*.

Middle English

The event which more than anything marks the end of the Old English period, and the beginning of the Middle English period, is the arrival of the Norman French in England, following their victory at Hastings under William the Conqueror in 1066. These French-speaking invaders proceeded to take over the whole of England. They became the ruling class, so that the language of the nobility, the government, the law and civilized behavior in England for the next two hundred years was French. It is the source of such modern terms as *army*, *court*, *defense*, *faith*, *prison* and *tax*.

Yet the language of the peasants remained English. The peasants worked on the land and reared *sheep*, *cows* and *swine* (words from Old English), while the French-speaking upper classes talked about *mutton*, *beef* and *pork* (words of French origin). Hence the different words in modern English to refer to these creatures 'on the hoof' as opposed to 'on the plate'.

Throughout this period, French (or, more accurately, an English version of French) was the prestige language and Chaucer tells us that one of his Canterbury pilgrims could speak it:

> *She was cleped Madame Eglentyne*
> *Ful wel she song the service dyvyne,*
> *Entuned in hir nose ful semely,*
> *And Frenshe she spak ful faire and fetisly.*

This is an example of Middle English, written in the late fourteenth century. It has changed substantially from Old English, but several changes were yet to take place before the language took on its modern form. Most significantly, the vowel sounds of Chaucer's time were very different from those we hear in similar words today. Chaucer lived in what would have sounded like a 'hoos', with his 'weef', and 'hay' would romance 'heer' with a bottle of 'weena', drunk by the light of the 'moan'. In the two hundred years, from 1400 to 1600, which separated Chaucer and Shakespeare, the sounds of English underwent a substantial change to form the basis of Modern English pronunciation. Whereas the types of borrowed words we have already noted are examples of external change in a language, many of the following examples can be seen as internal changes within the historical development of English.

Sound changes

One of the most obvious differences between Modern English and the English spoken in earlier periods is in the quality of the vowel sounds. Here are some examples of words, in phonetic transcription, whose general form has remained the same, but whose vowel sounds have changed considerably. (Note the use of the colon which indicates that the vowel sound is long.)

Old English	Modern English	
hu:s	haws	('house')
wi:f	wayf	('wife')
spo:n	spu:n	('spoon')
brɛ:k	bre:k	('break')
hɔ:m	hom	('home')

Not only did types of sounds change, but some sounds simply disappeared from the general pronunciation of English. One notable example is a voiceless velar fricative /x/ which was used in the Old English pronunciation of *nicht*, as [nɪxt] (close to the modern German pronunciation), but is absent in the present-day form *night*, as [nayt]. A number of other sound changes have been documented.

The change known as **metathesis** involves a reversal in position of two adjoining sounds. Examples are (from the Old English period):

acsian → ask   bridd → bird   brinnan → beornan (burn)
frist   → first   hros → horse   waeps → wasp

Indeed, the cowboy who pronounces the expression *pretty good* as something close to *purty good* is producing a similar example of metathesis as a dialect variant within Modern English. In some American English dialects, the form *aks*, as in *I aksed him*, can still be heard in place of *ask*.

The reversal of position in metathesis may actually occur between non-adjoining sounds. The Spanish form *palabra* was created from the Latin *parabola*, via the reversal of the [l] and [r] sounds. Notice that the pattern is repeated in the following set:

Latin	Spanish	
parabola	→ palabra	('word')
periculum	→ peligro	('danger')
miraculum	→ milagro	('miracle')

Another change involves the addition of a sound to the middle of a word, which is known as **epenthesis**. Examples are:

aemtig → empty   spinel → spindle   timr → timber

The addition of a [p] sound after the nasal [m], as in *empty*, can also be heard in some speakers' pronunciations of *something* as *sumpthing*. If you sometimes pronounce the word *film* as if it were *filum*, or *arithmetic* as *arithametic*, then you are producing examples of epenthesis in Modern English.

One other type of change worth noting, though not found in English, occurs in the development of other languages. It involves the addition of a sound to the beginning of a word and is called **prothesis**. It is very common in the change of pronunciation of some forms from Latin to Spanish, as in these examples:

schola → escuela ('school')
spiritus → espíritu ('spirit')

Indeed, speakers of Spanish who are learning English as a second language will often add a vowel sound to the beginning of some English words, so words like *strange* and *story* may sound like *estrange* and *estory*.

Syntactic changes

Some noticeable differences between the structure of sentences in Old and Modern English involve word order. In Old English texts, we find the subject-verb-object ordering most common in Modern English, but we can also find a number of different orders which are no longer possible. For example, the subject can follow the verb, as in *fĕrde he* ('he traveled'), and the object can be placed before the verb, as *hē hine geseah* ('he saw him'), or at the beginning of the sentence *him man ne sealde* ('no man gave [any] to him'). In this last example, the use of the negative also differs from Modern English, since the sequence *not gave* is no longer grammatical. A 'double-negative' construction was also possible, as in this example, with both 'not' and 'never'.

and   ne sealdest þū   mē   næfre ān ticcen
(and) (not) (gave) (you) (me) (never) (a) (kid)
    'and you never gave me a kid'

Perhaps the most sweeping change in the form of English sentences was the loss of a large number of inflectional affixes from many parts of speech. Notice that, in our examples, the verb forms *sealde* ('he gave') and *sealdest* ('you gave') are differentiated by inflectional suffixes which are no longer found in Modern English. Nouns, adjectives, articles and pronouns all took different inflectional forms according to their grammatical function in the sentence.

Lexical changes

The most obvious way in which Modern English differs lexically from Old English is in the number of borrowed words, particularly words of Latin and

Greek origin, which have come into the language since the Old English period. Less obviously, many words have ceased to be used. Since we no longer carry swords (most of us, at least), the word *foin*, meaning 'the thrust of a sword', is no longer everyday usage. A common Old English term for 'man' was *were*. This is no longer in general use, but within the domain of horror films, it has survived in the compound form, *werewolf*. A number of expressions, such as *lo*, *verily*, *egad*, are immediately recognized as belonging to a much earlier period of the language and, as has been pointed out by Langacker (1973), there is a certain medieval ring to some names – *Egbert*, *Percival* or *Bertha* – which makes them quite unfashionable in Modern English.

Perhaps more interesting are the two processes of broadening and narrowing of meaning. An example of **broadening** of meaning is the change from *holy day* as a religious feast to the very general break from work called a *holiday*. Another is the modern use of the word *dog*. We use it very generally, to refer to all breeds, but in its older form (Old English *docga*), it was only used for one particular breed.

The reverse process, called **narrowing**, has overtaken the Old English word *hund*, once used for any kind of dog, but now, as *hound*, used only for some specific breeds. Another example is *mete*, once used for any kind of food, which has in its modern form, *meat*, become restricted to only some specific types. The Old English version of the word *wife* could be used of any woman, but has narrowed in its application to only married women. A different kind of narrowing can lead to a negative meaning for words that previously were simply "ordinary" (= *vulgar*) or "worth noting" (= *naughty*).

The process of change

None of the changes described here happened overnight. They were gradual and probably difficult to discern while they were in progress. Although some changes can be linked to major social changes caused by wars, invasions and other upheavals, the most pervasive source of change in language seems to be in the continual process of cultural transmission. Each new generation has to find a way of using the language of the previous generation. In this unending process whereby each new language-user has to 'recreate' for him- or herself the language of the community, there is an unavoidable propensity to pick up some elements exactly and others only approximately. There is also the occasional desire to be different. Given this tenuous transmission process, it should be expected that languages will not remain stable, but that change and variation are inevitable.

In this chapter we have concentrated on variation in language viewed **diachronically**, that is, from the historical perspective of change through time. The type of variation which can be viewed **synchronically**, that is, in terms of differences within one language in different places and among different groups at the same time, is the subject of the final two chapters.

Study questions

1 What sound changes are illustrated by the following pairs?
   (a) *glimsian →glimpse*   (b) *scribere →escribir*   (c) *thridda →third*
2 How would you group the following languages into pairs which are closely related from a historical point of view: Romanian, Czech, Dutch, French, Gaelic, German, Russian, Welsh?
3 What are 'cognates'?
4 If you had the following data to work from, could you make a first guess at the probable proto-forms?

Languages

1	2	3		
cosa	chose	cosa	_____	('thing')
capo	chef	cabo	_____	('head')
capra	chèvre	cabra	_____	('goat')

5 From what you know of the influence of Norman French in the Middle English period, which of the following words would you guess was from Old English, and which from Old French:
   calf veal venison deer?

Discussion topics/projects

A Consider the following data:

Languages

1	2	3	4	5	6	7	
fem	pyat	cinco	piec	itsutsu	fünf	cinque	('five')
fire	chetyre	cuatro	cztery	yottsu	vier	quattro	('four')

(i)   There are six sets of examples from Indo-European languages here. Which one sample is most likely to be non-Indo-European?

(ii) The remaining six sets can be divided into three pairs of closely related languages. Which examples seem to go together as pairs?

(iii) With which pair would you associate the English language?

(iv) With which pair would you associate another language which has the cognates *quinque* and *quattuor*?

B With the following data to work from, complete the list of proto-forms, and describe three different processes of change which must have taken place in the development of this language set.

Languages

1	2	3	4	Proto-forms
lik	*ligu*	*ligu*	*liku*	_____ ('insect')
hip	*hiba*	*hiba*	*hipa*	_____ ('path')
rad	*radi*	*rathi*	*radi*	_____ ('cloud')
nam	*namu*	*namu*	*namu*	_____ ('dwelling')

C Some people maintain that English cannot be a Germanic language. They usually argue that English must be derived from Latin. How would you present an argument, and what evidence would you use, to convince such a person that English is best considered as a member of the Germanic branch of Indo-European? (You could consult any one of the following texts: Barber, 1993; Baugh & Cable, 1993; Williams, 1975.)

D Here are four versions of the same biblical event described in Matthew, Chapter 2. Can you provide an account of the different forms, structures and probable pronunciations to be found in these different versions?

Contemporary English
After they had gone, an angel of the Lord appeared to Joseph in a dream
Early Modern English (early seventeenth century)
And when they were departed, behold, the Angel of the Lord appeareth to Joseph in a dreame
Middle English (fourteenth century)
And whanne thei weren goon, lo, the aungel of the Lord apperide to Joseph in sleep
Old English (tenth century)
þā hī þā ferdon, þā ætȳwde Drihtnes engel Iosepe on swefnum

E You should be able to understand the following recipe for *Oystres in Gravey*, from the late Middle English period (15th century). Try to rewrite this text (quoted in Hughes, 1988) in contemporary English, noting all the differences (e.g. *hem*) and how you decided on your translations of unfamiliar words (e.g. *caste*).

Take almondes, and blanche hem, and grinde hem, and drawe hem thorgh a streynour with wyne, and with goode fressh broth into gode mylke, and sette hit

on the fire and lete boyle; and caste therto Maces, clowes, Sugar, pouder of
Ginger, and faire parboyled oynons mynced; And then take faire oystres, and par-
boyle hem togidre in faire water; And then caste hem thereto; And lete hem
boyle togidre til they ben yknowe; and serve hem forth for gode potage.

Further reading

Introductory treatments can be found in Chapter 9 of Finegan & Besnier
(1989) or Chapter 7 of O'Grady *et al.* (1993). Aitchison (1991) and McMahon
(1994) are basic textbooks, while more advanced surveys can be found in
Anttila (1989), Arlotto (1972), Bynon (1977), Hock (1991) and Lehman (1993).
A non-traditional perspective is presented in Thomason & Kaufman (1988).
Collections of papers are presented in Fisiak (1990) and Jones (1993). On Sir
William Jones, see Cannon (1990). For more on language families and numbers
of speakers, consult Crystal (1987). On the Indo-Europeans, try Renfrew
(1987), Gamkrelidze & Ivanov (1995), Mallory (1989) or Thieme (1958). There
are many texts on the history of English, including Barber (1993), Baugh &
Cable (1993), Bolton (1982) and Myers & Hoffman (1979). Burchfield (1985) is
a brief review and Crystal (1995) is encyclopedic. More specifically, on Old
English, see Hogg (1991), Mitchell & Robinson (1986) and Robinson (1992);
on Middle English, see Blake (1992) and Partridge (1982); on early Modern
English, see Gorlach (1991), Lass (1995) and Romaine (1995). If you would
like to hear how English was spoken during different historical periods, listen
to the recordings which accompany Finnie (1972).

20 Language varieties

Da history of da word pigeon is li'dis – Wen da French-speaking Normans wen conquer England in da year ten-six-six, dey wen bring along wit dem da word pigeon, for da type of bird it was. Da resident Anglo-Saxons used da word dove, or D-U-F-E, as dey used to spell'um, to mean da same bird. It just so happened dat terms in Norman-French wen blend wit Old English sentence structure, to form what we know as Middle English. In da process, da French word became da one dat referred to da pigeon as food. Today in England, if you look for dem, you can find recipes for pigeon pie.

Food for taught, eh – Even back den, da word pigeon wen blend with pigeon for get some moa pigeon.

So now days get pigeon by da zoo – get pigeon on da beach – get pigeon in town – get pigeon in coups – and no madda wat anybody try do, dey cannot get rid of pigeon – I guess wit such a wide blue sky, everyting deserves to fly.

Joseph Balaz (1988)

In many of the preceding chapters, we have treated languages, such as English, as if all speakers of the particular language used that language in a uniform way. That is, we have largely ignored the fact that every language will have more than one variety, especially in the way in which it is spoken. Yet this variation in speech is an important and well-recognized aspect of our daily lives as language-users in different regional and social communities. In this chapter we shall consider the type of variation which has been investigated via a form of 'linguistic geography', concentrating on regional varieties, and in the following chapter we shall consider the factors involved in social variation in language use. First, we should identify that particular variety which is normally meant when the general terms English, Italian, Japanese, Spanish, and so on are used.

The Standard Language

When we described the sounds, words and sentences of English, we were, in fact, concentrating on the features of only one variety, usually labeled **Standard English**. This is the variety which forms the basis of printed English in newspapers and books, which is used in the mass media and which is taught in schools. It is the variety we normally try to teach to those who want to learn English as a second language. It is clearly associated with education and broadcasting in public contexts and is more easily described in terms of the written language (i.e. vocabulary, spelling, grammar) than the spoken language.

If we are thinking of that general variety used in public broadcasting in the United States, we can refer more specifically to Standard American English or, in Britain, to Standard British English. There is no reason why other national varieties such as Standard Australian English, Standard Canadian English and Standard Indian English should not be recognized also.

Accent and dialect

Whether or not you think you speak a standard variety of English, you will certainly speak with an **accent**. It is a myth that some speakers have accents while others do not. Some speakers may have distinct or easily recognized types of accent while others do not, but every language-user speaks with an accent. The term accent, when used technically, is restricted to the description of aspects of pronunciation which identify where an individual speaker is from, regionally or socially. It is to be distinguished from the term **dialect** which describes features of grammar and vocabulary, as well as aspects of pronunciation. For example, the sentence *You don't know what you're talking about* will generally 'look' the same whether spoken with an American or a Scottish accent. Both speakers will be using Standard English forms, but have different pronunciations. However, this next sentence – *Ye dinnae ken whit yer haverin' aboot* – has the same meaning as the first, but has been written out in an approximation of what a person who speaks one dialect of Scottish English might say. There are, of course, differences in pronunciation (e.g. *whit, aboot*), but there are also examples of different vocabulary (*ken, haverin'*) and a different grammatical form (*dinnae*).

While differences in vocabulary are often easily recognized, dialect variations in the meaning of grammatical constructions are less frequently documented. Here is an example, quoted in Trudgill (1983), of an exchange between two British English speakers (B and C), and a speaker from

Ireland (A), which took place in Donegal, Ireland:

A: *How long are youse here?*
B: *Till after Easter.*
(Speaker A looks puzzled)
C: *We came on Sunday.*
A: *Ah. Youse're here a while then.*

It seems that the construction *How long are youse here?*, in speaker A's dialect, is used with a meaning close to the structure *How long have you been here?*, rather than with the future interpretation (*How long are you going to be here?*) made by speaker B.

Despite occasional difficulties of this sort, there is a general impression of mutual intelligibility among many speakers of different dialects, or varieties, of English. The important point to remember is that, from a linguistic point of view, no one variety is 'better' than another. They are simply different. From a social point of view, however, some varieties do become more prestigious. In fact, the variety which develops as the Standard Language has usually been one socially prestigious dialect, originally connected with a political or cultural center (e.g. London for British English, and Paris for French). Yet, there always continue to be other varieties of a language, spoken in different regions.

Regional dialects

The existence of different regional dialects is widely recognized and often the source of some humor for those living in different regions. Thus, in the United States, someone from Brooklyn may joke about the Southerner's definition of *sex* by telling you that *sex is fo' less than tin*, in his best imitation of someone from the Southern states. The Southerner can, in return, wonder what a *tree guy* is in Brooklyn, since he has heard Brooklyn speakers refer to *doze tree guys*. Some regional dialects clearly have stereotyped pronunciations associated with them.

Those involved in the serious investigation of regional dialects are fairly uninterested in such stereotypes, however, and have devoted a lot of research to the identification of consistent features of speech found in one geographical area rather than another. These dialect surveys often involved painstaking attention to detail and tended to operate with very specific criteria in identifying acceptable informants. After all, it is important to know if the person whose speech you are tape-recording really is a typical representative of the region's dialect. Consequently, the informants in many dialect surveys tended to be NORMS, or non-mobile, older, rural, male speakers. Such speakers were selected because it was believed that they were less likely to have influences from outside the region in their speech. One unfortunate consequence of using such criteria is that the dialect description which results is probably more accurate of a period well before the time of investigation. Nevertheless, the detailed information obtained has provided the basis for a number of Linguistic Atlases of whole countries (e.g. England) or of regions (e.g. the New England area of the United States).

Isoglosses and dialect boundaries

Let us take a look at some examples of regional variation found in one survey, that which resulted in the Linguistic Atlas of the Upper Midwest of the United States. One of the aims of such a survey is to find a number of significant differences in the speech of those living in different areas and to be able to chart where the boundaries are, in dialect terms, between those areas. If it is found, for example, that the vast majority of informants in one area say they take their groceries home in a *paper bag* while the majority in another area say they use a *paper sack*, then it is usually possible to draw a line across a map separating the two areas, as shown on the accompanying illustration. This line is called an **isogloss** and represents a boundary between the areas with regard to that one particular linguistic item. If a very similar distribution is found for another two items, such as a preference for *pail* to the north and for *bucket* to the south, then another isogloss, probably overlapping, can be drawn in. When a number of isoglosses come together in this way, a more solid line, indicating a **dialect boundary**, can be drawn.

In the accompanying illustration, the small circles indicate where *paper bag* was used and the plus sign (+) shows where *paper sack* was used. The broken line between the two areas represents an isogloss. Using this dialect boundary information, we find that in the Upper Midwest of the USA, there is a Northern dialect area which includes Minnesota, North Dakota, most of South Dakota, and Northern Iowa. The rest of Iowa and Nebraska show characteristics of the Midland dialect. Some of the noticeable pronunciation differences, and some vocabulary differences, are illustrated here:

	('t<u>au</u>ght')	('r<u>oo</u>f')	('cr<u>ee</u>k')	('grea<u>s</u>y')	
Northern:	[ɔ]	[ʊ]	[I]	[s]	
Midland:	[a]	[u]	[i]	[z]	
Northern:	*paper bag*	*pail*	*kerosene*	*slippery*	*get sick*
Midland:	*paper sack*	*bucket*	*coal oil*	*slick*	*take sick*

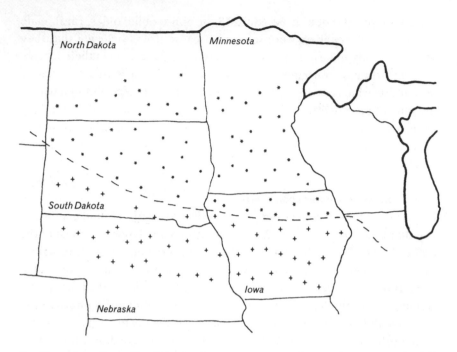

So, if an American English speaker pronounces the word *greasy* as [grizi] and takes groceries home in a *paper sack*, then he is not likely to have grown up and lived most of his life in Minnesota. It is worth noting that the characteristic forms listed here are not used by everyone living in the region. They are used by a significantly large percentage of the people interviewed in the dialect survey.

The dialect continuum

Another note of caution is required. The drawing of isoglosses and dialect boundaries is quite useful in establishing a broad view of regional dialects, but it tends to obscure the fact that, at most dialect boundary areas, one variety merges into another. Keeping this in mind, we can view regional variation as existing along a **continuum**, and not as having sharp breaks from one region to the next. A very similar type of continuum can occur with related languages existing on either side of a political border. As you travel from Holland into Germany, you will find concentrations of Dutch speakers giving way to areas near the border where the Dutch dialects and the German dialects are less clearly differentiated; then, as you travel into Germany, greater concentrations of distinctly German speakers occur.

Speakers who move back and forth across this border, using different varieties with some ease, may be described as **bidialectal** (i.e. 'speaking two dialects'). Most of us grow up with some form of bidialectalism, speaking one dialect 'in the street' and having to learn another dialect 'in the school'. However, if we want to talk about people knowing two distinct languages, we have to describe them as being **bilingual**.

Bilingualism

In many countries, regional variation is not simply a matter of two dialects of a single language, but a matter of two quite distinct and different languages. Canada, for example, is an officially bilingual country, with both French and English as official languages. This recognition of the linguistic rights of the country's French speakers, largely in Quebec, did not come about without a lot of political upheaval. For most of its history, Canada was essentially an English-speaking country, with a French-speaking minority group. In such a situation, bilingualism, at the individual level, tends to be a feature of the minority group. In this form of bilingualism, a member of a minority group grows up in one linguistic community, primarily speaking one language, such as Welsh in Wales, Gaelic in Scotland or Spanish in the United States, but learns another language, such as English, in order to take part in the larger, dominant, linguistic community.

Indeed, many members of linguistic minorities can live out their entire lives without ever seeing their native language appear in the public domain. Sometimes political activism can change that. It was only after English notices and signs were frequently defaced or replaced by scribbled Welsh-language versions that bilingual (English–Welsh) signs came into widespread use in Wales. One suspects that many *henoed* never expected to see their first language on public signs like this one, photographed recently in Wales. (But why, you might ask, are we being 'warned' about them?)

Individual bilingualism, however, doesn't have to be the result of political dominance by a group using a different language. It can simply be the result of having two parents who speak different languages. If a child simultaneously acquires the French spoken by her mother and the English spoken by her father, then the distinction between the two languages may not even be noticed. There will simply be two ways of talking according to the person being talked to. However, even in this type of bilingualism, one language tends eventually to become the dominant one, with the other in a subordinate role.

Language planning

Perhaps because bilingualism in Europe and North America tends to be found only among minority groups, a country like the United States is often assumed to be a single homogeneous speech community where everyone speaks English and all radio and television broadcasts and all newspapers use Standard English. It appears to be a **monolingual** country. This is a mistaken view. It ignores the existence of large communities for whom English is not the first language of the home. As one example, the majority of the population in San Antonio, Texas, are more likely to listen to radio broadcasts in Spanish than in English. This simple fact has quite large repercussions in terms of the organization of local representative government and the educational system. Should elementary school teaching take place in English or Spanish?

Consider a similar question in the context of Guatemala where, in addition to Spanish, there are twenty-six Mayan languages spoken. If, in this situation, Spanish is selected as the language of education, are all those Mayan speakers put at an early educational disadvantage within the society? Questions of this type require answers on the basis of some type of language planning. Government, legal and educational bodies in many countries have to plan which varieties of the languages spoken in the country are to be used for official business. In Israel, despite the fact that Hebrew was not the most widely used language among the population, it was chosen as the official government language. In India, the choice was Hindi, yet, in many non-Hindi-speaking regions, there were riots against this decision.

The process of language planning may be seen in a better light when the full series of stages is implemented over a number of years. A good modern example has been provided by the adoption of Swahili as the national language of Tanzania in East Africa. There still exist a large number of tribal languages as well as the colonial vestiges of English, but the educational, legal and government systems have gradually introduced Swahili as the official language. The process of 'selection' (choosing an official language) is followed by 'codification' in which basic grammars, dictionaries and written models are used to establish the Standard variety. The process of 'elaboration' follows, with the Standard variety being developed for use in all aspects of social life and the appearance of a body of literary work written in the Standard. The process of 'implementation' is largely a matter of government attempts to encourage use of the Standard, and 'acceptance' is the final stage when a substantial majority of the population have come to use the Standard and to think of it as the national language, playing a part in not only social, but also national, identity.

Pidgins and Creoles

In some areas, the Standard chosen may be a variety which originally had no native speakers. For example, in Papua New Guinea, most official business is conducted in Tok Pisin, a language sometimes described as Melanesian Pidgin. This language is now used by over a million people, but it began as a kind of 'contact' language called a Pidgin. A **Pidgin** is a variety of a language (e.g. English) which developed for some practical purpose, such as trading, among groups of people who had a lot of contact, but who did not know each other's languages. As such, it would have no native speakers. The origin of the term 'Pidgin' is thought to be from a Chinese Pidgin version of the English word 'business'.

There are several English Pidgins still used today. They are characterized by an absence of any complex grammatical morphology and a limited vocabulary. Inflectional suffixes such as -*s* (plural) and -*'s* (possessive) on nouns in Standard English are rare in Pidgins, while structures like *tu buk* ('two books') and *di gyal pleis* ('the girl's place') are common. Functional morphemes often take the place of inflectional morphemes found in the source language. For example, instead of changing the form of *you* to *your*, as in the English phrase *your book*, English-based Pidgins use a form like *bilong*, and change the word order to produce phrases like *buk bilong yu*.

The origin of many words in Pidgins can be phrases from other languages, such as one word used for 'ruin, destroy' which is *bagarimap* (derived from the English phrase "bugger him up"), or for 'lift' which is *haisimap* (from "hoist him up"), or for 'us' which is *yumi* (from "you" plus "me"). Original borrowings can be used creatively to take on new meanings such as the word *ars* which is used for 'cause' or 'source', as well as 'bottom', and originated in the English word *arse*.

The syntax of Pidgins can be quite unlike the languages from which terms were borrowed and modified, as can be seen in this example from an earlier stage of Tok Pisin:

Baimbai	hed	bilong yu	i-arrait	gain
(by and by)	(head)	(belong you)	(he-alright)	(again)

'Your head will soon get well again'

There are considered to be between six and twelve million people still using Pidgin languages and between ten and seventeen million using descendants from Pidgins called **Creoles**. When a Pidgin develops beyond its role as a trade language and becomes the first language of a social community, it is described as a Creole. Tok Pisin, for example, would more accurately be described nowadays as a Creole. Although still locally called 'pidgin', the language spoken by large numbers of people in Hawai'i is also a Creole. A Creole develops as the first language of the children of Pidgin speakers. Thus, unlike Pidgins, Creoles have large numbers of native speakers and are not restricted at all in their uses. A French-based Creole is spoken by the majority of the population in Haiti and English-based Creoles are used in Jamaica and Sierra Leone.

The separate vocabulary elements of a Pidgin can become grammatical elements in a Creole. The form *baimbai yu go* ('by and by you go') in early Tok Pisin gradually shortened to *bai yu go*, then to *yu bai go*, and finally to *yu bigo*, with a grammatical structure not unlike that of its English translation equivalent, *you will go*.

The Post-Creole continuum

In many contemporary situations where Creoles evolved, there is usually evidence of another process at work. Just as there was development from a Pidgin to a Creole, known as 'creolization', there is now often a retreat from the use of the Creole by those who have greater contact with a standard variety of the language. Where education and greater social prestige are associated with a 'higher' variety, used as a model (e.g. British English in Jamaica), many speakers will tend to use fewer Creole forms and structures. The process, known as 'decreolization', leads, at one extreme, to a variety that is closer to the external standard model and leaves, at the other extreme, a basic variety with more local Creole features. The more basic variety is called the **basilect** and the variety closer to the external model is called the **acrolect**. Between these two extremes may be a range of slightly different varieties, some with many and some with fewer Creole features, known as **mesolects**. This range of varieties, evolving after (= 'post') the Creole has been created, is called the **Post-Creole continuum**.

Thus, in Jamaica, one speaker may say *a fi mi buk dat* (basilect), another may put it as *iz mi buk* (mesolect) or yet another may choose *it's my book* (acrolect). It is also common for speakers to be able to use a range of features associated with different varieties and appropriate to different situations.

It is predictable that these differences will be tied very much to social values and identity. In the course of discussing language varieties in terms of regional differences, we have excluded, in a rather artificial way, the complex social factors which are also at work in determining language variation. In the final chapter, we shall go on to consider the influence of a number of these social variables.

Study questions
1   What is the difference between a dialect and an accent?
2   What are NORMS?
3   What does an isogloss represent?
4   What are the five stages in the complete language planning process?
5   What is the major difference between a Pidgin and a Creole?

Discussion topics/projects

A In studies of language variation, a large geographical barrier is often seen as a factor in the development of different varieties of a language. With the Atlantic Ocean as a fairly large barrier, we should not be surprised to find some variation between British and American English, particularly in their vocabularies. Can you identify the meanings of the following words in each variety? Are there other terms which belong to only one variety and not the other? Why do you think the variation is in fact not substantial even though the barrier is?

allowance baggage bill biscuits braces bonnet (of car) boot (of car) bum chips comforter dustman fanny first floor flat (n.) gas homely lay-by lift (n.) lorry lounge mean (adj.) mince nappy pants paraffin pavement petrol post rubber spanner surgery tights torch trailer sweets vest

B In some dialects of Britain (mainly northern England and Scotland) and of the USA (mainly southern, from Georgia to Louisiana), there is a grammatical construction that is not found in Standard English. It is called a 'double modal' construction, because two modal verbs are used together, as in I *might could* do it later. The basic English modals are: *can, could, may, might, must, ought to, shall, should, will, would.*
(i) If you have heard (or use) any double modal structures, what are they and which versions do you think are the most frequent?

(ii) What kind of meaning is communicated by the double modal (e.g. *might could*) that is not conveyed by a single modal?

(iii) Is it just an accident that these forms occur in two really separate regions (northern UK and southern USA) or do you think there might could be a connection?

C The following statistics regarding the population of Montreal in 1961 were published by the Royal Commission on Bilingualism and Biculturalism. You should be able to work out the percentage size of each group in terms of origin, whether bilingual or not, and whether monolingual or not.
(i) Is bilingualism or monolingualism more prevalent in any one group?

(ii) Consider which of the two official languages was more frequently learned by those in the group labeled 'Other'. Why do you think this happened in a Canadian city?

	British	French	Other
Population by ethnic origin:	377,625	1,353,480	378,404
Number of bilinguals by ethnic origin:	101,767	554,929	119,907
Number of individuals monolingual in each official language:	462,260	826,333	–

D Here are some examples of Hawai'i Creole English (from Bickerton, 1991) and their Standard English translations. What are the linguistic differences between these two varieties? (You might start with the ways in which past time and plurals are indicated.)

Us two bin get hard time raising dog	"The two of us had a hard time raising dogs"
John-them stay cockroach the kaukau	"John and his friends are stealing the food"
He lazy, 'a'swhy he no like play	"He doesn't want to play because he's lazy"
More better I bin go Honolulu for buy om	"It would have been better if I'd gone to Honolulu to buy it"
The guy gon' lay the vinyl bin quote me price	"The man who was going to lay the vinyl had quoted me a price"
Bin get one wahine she get three daughter	"There was a woman who had three daughters"
She no can go, she no more money, 'a'swhy	"She can't go because she hasn't any money"

E There is always controversy, in one form or another, with regard to different varieties of a language. In linguistic terms, there are only 'non-standard' varieties, but in social terms, there are 'bad' or 'substandard' varieties. The quotation at the beginning of this chapter is a subtle commentary on the fact that 'pidgin' (as used in Hawai'i) is viewed negatively by many people and is difficult to get rid of, but that it has a place in history and 'deserves to fly'. However, it is often argued that it is the duty of the school system to discourage the use of any non-standard varieties and to provide 'better' language for those children who don't have it.

(i)   Do you agree or disagree with this point of view?

(ii) Does the same argument apply to children entering the English-speaking school system with Spanish, Urdu, Vietnamese or a Creole as their home language?

(iii) Would it be better if English became the 'official' language of the USA? What would be the advantages and disadvantages of such a change? (You can consult Baron, 1990 or Crawford, 1992 for some ideas.)

Further reading

General introductions can be found in Downes (1984), Fasold (1990), Holmes (1992), Hudson (1990), Romaine (1994a) and Wardhaugh (1992). Regional variation is surveyed in section 20 of Crystal (1995). Other accessible readings on variation are collected in Ferguson & Heath (1981), Glowka & Lance (1993) and Milroy & Milroy (1988). On issues relating to the prestige of one variety over others, see Bailey (1991), Baron (1990), Crawford (1992) and Kachru (1986). On different Standard Englishes, read Trudgill & Hannah (1994). On dialect, there are textbooks such as Chambers & Trudgill (1980) or Francis (1983). Others include Davis (1983), Hughes & Trudgill (1979) or any of the books by Trudgill (1983; 1986; 1990; 1994) or Trudgill & Chambers (1991). Walters (1988) is one review, Labov (1991) is another, and Hendrickson (1986) is a collection. On the Dutch–German dialect continuum, and other aspects of German dialectology, see Barbour & Stevenson (1990). On dialect humor, try Blair & McDavid (1983) or Davies (1990). On regional dialect surveys, see Kurath (1972) for methods used, and Kurath et al. (1939–43) for a detailed example of the results. For more data on the Upper Midwest, see Allen (1973-6). On English and Welsh, see Coupland (1990). On bilingualism, see Hoffman (1991), Romaine (1994b) or Spolsky (1988). On language planning, see Christian (1988), Cooper (1990), Fishman (1993) and Kennedy (1984). On Pidgins and Creoles, see Bickerton (1991) or Hall (1959) for brief accounts, Romaine (1994b) or Todd (1990) for surveys and Holm (1989) for a more detailed review. Other, more technical, discussions can be found in Andersen (1983), Hancock (1985), Hymes (1971), Mühlhäusler (1986) and Valdman (1977). Literary work in Hawaiian Creole is surveyed in Romaine (1994c). The change in 'baimbai' (Tok Pisin) is documented in Sankoff & Laberge (1974). On basilects, see Bickerton (1975), and on Jamaican, see Roberts (1988). A critical appraisal of one post-Creole context is presented in Sato (1985).

21 Language, society and culture

When the anchorwoman Connie Chung was asked a fairly insensitive
question by a new co-worker about the relationship between her position as
an Asian-American woman and her rapid rise in the field, her response was
both pointed and humorous: "I pointed to the senior vice president and
announced, 'Bill likes the way I do his shirts.'" **Regina Barreca (1991)**

We have already noted that the way you speak may provide clues, in terms
of regional accent or dialect, to where you spent most of your early life.
However, your speech may also contain a number of features which are
unrelated to regional variation. Two people growing up in the same geographical area, at the same time, may speak differently because of a number
of social factors. It is important not to overlook this social aspect of
language because, in many ways, speech is a form of social identity and is
used, consciously or unconsciously, to indicate membership of different
social groups or different speech communities. A speech community is a
group of people who share a set of norms, rules and expectations regarding
the use of language. Investigating language from this perspective is known
as **Sociolinguistics**.

Sociolinguistics
In general terms, sociolinguistics deals with the inter-relationships between
language and society. It has strong connections to anthropology, through
the investigation of language and culture, and to sociology, through the
crucial role that language plays in the organization of social groups and
institutions. It is also tied to social psychology, particularly with regard to
how attitudes and perceptions are expressed and how in-group and

239

out-group behaviors are identified. All these connections are needed if we are to make sense of what might be described as 'social dialects'.

Social dialects

In modern studies of language variation, a great deal of care is taken to document, usually via questionnaires, certain details of the social backgrounds of speakers. It is as a result of taking such details into account that we have been able to make a study of **social dialects**, which are varieties of language used by groups defined according to class, education, age, sex, and a number of other social parameters.

Before exploring these factors in detail, it is important to draw attention to one particular interaction between social values and language use. The concept of 'prestige', as found in discussions about language in use, is typically understood in terms of **overt prestige**, that is, the generally recognized 'better' or positively valued ways of speaking in social communities. There is, however, an important phenomenon called **covert prestige**. This 'hidden' type of positive value is often attached to non-standard forms and expressions by certain sub-groups. Members of these sub-groups may place much higher value on the use of certain non-standard forms as markers of social solidarity. For example, schoolboys everywhere seem to attach covert prestige to forms of 'bad' language (swearing and 'tough' talk) that are not similarly valued in the larger community. It is, nevertheless, within the larger community that norms and expectations are typically established.

Social class and education

Two obvious factors in the investigation of social dialect are social class and education. In some dialect surveys, it has been found that, among those leaving the educational system at an early age, there is a greater tendency to use forms which are relatively infrequent in the speech of those who go on to college. Expressions such as those contained in *Them boys throwed somethin'* are much more common in the speech of the former group than the latter. It seems to be the case that a person who spends a long time going through college or university will tend to have spoken language features which derive from a lot of time spent working with the written language. The complaint that some professor "talks like a book" is possibly a recognition of an extreme form of this influence.

The social classes also sound different. A famous study by Labov (1972) combined elements from place of occupation and socio-economic status by looking at pronunciation differences among salespeople in three New York

City department stores, Saks (high status), Macy's (middle status) and Klein's (low status). Labov asked salespeople questions that elicited the expression *fourth floor*. He was interested in the pronunciation (or not) of the [r] sound after vowels. There was a regular pattern: the higher the socio-economic status, the more [r] sounds, and the lower the socio-economic status, the fewer [r] sounds were produced. So, the difference in a single consonant could mark high*er* versus low*ah* social class. That was in New York.

In Reading, England, Trudgill (1974) found that the same variable (i.e. [r] after a vowel) had the opposite social value. Upper middle class speakers in that area tended to pronounce fewer [r] sounds than lower/working class speakers. You may have encountered individuals who seem to have no [r] sound in "Isn't that mahvellous, dahling!"

Actually, a more stable indication of lower class and less education, throughout the English-speaking world, is the occurrence of [n] rather than [ŋ] at the end of words like *walking* and *going*. Pronunciations represented by *sittin'* and *drinkin'* are associated with lower social class.

Another social marker is [h]-dropping, which results in *'ouse* and *'ello*. In contemporary English, this is associated with lower social class and less education. For Charles Dickens, writing in the middle of the nineteenth-century, it was one way of marking a character's lower status, as in this example from Uriah Heep (in *David Copperfield*).

> '*I am well aware that I am the umblest person going*', said Uriah Heep, modestly; '*... My mother is likewise a very umble person. We live in a numble abode, Master Copperfield, but we have much to be thankful for. My father's former calling was umble.*'

Age and gender

Even within groups of the same social class, however, other differences can be found which seem to correlate with factors such as the age or gender of speakers. Many younger speakers living in a particular region often look at the results of a dialect survey of their area (conducted mainly with older informants) and claim that their grandparents may use those terms, but they do not. Variation according to **age** is most noticeable across the grandparent–grandchild time span.

Grandfather may still talk about the *icebox* and the *wireless*. He's unlikely to know what *rules*, what *sucks*, or what's *totally stoked*, and he doesn't use *like* to introduce reported speech, as his granddaughter might do: *We're get-*

ting ready, and he's like, Let's go, and I'm like, No way I'm not ready, and he splits anyway, the creep!

Variation according to the **gender** of the speaker has been the subject of a lot of recent research. One general conclusion from dialect surveys is that female speakers tend to use more prestigious forms than male speakers with the same general social background. That is, forms such as *I done it*, *it growed* and *he ain't* can be found more often in the speech of males, and *I did it*, *it grew* and *he isn't* in the speech of females.

In some cultures, there are much more marked differences between male and female speech. Quite different pronunciations of certain words in male and female speech have been documented in some North American Indian languages such as Gros Ventre and Koasati. Indeed, when Europeans first encountered the different vocabularies of male and female speech among the Carib Indians, they reported that the different sexes used different languages. What had, in fact, been found was an extreme version of variation according to the gender of the speaker.

In contemporary English, there are many reported differences in the talk of males and females. In same gender pairs having conversations, women generally discuss their personal feelings more than men. Men appear to prefer non-personal topics such as sport and news. Men tend to respond to an expression of feelings or problems by giving advice on solutions, while women are more likely to mention personal experiences that match or connect with the other woman's. There is a pattern documented in American English social contexts of women co-operating and seeking connection via language, whereas men are more competitive and concerned with power via language. In mixed-gender pairs having conversations, the rate of men interrupting women is substantially greater than the reverse. Women are reported to use more expressions associated with tentativeness, such as 'hedges' (*sort of, kind of*) and 'tags' (*isn't it?, don't you?*), when expressing an opinion: *Well, em, I think that golf is kind of boring, don't you?*

There have been noticeable changes in English vocabulary (e.g. *spokesperson, mail carrier* instead of *spokesman, mailman*) as part of an attempt to eliminate gender bias in general terms, but the dilemma of the singular pronoun persists. Is *a friend* to be referred to as *he or she*, *s/he*, or even *they* in sentences like: *Bring a friend if _____ can come.* In some contexts it appears that *they* is emerging as the preferred term (but you can be sure that somebody will complain that *they* don't like it!).

Ethnic background

In the quote that introduces this chapter, both the gender and the ethnicity of an individual are alluded to. The humorous response plays on the stereo-typed image of how a female member of one ethnic minority might succeed in society. In a more serious way, we can observe that, within any society, differences in speech may come about because of different **ethnic backgrounds**. In very obvious ways, the speech of recent immigrants, and often of their children, will contain identifying features. In some areas, where there is strong language loyalty to the original language of the group, a large number of features are carried over into the new language.

More generally, the speech of many African-Americans, technically known as **Black English Vernacular (BEV)**, is a widespread social dialect, often cutting across regional differences. When a group within a society undergoes some form of social isolation, such as the discrimination or seg-regation experienced historically by African-Americans, then social dialect differences become more marked. The accompanying problem, from a social point of view, is that the resulting variety of speech may be stigma-tized as "bad speech". One example is the frequent absence of the copula (forms of the verb 'to be') in BEV, as in expressions like *They mine* or *You crazy*. Standard English requires that the verb form *are* be used in such expressions. However, many other English dialects do not use the copula in such structures and a very large number of languages (e.g. Arabic, Russian) have similar structures without the copula. BEV, in this respect, cannot be "bad" any more than Russian is "bad" or Arabic is "bad". As a dialect, it sim-ply has features which are consistently different from the Standard.

Another aspect of BEV which has been criticized, sometimes by educa-tors, is the use of double negative constructions, as in *He don't know nothing* or *I ain't afraid of no ghosts*. The criticism is usually that such structures are 'illogical'. If that is so, then French, which typically employs a two-part neg-ative form, as exemplified by *il NE sait RIEN* ('he doesn't know anything'), and Old English, also with a double negative, as in *Ic NAHT singan NE cuðe* ('I didn't know how to sing'), must be viewed as equally 'illogical'. In fact, far from being illogical, this type of structure provides a very effective means of emphasizing the negative part of a message in this dialect. It is basically a dialect feature, present in one social dialect of English, sometimes found in other dialects, but not in the Standard Language.

Idiolect

Of course, aspects of all these elements of social and regional dialect variation are combined, in one form or another, in the speech of each individual. The term **idiolect** is used for the personal dialect of each individual speaker of a language. There are other factors, such as voice quality and physical state, which contribute to the identifying features in an individual's speech, but many of the social factors we have described determine each person's idiolect. From the perspective of the social study of language, you are, in many respects, what you say.

Style, register and jargon

All of the social factors we have considered so far are related to variation according to the user of the language. Another source of variation in an individual's speech is occasioned by the situation of use. There is a gradation of **style** of speech, from the very formal to the very informal. Going for a job interview, you may say to a secretary *Excuse me. Is the manager in his office? I have an appointment.* Alternatively, speaking to a friend about another friend, you may produce a much less formal version of the message: *Hey, is that lazy dog still in bed? I gotta see him about something.*

This type of variation is more formally encoded in some languages than others. In Japanese, for example, there are different terms used for the person you are speaking to, depending on the amount of respect or deference required. French has two pronouns (*tu* and *vous*), corresponding to singular *you*, with the first reserved for close friends and family. Similar distinctions are seen in the *you* forms in German (*du* and *Sie*) and in Spanish (*tu* and *usted*).

Differences in style can also be found in written language, with business letters (e.g. *I am writing to inform you ...*) versus letters to friends (*Just wanted to let you know ...*) as good illustrations. The general pattern, however, is that a written form of a message will inevitably be more formal in style than its spoken equivalent. If you see someone on the local bus, eating, drinking and playing a radio, you can say that what he's doing isn't allowed and that he should wait until he gets off the bus. Alternatively, you can draw his attention to the more formal language of the printed notice which reads:

The city has recently passed an ordinance that expressly prohibits the following while aboard public conveyances. Eating or Drinking. The Playing of Electronic Devices.

The formality of expressions such as *expressly prohibit*, *the following*, and *electronic devices* is more extreme than is likely to occur in the spoken language.

Variation according to use in specific situations is also studied in terms of **register**. There is a religious register in which we expect to find expressions not found elsewhere, as in *Ye shall be blessed by Him in times of tribulation*. In another register you will encounter sentences such as *The plaintiff is ready to take the witness stand*. The legal register, however, is unlikely to incorporate some of the expressions you are becoming familiar with from the linguistics register, such as *The morphology of this dialect contains fewer inflectional suffixes*.

It is obvious that one of the key features of a register is the use of special **jargon**, which can be defined as technical vocabulary associated with a special activity or group. In social terms, jargon helps to connect those who see themselves as 'insiders' in some way and to exclude 'outsiders'. If you are familiar with surfing talk, you'll know whether the following answer to an interview question was 'yes' or 'no'.

Q: *Would you ride a bodyboard if a shark bit off your legs?*
A: *Hey, if you can get tubed, nobody's bumming.*

The answer means, 'Yes, of course!'. Even when dictionaries are created for certain activities, the entries often explain jargon with other jargon, as in this example from *The New Hacker's Dictionary* (Raymond, 1991), compiled from the expressions used by those who spend a lot of time with computers.

juggling eggs. *Keeping a lot of state in your head while modifying a program. "Don't bother me now, I'm juggling eggs", means that an interrupt is likely to result in the program's being scrambled.*

You may actually feel that this idiom could apply equally well on many occasions in your daily life!

Diglossia

Taking all the preceding social factors into account, we might imagine that managing to say the right thing to the right person at the right time is a monumental social accomplishment. It is. It is a major skill which language-users must acquire over and above other linguistic skills such as pronunciation and grammar. In some societies, however, the choice of appropriate linguistic forms is made a little more straightforward because of **diglossia**. This term is used to describe a situation in which two very different varieties of language co-exist in a speech community, each with a distinct range of social functions. There is normally a 'High' variety, for formal or serious matters, and a 'Low' variety, for conversation and other informal uses.

A form of diglossia exists in most Arabic-speaking countries where the high, or classical, variety is used in lectures, religious speech and formal political talk, while the low variety is the local dialect of colloquial Arabic. In Greek, there is also a high and a low (or 'demotic') variety. In some situations, the high variety may be a quite separate language. Through long periods of Western European history, a diglossic situation existed with Latin as the high variety and local languages such as French and English as the low variety.

Language and culture

Many of the factors which give rise to linguistic variation are sometimes discussed in terms of cultural differences. It is not unusual to find linguistic features quoted as identifiable aspects of 'working class culture' or 'African-American culture', for example. In many respects, this view has been influenced by the work of anthropologists who tend to treat language as one element among others, such as beliefs, within the definition of **culture** as 'socially acquired knowledge'. Given the process of cultural transmission by which languages are acquired, it makes a lot of sense to emphasize the fact that linguistic variation is tied very much to the existence of different cultures.

In the study of the world's cultures, it has become clear that different groups not only have different languages, they have different world views which are reflected in their languages. In very simple terms, the Aztecs not only did not have a figure in their culture like Santa Claus, they did not have a word for this figure either. In the sense that language reflects culture, this is a very important observation and the existence of different world views should not be ignored when different languages or language varieties are studied. However, one quite influential theory of the connection between language and world view proposes a much more deterministic relationship.

Linguistic determinism

If two languages appear to have very different ways of describing the way the world is, then it may be that as you learn one of those languages, the way your language is organized will determine how you perceive the world being organized. That is, your language will give you a ready-made system of categorizing what you perceive, and as a consequence, you will be led to perceive the world around you only in those categories. Stated in this way, you have a theory of language which has been called **linguistic determinism** and which, in its strongest version, holds that "language determines thought". In short, you can only think in the categories which your language allows you to think in.

A much quoted example used to support this view is based on the (claimed) number of words the Eskimos have for what, in English, is described as *snow*. When you, as an English speaker, look at wintry scenes, you may see a single white entity called *snow*. The Eskimo, viewing similar scenes, may see a large number of different entities, and he does so, it is claimed, because his language allows him to categorize what he sees differently from the English speaker. We shall return to this example.

The Sapir-Whorf hypothesis

The general idea we are considering is part of what has become known as the **Sapir-Whorf hypothesis**. Edward Sapir and Benjamin Whorf produced arguments, in the 1930s, that the language of American Indians, for example, led them to view the world differently from those who spoke European languages. Let us look at an example of this reasoning. Whorf claimed that the Hopi Indians of Arizona perceived the world differently from other tribes (e.g. the English-speaking tribe) because their language led them to do so. In the grammar of Hopi, there is a distinction between 'animate' and 'inanimate', and among the set of entities categorized as 'animate' were clouds and stones. Whorf concluded that the Hopi believe that clouds and stones are animate (living) entities and that it is their language which leads them to believe this. Now, English does not mark in its grammar that clouds and stones are animate, so English speakers do not see the world in the same way as the Hopi. In Whorf's words, "We dissect nature along lines laid down by our native languages."

A number of arguments have been presented against this view. Here is one from Sampson (1980). Imagine a tribe which has a language in which differences in sex are marked grammatically, so that the terms used for females have special markings in the language. Now, you find that these 'female markings' are also used with the terms for *stone* and *door*. We may then conclude that this tribe believes that stones and doors are female entities in the same way as girls and women. This tribe is probably not unfamiliar to you. They use the terms *la femme* ('woman'), *la pierre* ('stone') and *la porte* ('door'). It is the tribe which lives in France. Do you think that the

French believe that stones and doors are 'female' in the same way as women?

The problem with the conclusions in both these examples is that there is a confusion between linguistic categories ('animate', 'feminine') and biological categories ('living', 'female'). Of course, there is frequently a correspondence in languages between these categories, but there does not have to be. Moreover, the linguistic categories do not force you to ignore biological categories. While the Hopi language has a particular linguistic category for 'stone', it does not mean that a Hopi truck driver thinks he has killed a living creature when he runs over a stone with his truck.

Returning to the Eskimos and 'snow', we realize that English does not have a large number of single terms for different kinds of snow. However, English speakers can create expressions, by manipulating their language, to refer to *wet snow*, *powdery snow*, *spring snow*, and so on. The average English speaker probably does have a very different view of 'snow' from the average Eskimo speaker. That is a reflection of their different experiences in different cultural environments. The languages they have learned reflect the different cultures. In Tuvaluan (spoken in some central Pacific islands), they have many different words for types of coconut. In another Pacific culture, that of Hawai'i, the traditional language had a very large number of words for different kinds of rain. Our languages reflect our concerns.

The notion that language determines thought may be partially correct, in some extremely limited way, but it fails to take into account the fact that users of a language do not inherit a fixed set of patterns to use. They inherit the ability to manipulate and create with a language, in order to express their perceptions. If thinking and perception were totally determined by language, then the concept of language change would be impossible. If a young Hopi boy had no word in his language for the object known to us as a *computer*, would he fail to perceive the object? Would he be unable to think about it? What the Hopi does when he encounters a new entity is to change his language to accommodate the need to refer to the new entity. The human manipulates the language, not the other way around.

Language universals

While many linguists have recognized the extent to which languages are subject to variation, they have also noted the extent to which all languages have certain common properties. Those common properties, called **language universals**, can be described, from one point of view, as those definitive features of language which we investigated in Chapter 3.

Specifically, every human language can be learned by children, employs an arbitrary symbol system, and can be used to send and receive messages by its users. From another point of view, every language has nounlike and verblike components which are organized within a limited set of patterns to produce complex utterances. At the moment, much of what is known about the general character of languages is in the form of certain established relationships. For example, if a language uses fricative sounds, it invariably also uses stops. If a language places objects after verbs, it will also use prepositions. By discovering universal patterns of this type, it may be possible one day to describe, not just the grammars of all languages, but the single grammar of human language.

Study questions

1 How would you define 'a speech community'?
2 How would you describe the constructions used in these two examples from one English dialect: (a) *We ain't got none.* (b) *He just lazy?*
3 What is meant by the term 'idiolect'?
4 What is diglossia?
5 What is the strong version of 'linguistic determinism'?

Discussion topics/projects

A Below is a graphic representation of some findings of Labov (1972) concerning the use of [n] (e.g. *walkin'*) as opposed to [ŋ] (*walking*) in different speech styles by different social groups.

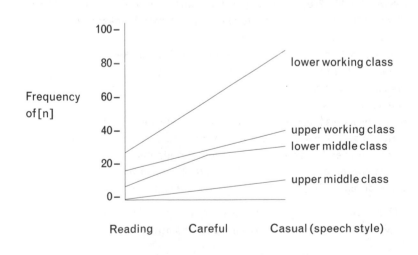

(i) How would you interpret these findings? For example, which group uses [n] (*-in'* as opposed to *-ing*) most frequently and in which speech style?

(ii) Which group uses it least often, and when?

(iii) Say you wanted to investigate the occurrence of this feature in your speech community, how would you go about it?

B Forms of address in English seem to differ according to a number of the features we considered. Work through the diagram below several times. taking different combinations of choices, to arrive at different ways of addressing people.

sex →	age →	name →	setting →	status
male	older	known	formal	higher
female	younger	unknown	informal	lower

(i) Are there other forms of address not captured by these sets of features?

(ii) What actually happens when an inappropriate form of address is used?

(iii) Does the concept of 'appropriate' actually depend on complex cultural assumptions? For example, what?

C The following extracts are from the 'Personals', a section in most US daily newspapers, where individuals who are 'seeking' other individuals can place advertisements.

(1) DWM, 46, 5' 11", 200 pounds, enjoys hunting, fishing, golf. Desires S/DWF, 30-40, with sense of humor, for fun and commitment. Smoker okay.

(2) Hard-working, honest, professional SBM, 24, 5' 3", caring, enjoys travel. Needs attention from attractive slender lady. Nonsmoker, no drugs.

(3) Cute SBF, 20, full-figured, college student, seeks sincere, intelligent gentleman, 6' plus, financially secure, 25-30, for possible relationship. No games.

(4) Sunshine seeks the moon and stars to complete her day. NS, DWF, mature, nature-loving Scorpio, looking for sensitive companion for conversation, friendship and fine wine. Only serious-minded need apply.

(5) Fun-loving, outgoing, open-minded, SWF, 22, enjoys movies, puzzles, social drinking. Copes with ambiguity. Seeks same for friendship.

(i) This seems to be a special register. What special terminology, abbreviations and structures have to be known in order to make sense of these texts? (For example, how would you explain 'full-figured' and 'no games'?)

(ii)   As an exercise in the analysis of social expectations (as expressed in language), try to list the qualities being sought in a woman (examples 1 and 2) with the qualities offered by women (examples 3, 4 and 5). Any mismatches?

(iii) If you can find other examples of this type of language, what additional linguistic features would you propose as representative of this social phenomenon?

D   Socio-cultural variation is not only found in language, it is also present in 'paralanguage' (physical and vocal gestures accompanying or in place of language use). Consider the following analysis from Poyatos (1993: 368–9).

As one moves up the social ladder, *uncontrolled involuntary belching* is a taboo in most advanced cultures under any circumstances unless due to illness, and even then one is supposed to minimize it and shield the mouth with one hand (unless unable to control it), while its sound is considered embarrassing and offensive if it is not repressed. However, we find double standards for men and women in many cultures: an Australian male informant assures me that "it is all right for men to belch in bars, but never in a restaurant", while the Chinese tell me that women should refrain from belching, but that "it is all right for men".

(i)   What different patterns exist, in your experience, regarding this type of 'paralanguage'?

(ii)   Do the same expectations apply equally to shouting, crying, laughing, yawning, spitting, and sneezing (in public)?

(iii) What different things do people ritually say (e.g. *Bless you*) in different situations, in reaction to any of the behaviors listed above?

E   In a recent study, equal numbers of male and female students (at a university in California) were recorded performing problem-solving tasks. The Table below lists the number of "intensifiers" used by the different sexes in the tasks. (The word *really* is an intensifier in the phrase, *that's a really difficult problem*.)

	male	female		male	female
Absolutely	1	2	Quite	1	1
Complete	3	0	Real	64	29
Completely	1	1	Really	246	456
Definitely	28	14	So	163	272
Extremely	5	2	Such a	12	24
Fucking	1	0	Super	3	7
Fully	2	0	Total	6	4
Lots	1	0	Totally	26	32
Mega	0	1	Very	61	42
Overly	0	1	Way	3	0

(i)   Does one of the two groups use many more intensifiers than the other?

(ii)   Would you propose that there are some intensifiers that are 'more male' and others that are 'more female'?

(iii)   Why do you think these patterns are present in the speech of males and females? Is the same pattern present in your speech community?
(If you want to know more about the study, consult Bradac *et al.*, 1995.)

Further reading
Many of the introductory texts listed for Chapter 20 also contain sections on the issues explored here; see Downes (1984), Holmes (1992), Hudson (1990), Romaine (1994a) and Wardhaugh (1992). More technical treatments can be found in Chambers (1994), Giglioli (1972), Labov (1972), Guy (1988), Milroy (1987a; 1987b), Pride & Holmes (1972) and Scherer & Giles (1979). On the general topic of socially preferred talk, see Allan & Burridge (1991), Burgess (1992), Cameron (1995), Crowley (1991), Heath (1983), Honey (1989) and Quirk (1995). The marking of social dialect in Dickens is among the things analyzed by Mugglestone (1995). On some socially non-preferred talk, see Jay (1992) and Spears (1990). On language and age, see Coupland *et al.* (1991) and Romaine (1984). On the age-distinguishing uses of 'like', see Blyth *et al.* (1990). On language and gender, see Baron (1986), Cameron (1990; 1992), Coates (1993), Coates & Cameron (1989), Crawford (1995), Graddol & Swann (1989), Holmes (1995), Lakoff (1975; 1990), Penelope (1990), Philips *et al.* (1987) or Thorne *et al.* (1983). The work of Tannen (1986; 1990; 1993; 1994) is particularly relevant to gender issues in interaction. On language and cross-cultural communication, two surveys are provided by Clyne (1994) and Scollon & Scollon (1995). On the importance of sociolinguistics in second-language studies, see

Preston (1989) or Wolfson (1989). On ethnicity, see Baugh (1983; 1988), Fishman (1989) and Goodwin (1990). On style and register, see Biber & Finegan (1994) or Gregory & Carroll (1978). On jargon, try Nash (1993). On language and the law, see Gibbons (1994). On diglossia, try Ferguson (1959) and Fishman (1971) for earlier perspectives and Hudson (1992) for recent work. On Sapir-Whorf, see Carroll (1956), on Eskimos and snow, see Pullum (1991), on coconuts in Tuvaluan, see Finegan & Besnier (1989) and on rain in Hawaiian, see Kent (1986). On language universals, see Comrie (1989) or Greenberg (1966).

Appendix

Suggested answers to Study questions

1 The origins of language
1 The sounds produced by humans when exerting physical effort (grunts), especially when co-operating with other humans, may be the origins of speech sounds ("yo-heave-ho").
2 The patterns of movement in articulation (of tongue, lips) would be the same as gestural movement (of hands), hence waving tongue would develop from waving hand.
3 Human teeth are upright and roughly even in height; human lips are very flexible because of their intricate muscle interlacing.
4 The larynx moved lower, making it easier for the human (unlike a monkey) to choke on pieces of food.
5 They are "interactional", which is mainly a social function of language, and "transactional", which is mainly a function involving the communication of knowledge and information.

2 The development of writing
1 China.
2 The Cyrillic alphabet.
3 Japanese.
4 An extremely large number of separate symbols are involved, so there are problems in learning all the symbols and also in remembering them.
5 Rebus writing involves a process whereby the symbol used for an entity comes to be used for the sound of the spoken word used for that entity.

3 The properties of language
1 Linguistic forms are described as arbitrary because there is generally no natural connection between the form and its meaning.

2 Displacement.
3 No, because many animal communication systems use the vocal-auditory channel for signaling and for no other purpose.
4 Duality.
5 For example, a child with genetic features from its natural parents (e.g. Korean) will learn the language of the culture of its adopting parents (e.g. English).

4 Animals and human language

1 It's unlikely. Viki produced versions of three English words, but it is not clear that she actually produced human speech sounds; the problem is that no other creature is physiologically equipped to produce human speech sounds.
2 Arbitrariness.
3 After careful examination of the filmed record, Terrace concluded that chimpanzees were performing tricks to get food rewards.
4 They designed an experiment in which no humans could provide cues and Washoe still produced correct signs.
5 Early exposure to language in use.

5 The sounds of language

1 (a) glottal (b) labio-dental (c) alveolar (d) bilabial (e) alveo-palatal
   (f) dental (g) velar (h) alveolar
2 (a), (c), (f) are voiceless; (b), (d), (e) are voiced
3 (a) fricative (b) stop (c) affricate (d) nasal (e) stop (f) approximant
   (g) approximant (liquid) (h) fricative
4 (a) king (b) face (c) sheep (d) the (e) who (f) back (g) bought (h) how
5 (a) ši/šiy (b) tep (c) dop (d) wɔk (e) say (f) fɛl (g) ðiz (h) ɵɔt

6 The sound patterns of language

1 If we substitute one sound for another in a word and we get a change of meaning, then the two sounds must be phonemes.
2 Pat – fat; pat – pit; heat – heel; tape – tale; bun – ban; fat – far; bell – bet; meal – heel.
3 Substituting phonemes changes meaning and sound; substituting allophones only changes sound.
4 An open syllable ends with a vowel whereas a closed syllable ends with a consonant (as coda).
5 (i) /t/ (ii) /n/ (iii) /d/ (iv) /p/

7 Words and word-formation processes

1 (a) is a 'calque', because the elements are directly translated; (b) and (c) are 'borrowings'
2 Coinage.

3   Un-, re-, dis- are prefixes; -ful, -less, -ness, -able are suffixes.
4   (a) conversion (b) acronym (c) blending (d) infixing.
5   (a) clipping from 'telephone' to 'phone', then compounding; (b) compound-
    ing of 'foot' and 'ball', then derivation with '-er'; (c) compounding of 'blue'
    and 'print', then conversion to a verb; (d) blending of 'car' and 'hijack', then
    derivation with '-ing'.

8 Morphology

1   (a) mis-, -s; pre-, -er; -en, -ed; un-, -er; -less, -ly (b) atypical.
2   The, on, a, and, them, of.
3   (a) -'s, -s (b) -ing (c) -est (d) -ed.
4   -s, -en, Ø, -es, -a.
5   bibili; kəǰi; sal; abalongo; táwa; tiap; kumain.

9 Phrases and sentences: grammar

1   'The' (article); 'boy' (noun); 'rubbed' (verb); 'the' (article); 'magic' (adjec-
    tive); 'lamp' (noun); 'and' (conjunction); 'suddenly' (adverb); 'a' (article);
    'genie' (noun); 'appeared' (verb); 'beside' (preposition); 'him' (pronoun).
2   (a) You must not end a sentence with a preposition.
    (b) You must not split an infinitive.
3   The descriptive approach has, as a general principle, a procedure which
    involves describing the regular structures actually found in the particular
    language being analyzed.
5   (a) The small boy hit the black dog. (b) The dog saw the big man.
4
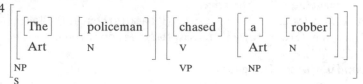

10 Syntax

1   (a) "a teacher of American history" or "an American who teaches history"
    (b) "planes which are flying" or "when a person flies in a plane" (c) "parents
    of the bride, plus the groom" or "the parents of both the bride and the
    groom".
2   (a) The police arrested Lara. (b) She took off her coat. (c) My bicycle was
    stolen. (d) I told him to turn the volume down.
3   All of them.
4   (a), (b) and (c) can be changed; (d) cannot, because here "in" is a preposition
    and not a particle.

5 (a)

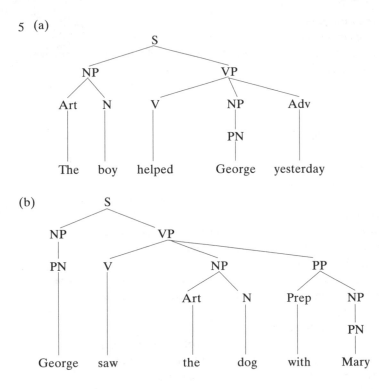

(b)

11 Semantics

1 (a) antonymy (b) synonymy (c) homophony (d) hyponymy (e) antonymy
   (f) hyponymy.
2 (a) The verb "drink" requires a subject with the feature '+animate', but "television" has the feature '−animate'. (b) The verb "write" requires a subject
   with the feature '+human', and the noun "dog" has the feature '−human'.
3 Instrument (golf club), Agent (Fred), Theme (the ball), Source (the woods),
   Goal (the grassy area), Location (the river), Experiencer (he)
4 (a), (d) = non-gradable; (b), (e) = gradable; (c), (f) = reversive
5 (a), (d) = polysemy; (b), (c), (e) = metonymy

12 Pragmatics

1 "I", "now", "you", "that", "here", "come", "tomorrow".
2 (a) He bought the beer. (b) You have a watch. (c) We bought the car.
3 she, him, it
4 (a) The name of a writer can be used to refer to a book by that writer. (b) A
   person with an injury in hospital can be identified by the name of that injury.
5 (a) direct (b) indirect (c) indirect (d) direct

13 Discourse analysis

1   The ties and connections which exist across sentences in texts.
2   Motorist requests mechanic to perform action; mechanic states reason why he cannot comply with request.
3   It describes the observed fact that people take turns at speaking, one at a time, in conversation.
4   Quantity, Quality, Relation, Manner.
5   Quality – since the speaker is stressing the 'honesty' of what he says.

14 Language and machines

1   Spoken language produced electronically.
2   Speaking involves having something to say (a mental process) whereas artic- ulation is simply the activity of saying (a physical process).
3   Modeling human intelligence via machines, or the science of making machines do what would require intelligence if done by humans.
4   Syntactic analysis, primarily.
5   It is computationally impossible to give the machine all world-knowledge, but the machine can be very knowledgeable within a small, limited world.

15 Language and the brain

1   Broca's area, Wernicke's area, the motor cortex and the arcuate fasciculus.
2   Aphasia is an impairment of language function due to localized cerebral damage which leads to difficulty in understanding or producing language.
3   In a dichotic listening test, a person sits with a set of earphones on, and through each earphone, simultaneously, comes a different sound.
4   For most people, the left hemisphere is specialized for language sounds and the right hemisphere for environmental sounds.
5   Genie did not learn language during the critical period, and when she did begin using language, she appeared to have a right-hemisphere specializa- tion.

16 First language acquisition

1   Caretaker speech has frequent questions, exaggerated intonation, simple sentence structures, a lot of repetition, and simple vocabulary.
2   By the age of two, five times as many words are understood as are produced and the child will have reached the 'two-word' stage.
3   The order would be: -ing; -s (plural); – 's; -ed.
4   The more advanced form is (a) since the negative element is no longer stuck on the front of the sentence, as in (b).
5   Overextension.

17 Second language acquisition/learning

1   An L2 is mostly learned in teenage or adult years, in brief periods at school,

while the learners are busy with other things, and already have an L1 to use
for communicative purposes.
2 The ability of adults to master aspects of the written language, but still
   speaking with a foreign accent.
3 There are many features which do not match the target language and there is
   no further development.
4 It may provide clear and simple examples of the basic structure of the L2, as
   well as communicative success, for the beginning learner.
5 Grammatical, sociolinguistic and strategic competence.

18 Sign language
1 English, Spanish, Italian, ASL.
2 To have deaf students produce English speech and to lipread, in order to
   make them members of the hearing community.
3 Signed English is essentially the English language, in a shorthand version,
   employing signs for vocabulary; ASL is a separate language, with a quite different structural organization from English.
4 Shape, orientation, location and movement.
5 (i) Did it happen last night? (ii) The boy isn't/wasn't walking with
   pleasure/enjoyment.

19 Language history and change
1 (a) epenthesis (b) prothesis (c) metathesis
2 Romanian and French; Czech and Russian; Dutch and German; Gaelic and
   Welsh.
3 Cognates are two words in different languages which are similar in form and
   meaning.
4 Proto-forms: cosa – capo – capra.
5 'Calf' and 'deer' are from Old English; 'veal' and 'venison' are from Old
   French.

20 Language varieties
1 The term 'accent' is used only to describe pronunciation, whereas 'dialect'
   covers grammar, vocabulary and pronunciation.
2 Non-mobile, older, rural, male, speakers.
3 It represents the limit of an area in which a particular linguistic feature is
   used.
4 Selection, codification, elaboration, implementation and acceptance.
5 A Creole has native speakers, a Pidgin has none.

21 Language, society and culture
1 A speech community is a group of people who share a set of norms, rules and
   expectations regarding the use of language.

2 (a) double-negative construction (b) absence of copula.
3 The personal dialect of an individual speaker.
4 Diglossia describes a situation in which two distinct varieties of a language, a 'high' and a 'low', are used, each with separate social functions.
5 Briefly, that your language determines the way you think.

References

Abercrombie, D. (1967) *Elements of General Phonetics* Edinburgh University Press

Adams, V. (1973) *An Introduction to Modern English Word-Formation* Longman

Ainsworth, W. (1988) *Speech Recognition by Machine* Peter Peregrinus

Aitchison, J. (1989) *The Articulate Mammal* Routledge

Aitchison, J. (1991) *Language Change: Progress or Decay?* (2nd edition) Cambridge University Press

Aitchison, J. (1994) *Words in the Mind* (2nd edition) Blackwell

Akmajian, A., Demers, R. A., Farmer, A. K. & Harnish, R. M. (1990) *Linguistics: An Introduction to Language and Communication* (3rd edition) MIT Press

Akmajian, A. & Heny, F. (1975) *An Introduction to the Principles of Transformational Syntax* MIT Press

Alexander, L.G. (1988) *Longman English Grammar* Longman

Algeo, A. (ed.) (1991) *Fifty Years among the New Words: A Dictionary of Neologisms* Cambridge University Press

Allan, K. (1986) *Linguistic Meaning* (2 Volumes) Routledge

Allan, K. & Burridge, K. (1991) *Euphemism & Dysphemism* Oxford University Press

Allen, H. B. (1973–6) *The Linguistic Atlas of the Upper Midwest* (3 Volumes) University of Minnesota Press

Allen, J. (1987) *Natural Language Understanding* Benjamin Cummings

Allen, J., Hunnicutt, M. & Klatt, D. (1987) *From Text to Speech: The MITalk System* Cambridge University Press.

Allen, J. P. B. & van Buren, P. (1971) *Chomsky. Selected Readings* Oxford University Press

Allott, R. (1989) *The Motor Theory of Language Origin* The Book Guild

Allport, D. A. & Funnel, E. (1981) Components of the mental lexicon. In *The Psychological Mechanisms of Language* The Royal Society and the British Academy

Andersen, R. W. (1983) *Pidginization and Creolization as Language Acquisition* Newbury House

Anderson, A. H., Brown, G., Shillcock, R., & Yule, G. (1984) *Teaching Talk: Strategies for Production and Assessment* Cambridge University Press

Anderson, R. C., Reynolds. R. E., Schallert, D. L. & Goetz, E.T. (1977) Frameworks for comprehending stories. *American Educational Research Journal* 14: 367–81

Anderson, S. R. (1985) *Phonology in the Twentieth Century* University of Chicago Press

Anderson, T. (1994) Quoted in *Beavis and Butt-head's Greatest Hits* Marvel Comics

Andrews, A. (1985) The major functions of the noun phrase. In Shopen (ed.)

Anttila, R. (1989) *Historical and Comparative Linguistics* (2nd edition) John Benjamins

Appelt, D. (1992) *Planning English Sentences* Cambridge University Press

Arbib, M., Caplan, D. & Marshall, J. (eds.) (1982) *Neural Models of Language Processes* Academic Press

Arlotto, A. (1972) *Introduction to Historical Linguistics* Houghton Mifflin

Armstrong, D. F., Stokoe, W. C. & Wilcox, S. E. (1995) *Gesture and the Nature of Language* Cambridge University Press

Aronoff, M. (1976) *Word Formation in Generative Grammar* MIT Press

Atkinson, M. & Heritage, J. (eds.) (1984) *Structures of Social Action* Cambridge University Press

Atkinson, M., Kilby, D. & Roca, I. (1988) *Foundations of General Linguistics* (2nd edition) Allen & Unwin

Austin, J. L. (1962) *How to do Things with Words* Clarendon Press

Avery, P. & Ehrlich, S. (1992) *Teaching American English Pronunciation* Oxford University Press

Bailey, R. W. (1991) *Images of English: A Cultural History of the Language* Cambridge University Press

Baker, C. & Cokely, D. (1980) *American Sign Language* T. J. Publishers

Balaz, J. P. (1988) Da history of pigeon. Quoted in Romaine (1988)

Baldwin, J. & French, P. (1990) *Forensic Phonetics* Pinter

Barber, C. (1993) *The English Language. A Historical Introduction* Cambridge University Press

Barbour, S. & Stevenson, P. (1993) *Variation in German* Cambridge University Press

Barnhart, R. K. (ed.) (1988) *The Barnhart Dictionary of Etymology* H.W. Wilson

Barnhart, R. K., Steinmetz, S. & Barnhart, C. L. (eds.) (1990) *Third Barnhart Dictionary of New English* H. W. Wilson

Baron, D. (1986) *Grammar and Gender* Yale University Press

Baron, D. (1990) *The English-Only Question: An Official Language for Americans?* Yale University Press

Barreca, R. (1991) *They Used to Call Me Snow White ... But I Drifted* Viking Press

Barrett, M.D. (ed.) (1985) *Children's Single-Word Speech* John Wiley

Bartlett, F.C. (1932) *Remembering* Cambridge University Press

Barton, D. (1994) *Literacy: An Introduction to the Ecology of Written Language* Blackwell

Bates, E., Bretherton, I. & Snyder, L. (1988) *From First Words to Grammar* Cambridge University Press

Bauer, L. (1983) *English Word-Formation* Cambridge University Press

Bauer, L. (1988) *Introducing Linguistic Morphology* Edinburgh University Press

Baugh, A. C. & Cable, T. (1993) *A History of the English Language* (4th edition) Routledge

Baugh, J. (1983) *Black Street Speech* University of Texas Press

Baugh, J. (1988) Language and race. In Newmeyer (ed.)

Beebe, L., Takahashi, T. & Uliss-Weltz, R. (1990) Pragmatic transfer in ESL refusals. In Scarcella *et al.* (eds.)

Bell, A. G. (1883) *Memoir upon the Formation of a Deaf Variety of the Human Race* (reprinted 1969) Alexander Graham Bell Association

Bellugi. U. (1970) Learning the language. *Psychology Today* 4: 32–5

Bever, T. G. & Rosenbaum, P. S. (1971) Some lexical structures and their empirical validity. In Steinberg, D. & Jakobovits, L.A. (eds.) *Semantics* Cambridge University Press

Biber, D. (1991) *Variation Across Speech and Writing* Cambridge University Press

Biber, D. & Finegan, E. (eds.) (1994) *Sociolinguistic Perspectives on Register* Oxford University Press

Bickerton, D. (1975) *Dynamics of a Creole System* Cambridge University Press

Bickerton, D. (1981) *The Roots of Language* Karoma

Bickerton, D. (1990) *Language and Species* University of Chicago Press

Bickerton, D. (1991) Creole languages. In Wang (ed.)

Blair, W. & McDavid, R. (1983) *The Mirth of a Nation: America's Great Dialect Humor* University of Minnesota Press

Blake, N. F. (ed.) (1992) *The Cambridge History of the English Language Volume 2 (1066–1476)* Cambridge University Press

Blakemore, D. (1992) *Understanding Utterances* Blackwell

Bloom, L. (1991) *Language Development from Two to Three* Cambridge University Press

Bloom, L. (1993) *The Transition from Infancy to Language* Cambridge University Press

Bloomfield, L. (1933) *Language* Holt, Rinehart & Winston

Blumstein, S.E. (1988) Neurolinguistics: an overview of language–brain relations. In Newmeyer (ed.)

Blyth, C., Recktenwald, S. & Wang, J. (1990) I'm like, "Say what?!": a new quotative in American oral narrative *American Speech* 65: 215–27

Boas, F. (1911) *Handbook of American Indian Languages* Smithsonian Institution

Bobrow, D. G., Kaplan, R. M., Kay, M., Norman, D. A., Thompson, H. & Winograd, T. (1977) GUS, a frame-driven dialog system. *Artificial Intelligence* 8:155–73

Boden, M. A. (1987) *Artificial Intelligence and Natural Man* MIT Press

Boden, M.A. (1988) *Computer Models of Mind* Cambridge University Press

Bolinger D. (1975) *Aspects of Language* Harcourt, Brace, Jovanovich

Bolinger, D. (1980) *Language: The Loaded Weapon* Longman

Bolton, W. F. (1982) *A Living Language* Random House

Borden, G. J., Harris, K. S. & Raphael, L. J. (1994) *Speech Science Primer* (3rd edition) Williams & Wilkins

Bornstein, H., Saulnier, K. L. & Hamilton, L. B. (eds.) (1983) *The Comprehensive Signed English Dictionary* Kendall Green

Borsley, R. D. (1991) *Syntactic Theory* Edward Arnold

Bouton, C. (1991) *Neurolinguistics* Plenum Press

Bradac, J. J., Mulac, A. & Thompson, S. (1995) Men's and women's use of intensifiers and hedges in problem-solving interaction: molar and molecular analyses. *Research on Language and Social Interaction* 28: 93–116

Braine, M. D. S. (1971) The acquisition of language in infant and child. In Reed, C. E. (ed.) *The Learning of Language* Appleton-Century-Crofts

Bridge, D. & Harlow, S. (1996) *An Introduction to Computational Linguistics* Blackwell

Brown, E. K. & Miller, J. E. (1991) *Syntax: A Linguistic Introduction to Sentence Structure* (2nd edition) Harper Collins

Brown, G. (1990) *Listening to Spoken English* (2nd edition) Longman

Brown, G. & Yule, G. (1983a) *Discourse Analysis* Cambridge University Press

Brown, G. & Yule, G. (1983b) *Teaching the Spoken Language* Cambridge University Press

Brown, P. & Levinson, S. (1987) *Politeness* Cambridge University Press

Brown, R. (1973) *A First Language: The Early Stages* Harvard University Press

Brown, R. & McNeill, D. (1966) The 'tip of the tongue' phenomenon. *Journal of Verbal Learning and Verbal Behavior* 5: 325–37

Bryden, M. (1982) *Laterality: Functional Assymetry in the Intact Brain* Academic Press

Bryson, B. (1990) *The Mother Tongue* William Morrow

Bryson, B. (1994) *Made in America* William Morrow

Buckingham, H. W. (1982) Neuropsychological models of language. In Lass *et al.*

Buckingham, H. W. (1992) The mechanisms of phonemic paraphasia. *Clinical Linguistics and Phonetics* 6: 41–63

Budge, W. (1913) *The Book of the Dead* (2 Volumes) The Medici Society

Budge, W. (1983) *Egyptian Language* Dover Publications

Burchfield, R. (1985) *The English Language* Oxford University Press

Burgess, A. (1992) *A Mouthful of Air* William Morrow

Burton-Roberts, N. (1986) *Analysing Sentences* Longman

Butler, C. (1985) *Computers in Linguistics* Blackwell

Bybee, J. (1985) *Morphology* John Benjamins

Bynon, T. (1977) *Historical Linguistics* Cambridge University Press

Calvert, D. M. (1992) *Descriptive Phonetics* (2nd edition) Thieme

Cameron, D. (1990) *The Feminist Critique of Language* Routledge

Cameron, D. (1992) *Feminism and Linguistic Theory* (2nd edition) St. Martin's Press

Cameron, D. (1995) *Verbal Hygiene* Routledge

Campbell, J. (1982) *Grammatical Man* Simon & Schuster

Campbell, R. & Wales, R. (1970) The study of language acquisition. In Lyons (ed.)

Canale, M. & Swain, M. 1980. Theoretical bases of communicative approaches to second language teaching and testing. *Applied Linguistics* 1: 1–47.

Cannon, G. H. (1990) *The Life and Times of Oriental Jones* Cambridge University Press

Caplan, D. (1987) *Neurolinguistics and Linguistic Aphasiology* Cambridge University Press

Caramazza, A. & Berndt, R. S. (1982) A psycholinguistic assessment of adult aphasia. In S. Rosenberg (ed.) *Handbook of Applied Psycholinguistics* Lawrence Erlbaum

Carr, P. (1993) *Phonology* MacMillan

Carroll, J. B. (ed.) (1956) *Language, Thought and Reality; Selected Writings of Benjamin Lee Whorf* MIT Press

Carver, C. M. (1991) *A History of English in Its Own Words* HarperCollins

Catford, J. C. (1988) *A Practical Introduction to Phonetics* Clarendon Press

Cazden, C. (1972) *Child Language and Education* Holt

Cazden, C. (1988) *Classroom Discourse* Heineman

Celce-Murcia, M., Brinton, D. & Goodwin, J. (1996) *Teaching Pronunciation* Cambridge University Press

Celce-Murcia, M. & Larsen-Freeman, D. (1983) *The Grammar Book* Newbury House

Chafe, W. (1994) *Discourse, Consciousness and Time* University of Chicago Press

Chambers, J. K. (1994) *Sociolinguistic Theory* Blackwell

Chambers, J. K. & Trudgill, P. (1980) *Dialectology* Cambridge University Press

Chaudron, C. 1988. *Second Language Classrooms* Cambridge University Press.

Cheney, D. L. & Seyfarth, R. M. (1990) *How Monkeys See the World* University of Chicago Press

Cheney, D. L. & Seyfarth, R. M. (1991) Truth and deception in animal communication. In Ristau, C. A. (ed.) *Cognitive Ethology. The Minds of Other Animals* Lawrence Erlbaum

Chierchia, G. & McConnel-Ginet, S. (1990) *Meaning and Grammar* MIT Press

Chomsky, N. (1957) *Syntactic Structures* Mouton

Chomsky, N. (1965) *Aspects of the Theory of Syntax* MIT Press

Chomsky, N. (1972) *Language and Mind* Harcourt, Brace, Jovanovich

Chomsky, N. (1983) An interview (by John Gliedman) *Omni* 6:112–18

Chomsky, N. (1988) *Language and Problems of Knowledge: The Managua Lectures* MIT Press

Chomsky, N. & Halle. M. (1991) *The Sound Pattern of English* Harper & Row

Christian, D. (1988) Language planning. In Newmeyer (ed.)

Claiborne, R. (1974) *The Birth of Writing* Time-Life Books

Clark, E. V. (1982) The young word-maker. In Wanner & Gleitman (eds.)

Clark, E. V. (1993) *The Lexicon in Acquisition* Cambridge University Press

Clark, E. V. & Clark, H. H. (1979) When nouns surface as verbs. *Language* 55: 767–811

Clark, J. & Yallop, C. (1995) *An Introduction to Phonetics and Phonology* (2nd edition) Blackwell

Clyne, M. (1994) *Inter-cultural Communication at Work* Cambridge University Press

Coates, J. (1993) *Women, Men and Language* (2nd edition) Longman

Coates, J. & Cameron, D. (1989) *Women in their Speech Communities* Longman

Codrescu, A. (1989) *Raised by Puppets* Addison-Wesley

Collins, H. M. (1990) *Artificial Experts* MIT Press

Comrie, B. (1989) *Language Universals and Linguistic Typology* (2nd edition) University of Chicago Press

Condillac, E. (1746/1947) *Essai sur l'origine des connoissances humaines* Presses Universitaires de France

Cook, B. F. (1987) *Greek Inscriptions* University of California Press

Cook, G. (1989) *Discourse* Oxford University Press

Cook, V. J. (1988) *Chomsky's Universal Grammar* Blackwell

Cook, V. J. (1993) *Linguistics and Second Language Acquisition* St. Martin's Press

Cook, W. (1989) *Case Grammar Theory* Georgetown University Press

Cooper, R. L. (1990) *Language Planning and Social Change* Cambridge University Press

Corballis, M. C. (1991) *The Lopsided Ape* Oxford University Press

Corbett, G. G. (1991) *Gender* Cambridge University Press

Corder, S. P. (1981) *Error Analysis and Interlanguage* Oxford University Press

Coulmas, F. (1989) *The Writing Systems of the World* Blackwell

Coulter, G. R. (ed.) (1993) *Current Issues in ASL Phonology* Academic Press

Coulthard, M. (1985) *An Introduction to Discourse Analysis* Longman

Coupland, D. (1991) *Generation X: Tales for an Accelerated Culture* St. Martin's Press

Coupland, N. (ed.) (1990) *English in Wales* Multilingual Matters

Coupland, N., Coupland, J. & Giles, H. (1991) *Language, Society and the Elderly* Blackwell

Cowan, W. & Rakusan, J. (1985) *Source Book for Linguistics* John Benjamins

Crawford, J. (1992) *Hold Your Tongue – Bilingualism and the Politics of "English Only"* Addison-Wesley

Crawford, M. (1995) *Talking Difference* Sage Publications

Crowley, T. (ed.) (1991) *Proper English? Readings in Language, History and Cultural Identity* Routledge

Cruse, D. (1986) *Lexical Semantics* Cambridge University Press

Crystal, D. (1987) *The Cambridge Encyclopedia of Language* Cambridge University Press

Crystal, D. (1991) *A Dictionary of Linguistics and Phonetics* (3rd edition) Blackwell

Crystal, D. (ed.) (1995) *The Cambridge Encyclopedia of the English Language* Cambridge University Press

Curtiss, S. (1977) *Genie. A Psycholinguistic Study of a Modern-day Wild Child* Academic Press

Cutler, A. (ed.) (1982) *Slips of the Tongue and Language Production* Mouton

Dalton, C. & Seidlhofer, B. (1994) *Pronunciation* Oxford University Press

Daniels, P.T. & Bright, W. (eds.) (1995) *The World's Writing Systems* Oxford University Press

Davies, C. (1990) *Ethnic Humor Around the World* Indiana University Press

Davies, W. V. (1987) *Egyptian Hieroglyphics* University of California Press

Davis, L. M. (1983) *English Dialectology: An Introduction* University of Alabama Press

Davis, S. (ed.) (1991) *Pragmatics. A Reader* Oxford University Press

de Beaugrande, R. & Dressler, W. U. (1981) *Introduction to Text Linguistics* Longman

DeFrancis, J. (1989) *Visible Speech* University of Hawaii Press

de Grollier, E. (1983) *Glossogenetics. The Origin and Evolution of Language* Harwood Academic

Demers, R. A. (1988) Linguistics and animal communication. In Newmeyer (ed.)

Denes, P. B. & Pinson, E. N. (1993) *The Speech Chain* (2nd edition) W. H. Freeman

Deninger, P. L. & Schmid, C. W. (1976) Thermal stability of human DNA and chimpanzee DNA heteroduplexes *Science* 194: 846–8

Desmond, C. J. (ed.) (1991) *Cultural Beginnings: Approaches to Understanding Early Hominid Life-Ways in the African Sahara* Habelt

Deuchar, M. (1984) *British Sign Language* Routledge

Diamond, A. S. (1965) *The History and the Origin of Language* Citadel Press

Dingwall, W. D. (1988) The evolution of human communicative behavior. In Newmeyer (ed.)

Diringer, D. (1968) *The Alphabet* (2 Volumes) (3rd edition) Hutchinson

Di Sciullo, A-M. & Williams, E. (1987) *On the Definition of Word* MIT Press

Downes, W. (1984) *Language and Society* Fontana Paperbacks

Downing, A. & Locke, P. (1992) *A University Course in English Grammar* Prentice–Hall

Downing, B. & Fuller, J. (1984) Cultural contact and the expansion of the Hmong lexicon. Unpublished manuscript, Linguistics Department, University of Minnesota

Downing, P., Lima, S. & Noonan, M. (eds.) (1992) *The Linguistics of Literacy* John Benjamins

Drew, P. & Heritage, J. (eds.) (1992) *Talk at Work* Cambridge University Press

Dreyfus, H. L. & Dreyfus, S. E. (1986) *Mind Over Machine* The Free Press

Edwards, H. T. (1992) *Applied Phonetics* Singular Publishing

Edwards, M. L. & Shriberg, L. D. (1983) *Phonology* College Hill Press

Efron, R. (1990) *The Decline and Fall of Hemispheric Specialization* Lawrence Erlbaum

Elliot, A. J. (1981) *Child Language* Cambridge University Press

Ellis, R. (1986) *Understanding Second Language Acquisition* Oxford University Press

Espy, W. R. (1978) *O Thou Improper, Thou Uncommon Noun* Potter

Evans, W. E. & Bastain. J. (1969) Marine mammal communication: social and ecological factors. In H. T. Anderson (ed.) *The Biology of Marine Mammals* Academic Press

Fano, G. (1992) *The Origins and Nature of Language* Indiana University Press

Fant, L. (1977) *Sign Language* Joyce Media

Fasold, R. (1990) *The Sociolinguistics of Language* Blackwell

Fauconnier, G. (1994) *Mental Spaces* Cambridge University Press

Fay, D. & Cutler, A. (1977) Malapropisms and the structure of the mental lexicon. *Linguistic Inquiry* 8: 505–20

Ferguson, C. A. (1959) Diglossia. *Word* 15: 325–40

Ferguson, C. A. & Heath, S. B. (eds.) (1981) *Language in the USA* Cambridge University Press

Fillmore, C. (1975) *Santa Cruz Lectures on Deixis* Indiana University Linguistics Club

Finegan, E. & Besnier, N. (1989) *Language. Its Structure and Use* Harcourt Brace Jovanovich

Finnie, W. B. (1972) *The Stages of English* Houghton Mifflin

Fischer, S. D. & Siple, P. (eds.) (1990) *Theoretical Issues in Sign Language Research* (2 Volumes) University of Chicago Press

Fishman, J. A. (1971) *Sociolinguistics: A Brief Introduction* Newbury House

Fishman, J. (1989) *Language and Ethnicity in Minority Sociolinguistic Perspective* Multilingual Matters

Fishman, J. A. (ed.) (1993) *The Earliest Stage of Language Planning* Mouton de Gruyter

Fisiak, J. (ed.) (1990) *Historical Linguistics and Philology* Mouton de Gruyter

Flanagan, J. L. (1972) The synthesis of speech. *Scientific American* 226: 48–58

Fletcher, P. (1985) *A Child's Learning of English* Blackwell

Fletcher, P. & Garman, M. (eds.) (1986) *Language Acquisition* Cambridge University Press

Fouts, R. S., Fouts, D. H. & Van Cantford, T. E. (1989) The infant Loulis learns signs from cross-fostered chimpanzees. In Gardner *et al.* (eds.)

Fox, B. (1993) *Discourse Structure and Anaphora* Cambridge University Press

Francis, W. N. (1983) *Dialectology* Longman

Frank, M. (1993) *Modern English* (2nd edition) Regents

Franklin, M. & Barten, S. (eds.) *Child Language: A Reader* Oxford University Press

Freidin, R. (1992) *Foundations of Generative Syntax* MIT Press

Friedman, L. A. (ed.) (1977) *On the Other Hand* Academic Press

Fromkin, V. A. (ed.) (1973) *Speech Errors as Linguistic Evidence* Mouton

Fromkin, V. A. (ed.) (1985) *Phonetic Linguistics* Academic Press

Fromkin, V. A. (1988) Grammatical aspects of speech errors. In Newmeyer (ed.)

Fromkin, V. & Rodman. R. (1993) *An Introduction to Language* (5th edition) Harcourt Brace Jovanovich

Fry, D. B. (1979) *The Physics of Speech* Cambridge University Press

Gallaway, C. & Richards, B. (eds.) (1994) *Input and Interaction in Language Acquisition* Cambridge University Press

Gamkrelidze, T. V. & Ivanov, V. V. (eds.) (1995) *Indo-European and the Indo-Europeans* Mouton de Gruyter

Gardner, B. T. (1981) Project Nim: who taught whom? *Contemporary Psychology* 26: 425–6

Gardner, H. (1986) *The Mind's New Science* Basic Books

Gardner, R. A. & Gardner, B. T. (1969) Teaching sign language to a chimpanzee *Science* 165: 664–72

Gardner, R. A. & Gardner, B. T. (1978) Comparative psychology and language acquisition *Annals of the New York Academy of Sciences* 309: 37–76

Gardner, R. A., Gardner, B. T. & Van Cantfort, T. E. (eds.) (1989) *Teaching Sign Language to Chimpanzees* State University of New York Press

Garfield, J. & Kitely, M. (eds.) (1991) *Meaning and Truth: Essential Readings in Modern Semantics* Paragon House

Gass, S. & Selinker, L. (1994) *Second Language Acquisition* Lawrence Erlbaum.

Gelb, I. J. (1963) *A Study of Writing* University of Chicago Press

Geschwind, N. (1972) Language and the brain. *Scientific American* 226: 76–83

Geschwind, N. (1979) Specializations of the human brain. In Wang (ed.)

Gibbons, J. (ed.) (1994) *Language and the Law* Longman

Gibson, K. R. & Ingold, T. (eds.) (1993) *Tools, Language and Cognition in Human Evolution* Cambridge University Press

Giegerich, H. J. (1992) *English Phonology* Cambridge University Press

Giglioli, P. P. (ed.) (1972) *Language and Social Context* Penguin Books

Gimson, A. C. (1994) *An Introduction to the Pronunciation of English* (5th edition, revised by A. Cruttenden) Edward Arnold

Givon, T. (1989) *Mind, Code and Context: Essays in Pragmatics* Erlbaum

Givon, T. (1990) *Syntax* (2 Volumes) John Benjamins

Givon, T. (1993) *English Grammar* (2 Volumes) John Benjamins

Gleason, H. A. (1955) *Workbook in Descriptive Linguistics* Holt, Rinehart & Winston

Gleason, H. A. (1961) *An Introduction to Descriptive Linguistics* Holt, Rinehart & Winston

Gleason, J.B. (ed.) (1989) *The Development of Language* Merrill

Glowka, A. W. & Lance, D. M. (eds.) (1993) *Language Variation in North American English* Modern Language Association

Goldsmith, J. (ed.) (1994) *The Handbook of Phonology* Blackwell

Goodall, J. (1986) *The Chimpanzees of Gombe* Harvard University Press

Goodglass, G. & Kaplan, E. (1983) *The Assessment of Aphasia and Related Disorders* Lea and Febiger

Goodluck, H. (1991) *Language Acquisition* Blackwell

Goodwin, C. (1981) *Conversational Organization* Academic Press

Goodwin, M. H. (1990) *He-said-she-said. Talk as Social Organization among Black Children* Indiana University Press

Goody, J. (1986) *The Logic of Writing and the Organization of Society* Cambridge University Press

Goody, J. (1987) *The Interface between the Written and the Oral* Cambridge University Press

Gordon, P. (1985) Level-ordering in lexical development *Cognition* 21: 73–93

Gorlach, M. (1991) *An Introduction to Early Modern English* Cambridge University Press

Gould, J. L. & Marler, P. (1991) Learning by instinct. In Wang (ed.)

Graddol, D. & Swann, J. (1989) *Gender Voices* Blackwell

Green, G. (1989) *Pragmatics and Natural Language Understanding* Erlbaum

Green, J. (1991) *Neologisms. New Words Since 1960* Bloomsbury

Greenberg, J. H. (1966) *Language Universals* Mouton

Gregory, M. & Carroll, S. (1978) *Language and Situation: Language Varieties and their Social Contexts* Routledge & Kegan Paul

Gregory, S. & Taylor, J. (eds.) (1991) *Being Deaf* Pinter

Grice, H. P. (1975) Logic and conversation. In Cole, P. & Morgan, J.P. (eds.) *Syntax and Semantics 3: Speech Acts* Academic Press

Grice, H. P. (1989) *Studies in the Way of Words* Harvard University Press

Griffin, D. (1984) *Animal Thinking* Harvard University Press

Grishman, R. (1986) *Computational Linguistics* Cambridge University Press

Groce, N. E. (1985) *Everyone Here Spoke Sign Language* Harvard University Press

Guiora, A. Z., Beit-Hallahmi, B., Brannon, R. C. L., Dull, C. Y. & Scovel, T. (1972) The effects of experimentally induced change in ego states on pronunciation ability in a second language: an exploratory study. *Comprehensive Psychiatry* 13: 5–23

Gumperz, J. J. (1982) *Discourse Strategies* Cambridge University Press

Guy, G. R. (1988) Language and social class. In Newmeyer (ed.)

Haegeman, L. (1991) *Introduction to Government and Binding Theory* Blackwell

Hall, R. A. (1959) Pidgin languages. *Scientific American* 200: 124–34

Halle, M. (1990) Phonology. In Osherson & Lasnik (eds.)

Halle, M. & Clements, G. N. (1983) *Problem Book in Phonology: A Workbook for Introductory Courses* MIT Press

Halliday, M. A. K. (1989) *Spoken and Written Language* Oxford University Press

Halliday, M. A. K. & Hasan, R. (1976) *Cohesion in English* Longman

Hamilton, H. E. (1994) *Conversations with an Alzheimer's Patient* Cambridge University Press

Hancock, I. (ed.) (1985) *Diversity and Development in English-Related Creoles* Karoma

Hardcastle, W. J. & Laver, J. (1995) *Handbook of Phonetic Sciences* Blackwell

Harnad, S. R., Steklis, H. D., & Lancaster, J. (eds.) (1976) Origins and Evolution of Language and Speech. *Annals of the New York Academy of Sciences* 280

Harris, J. (1994) *English Sound Structure* Blackwell

Harris, R. (1986) *The Origin of Writing* Open Court

Hatch, E. (1992) *Discourse and Language Education* Cambridge University Press

Hawkins, J. & Gell-Mann, M. (eds.) (1992) *The Evolution of Human Languages* Addison-Wesley

Hawkins, P. (1984) *Introducing Phonology* Routledge

Hayes, C. (1951) *The Ape in our House* Harper

Healey, J. F. (1990) *The Early Alphabet* University of California Press

Heath, S. B. (1983) *Ways With Words* Cambridge University Press

Hendrickson, R. (1986) *American Talk: The Words and Ways of American Dialects* Viking Press

Hendrix, G. G. & Sacerdoti, E. D. (1981) Natural-language processing. *Byte* 6: 30–52

Hewes, G. W. (1973) Primate communication and the gestural origin of language *Current Anthropology* 14: 5–24

Hinton, L., Nichols, J. & Ohala, J. (eds.) (1994) *Sound Symbolism* Cambridge University Press

Hock, H. H. (1991) *Principles of Historical Linguistics* (2nd edition) Mouton de Gruyter

Hockett, C. (1954) Two models of grammatical description. *Word* 10: 21–31

Hockett, C. (1958) *A Course in Modern Linguistics* Macmillan

Hockett, C. (1960) The origin of speech *Scientific American* 203: 89–96

Hockett, C. (1963) The problem of universals in language. In J. H. Greenberg (ed.) *Universals of Language* MIT Press

Hoffman, C. (1991) *An Introduction to Bilingualism* Longman

Hogg, R. & McCully, C. (1987) *Metrical Phonology* Cambridge University Press

Hogg, R. M. (ed.) (1991) *The Cambridge History of the English Language Volume 1 (The beginnings to 1066)* Cambridge University Press

Hollien, H. (1990) *The Acoustics of Crime: The New Science of Forensic Phonetics* Plenum Press

Holm, J. (1989) *Pidgins and Creoles* (2 Volumes) Cambridge University Press

Holmes, J. (1992) *An Introduction to Sociolinguistics* Longman

Holmes, J. (1995) *Women, Men and Politeness* Longman

Honey, J. (1989) *Does Accent Matter?* Faber & Faber

Hooker, J. T. (ed.) (1990) *Ancient Writing from Cuneiform to the Alphabet* University of California Press

Houston, S. D. (1989) *Maya Glyphs* University of California Press

Howard, D. & Franklin, S. (1988) *Missing the Meaning?* MIT Press

Howard, P. (1990) *A Word in Time* Sinclair-Stevenson

Howatt, A. P. R. (1984) *A History of English Language Teaching* Oxford University Press

Huddleston, R. (1976) *An Introduction to English Transformational Syntax* Longman

Huddleston, R. (1984) *Introduction to the Grammar of English* Cambridge University Press

Huddleston, R. (1988) *English Grammar. An Outline* Cambridge University Press

Hudson, A. (1992) Diglossia: A bibliographic review. *Language in Society* 21: 611–74

Hudson, R. A. (1990) *Sociolinguistics* Cambridge University Press

Hughes, A. & Trudgill P. (1979) *English Accents and Dialects* Edward Arnold

Hughes, G. (1988) *Words in Time* Blackwell

Hughes, J. P. (1962) *The Science of Language* Random House

Hurford, J. (1994) *Grammar. A Student's Guide* Cambridge University Press

Hurford, J. R. & Heasley, B. (1983) *Semantics. A Coursebook* Cambridge University Press

Hyman, L. M. (1975) *Phonology: Theory and Analysis* Holt, Rinehart & Winston

Hymes, D. (1964) Toward ethnographies of communicative events. In Giglioli (ed.) (1972)

Hymes, D. (ed.) (1971) *Pidginisation and Creolisation of Languages* Cambridge University Press

Iaccino, J. (1993) *Left Brain – Right Brain Differences* Erlbaum

Ingram, D. (1989) *First Language Acquisition* Cambridge University Press

Jackendoff, R. (1983) *Semantics and Cognition* MIT Press

Jackendoff, R. (1994) *Patterns in the Mind* Basic Books

Jackson, H. (1985) *Discovering Grammar* Pergamon

Jacobs, R. (1995) *English Syntax* Oxford University Press

Jarvella, R. & W. Klein (eds.) (1982) *Speech, Place and Action: Studies in Deixis and Related Topics* John Wiley

Jay, T. (1992) *Cursing in America* John Benjamins

Jeffery, L. H. (1961) *The Local Scripts of Archaic Greece* Clarendon Press

Jensen, H. (1969) *Sign, Symbol and Script* Allen & Unwin

Jensen, J. T. (1990) *Morphology* John Benjamins

Jensen, J. T. (1993) *English Phonology* John Benjamins

Jespersen, O. (1921) *Language: Its Nature, Development and Origin* Macmillan

Jespersen, O. (1924) *The Philosophy of Grammar* Allen & Unwin

Jolly, A. (1985) A new science that sees animals as conscious beings *Smithsonian* 15 (12): 66–75

Jones, C. (1989) *A History of English Phonology* Longman

Jones, C. (ed.) (1993) *Historical Linguistics* Longman

Kachru, B. (1986) *The Alchemy of English* Pergamon

Kasper, G. & Blum-Kulka, S. (eds.) (1993) *Interlanguage Pragmatics* Oxford University Press.

Kasper, G. & Kellerman, E. (eds.) (1996) *Advances in Communication Strategy Research* Longman

Katamba, F. (1989) *An Introduction to Phonology* Longman

Katamba, F. (1993) *Morphology* St. Martin's Press

Kaye, J. (1988) *Phonology: A Cognitive View* Erlbaum

Kean, M-L. (ed.) (1985) *Agrammatism* Academic Press

Kellerman, E., Ammerlan, T., Bongaerts, T. & Poulisse, N. (1990) System and hierarchy in L2 compensatory strategies. In Scarcella *et al.* (eds.)

Kellerman, E. & Sharwood-Smith, M. (eds.) (1986) *Cross-linguistic Influence in Second Language Acquisition* Pergamon Press

Kellogg, W. N. & Kellogg, L. A. (1933) *The Ape and the Child* McGraw-Hill

Kempson, R. (1977) *Semantic Theory* Cambridge University Press

Kendon, A. (1988) *Sign Languages of Aboriginal Australia* Cambridge University Press

Kennedy, C. (ed.) (1984) *Language Planning and Language Education* George Allen & Unwin

Kent, H. W. (1986) *Treasury of Hawaiian Words in One Hundred and One Categories* University of Hawai'i Press

Kimura, D. (1973) The asymmetry of the human brain *Scientific American* 228:70–8

King, M. (ed.) (1983) *Parsing Natural Language* Academic Press

King, M-C. & Wilson, A. C. (1975) Evolution at two levels in humans and chimpanzees *Science* 188: 107–15

Klaiman, M. H. (1991) *Grammatical Voice* Cambridge University Press

Klima, E. S. & Bellugi, U. (1966) Syntactic regularities in the speech of children. In Lyons, J. & Wales, R. J. (eds.) *Psycholinguistic Papers* Edinburgh University Press

Klima, E. S. & Bellugi, U. (1979) *The Signs of Language* Harvard University Press

Krashen, S. 1985. *The Input Hypothesis* Longman

Krashen, S. & Terrell, T. (1983) *The Natural Approach* Pergamon Press

Kreidler, C. W. (1989) *The Pronunciation of English* Blackwell

Kurath, H. (1972) *Studies in Area Linguistics* Indiana University Press

Kurath, H., Hanley, M., Bloch, B. & Lowman, G. S. (1939–43) *Linguistic Atlas of New England* (3 Volumes) Brown University Press

Kyle, J. G. (ed.) (1987) *Sign and School* Multilingual Matters

Kyle, J. G. & Woll, B. (eds.) (1983) *Language in Sign* Croom Helm

Kyle, J. G. & Woll, B. (eds.) (1985) *Sign Language: The Study of Deaf People and Their Language* Cambridge University Press

Labov, W. (1972) *Sociolinguistic Patterns* University of Pennsylvania Press

Labov, W. (1991) The three dialects of English. In Eckart, P. (ed.) *New Ways of Analyzing Sound Change* Academic Press

Ladefoged, P. (1992) *A Course in Phonetics* (3rd edition) Harcourt, Brace, Jovanovich

Ladefoged, P. & Maddieson, I. (1995) *The Sounds of the World's Languages* Blackwell

Lakoff, G. (1987) *Women, Fire and Dangerous Things* University of Chicago Press

Lakoff, R. (1975) *Language and Woman's Place* Harper & Row

Lakoff, R. (1990) *Talking Power* Basic Books

Landsberg, M. E. (ed.) (1988) *The Genesis of Language* Mouton de Gruyter

Lane, H. L. (1980) A chronology of the oppression of Sign Language in France and the United States. In Lane & Grosjean (eds.)

Lane, H. L. (1984) *When the Mind Hears: A History of the Deaf* Random House

Lane, H. L. (1992) *The Mask of Benevolence: Disabling the Deaf Community* Knopf

Lane, H. L. & Grosjean, F. (eds.) (1980) *Recent Perspectives on American Sign Language* Lawrence Erlbaum

Langacker, R. W. (1973) *Language and its Structure* (2nd edition) Harcourt, Brace, Jovanovich

Larsen-Freeman, D. & Long, M. (1991) *An Introduction to Second Language Acquisition Research* Longman

Larson, G. (1989) *The PreHistory of the Far Side* Andrews and McMeel

Lasnik, H. (1990) Syntax. In Osherson & Lasnik (eds.)

Lass, N., McReynolds, L., Northern, J. & Yoder, D. (eds.) (1982) *Speech, Language and Hearing. Volume 1* W.B. Saunders

Lass, R. (1984) *Phonology* Cambridge University Press

Lass, R. (ed.) (1995) *The Cambridge History of the English Language Volume 3 (1476–1776)* Cambridge University Press

Laver, J. (ed.) (1991) Speaker characterization in speech technology. Special issue of *Speech Communication* 10 (5–6)

Laver, J. (1994) *Principles of Phonetics* Cambridge University Press

Lee, K-F. (1989) *Automatic Speech Recognition* Kluwer

Leech, G. N. (1974) *Semantics* Penguin Books

Leech, G. N. (1983) *Principles of Pragmatics* Longman

Leech, G. N. & Svartvik, J. (1994) *A Communicative Grammar of English* (2nd edition) Longman

Lehman, W. P. (1993) *Historical Linguistics* (3rd edition) Routledge

Lehrer, A. (1985) Markedness and antonymy *Journal of Linguistics* 21: 397–429

Le May, H., Lerner, S. & Taylor, M. (1988) *New New Words Dictionary* Ballantine

Lemonick, M. (1993) Not-so-stupid pet tricks *Time* (March 22nd)

Lenneberg, E. H. (1967) *Biological Foundations of Language* Wiley

Lesser, R, & Milroy, L. (1993) *Linguistics and Aphasia* Longman

Levelt, W. (1989) *Speaking* MIT press

Levi, J. (1978) *The Syntax and Semantics of Complex Nominals* Academic Press

Levine, J. (1990) PRAGMA: A flexible bi-directional dialogue system. In *Proceedings of the Eighth National Conference on Artificial Intelligence* MIT Press

Levinson, S. (1983) *Pragmatics* Cambridge University Press

Liddell, S. K. (1980) *American Sign Language Syntax* Mouton

Lieberman, P. (1975) *On the Origins of Language* Macmillan

Lieberman, P. (1984) *The Biology and Evolution of Language* Harvard University Press

Lieberman, P. (1991) *Uniquely Human* Harvard University Press

Lieberman, P. & Blumstein, S. (1988) *Speech Physiology, Speech Perception and Acoustic Phonetics* Cambridge University Press

Lightbown, P. & Spada, N. (1993) *How Languages are Learned* Oxford University Press

Linden, E. (1976) *Apes, Men and Language* Penguin Books

Linden, E. (1987) *Silent Partners: The Legacy of the Ape Language Experiments* Ballantine

Lipka, L. (1990) *An Outline of English Lexicology* Max Niemeyer Verlag

Lodge, K. (1984) *Studies in the Phonology of Colloquial English* Croom Helm

Long, M. (1996) *Task Based Language Teaching* Blackwell

Love, R. & Webb, W. (1992) *Neurology for the Speech Language Pathologist* Butterworth-Heinemann

Lowe, R. J. (1994) *Phonology* Williams & Wilkins

Lucas, C. (ed.) (1989) *The Sociolinguistics of the Deaf Community* Academic Press

Lucas, C. (ed.) (1990) *Sign Language Research: Theoretical Issues* Gallaudet University Press

Lucas, C. & Valli, C. (1992) *Language Contact in the American Deaf Community* Academic Press

Lyons, J. (1968) *Introduction to Theoretical Linguistics* Cambridge University Press

Lyons, J. (ed.) (1970) *New Horizons in Linguistics* Penguin Books

Lyons, J. (1977) *Semantics* (2 Volumes) Cambridge University Press

Lyons, J. (1991) *Noam Chomsky* (3rd edition) Fontana

MacKay, D. G. (1970) Spoonerisms: the structure of errors in the serial order of speech. *Neuropsychologia* 8: 323–50

MacKay, I. R. (1987) *Phonetics: The Science of Speech Production* (2nd edition) Little, Brown

MacNeilage, P., Studdert-Kennedy, M. & Lindblom, B. (1988) Primate handedness: A foot in the door *Behavioral and Brain Sciences* 11: 737–44

MacNeilage, P., Studdert-Kennedy, M. & Lindblom, B. (1993) Hand signals: Right side, left brain and the origin of language *The Sciences* (Jan–Feb): 32–7

Maddieson, I. (1984) *Patterns of Sounds* Cambridge University Press

Madsen, W. J. (1982) *Intermediate Conversational Sign Language* Gallaudet Press

Mallory, J. P. (1989) *In Search of the Indo-Europeans* Thames and Hudson

Marchand, H. (1969) *The Categories and Types of Present-Day English Word Formation* (2nd edition) Beck

Marshack, A. (1991) The origin of language: An anthropological approach. In Wind *et al.* (eds.)

Martin, R. (1987) *The Meaning of Language* MIT Press

Martinet, A. (1964) *Elements of General Linguistics* University of Chicago Press

Matthews, P. H. (1981) *Syntax* Cambridge University Press

Matthews, P. H. (1991) *Morphology* Cambridge University Press

McArthur, T. (ed.) (1992) *The Oxford Companion to the English Language* Oxford University Press

McCarthy, M. (1991) *Discourse Analysis for Language Teachers* Cambridge University Press

McCarthy, R. & Warrington, E. (1990) *Cognitive Neuropsychology* Academic Press

McCawley, J. D. (1988) *The Syntactic Phenomena of English* (2 Volumes) University of Chicago Press

McCorduck, P. (1979) *Machines Who Think* Freeman

McLaughlin, B. (1987) *Theories of Second Language Learning* Edward Arnold

McMahon, A. M. (1994) *Understanding Language Change* Cambridge University Press

McMillan, J. B. (1980) Infixing and interposing in English *American Speech* 55: 163–83

McNeill, D. (1966) Developmental psycholinguistics. In Smith & Miller (eds.)

Mellor, D. H. (ed.) (1990) *Ways of Communicating* Cambridge University Press

Merrifield, W. R., Naish, C. M., Rensch, C. R. & Story, G. (1962) *Laboratory Manual for Morphology and Syntax* Summer Institute of Linguistics

Messer, D. J. & Turner, G.J. (eds.) (1993) *Critical Influences on Child Language Acquisition and Development* St. Martin's Press

Mey, J. L. (1993) *Pragmatics* Blackwell

Miller, D. G. (1994) *Ancient Scripts and Phonological Knowledge* John Benjamins

Miller, G. (1991) *The Science of Words* Scientific American Library

Miller, G. & Gildea, P. (1991) How children learn words. In Wang (ed.)

Milroy, J. & Milroy, L. (eds.) (1988) *Regional Variation in British English Syntax* ESRC

Milroy, L. (1987a) *Observing and Analyzing Natural Language* Blackwell

Milroy, L. (1987b) *Language and Social Networks* (2nd edition) Blackwell

Minsky, M. L. (1968) *Semantic Information Processing* MIT Press

Mish, F. C. (1986) *12,000 Words* Merriam-Webster

Mitchell, B. & Robinson, F. (1986) *A Guide to Old English* Blackwell

Morenberg, M. (1991) *Doing Grammar* Oxford University Press

Moskowitz, B. A. (1991) The acquisition of language. In Wang (ed.)

Mossman, J. (ed.) (1993) *Acronyms, Initialisms & Abbreviations Dictionary* (17th edition) Gale Research

Mugglestone, L. (1995) *Talking Proper: The Rise of Accent as Social Symbol* Clarendon Press

Mühlhäusler, P. (1986) *Pidgin and Creole Linguistics* Blackwell

Myers, L. M. & Hoffman, R. L. (1979) *The Roots of Modern English* Little, Brown

Nakanishi, A. (1990) *Writing Systems of the World* Charles E. Tuttle Company

Nash, W. (1993) *Jargon* Blackwell

Neisser, A. (1983) *The Other Side of Silence* Alfred Knopf

Nelson, K. (ed.) (1989) *Narratives from the Crib* Harvard University Press

Newmeyer, F. (ed.) (1988) *Linguistics: The Cambridge Survey* (4 Volumes) Cambridge University Press

Nolan, F. (1983) *The Phonetic Basis of Speaker Recognition* Cambridge University Press

Nunan, D. (1991) *Language Teaching Methodology* Prentice-Hall

Nunan, D. (1995) Closing the gap between learning and instruction *TESOL Quarterly* 29: 133–58

Nuyts, J. & Verschueren, J. (eds.) (1987) *A Comprehensive Bibliography of Pragmatics* John Benjamins

Ochs, E. (1988) *Culture and Language Development* Cambridge University Press

Odlin, T. 1989. *Language Transfer* Cambridge University Press

O'Grady, W., Dobrovolsky, M. & Aronoff, M. (1993) *Contemporary Linguistics* (2nd edition) St. Martin's Press

Oh, C-K. & Dineen, D. (eds.) (1979) *Syntax and Semantics Volume 11: Presupposition* Academic Press

Olson, D. R. (1994) *The World on Paper* Cambridge University Press

Olson, D. R. & Torrance, N. (eds.) (1991) *Literacy and Orality* Cambridge University Press

Osherson, D.N. & Lasnik, H. (eds.) (1990) *Language* MIT Press

Overstreet, M. (1995) Pillow Talk. Unpublished data

Paget, R. (1930) *Human Speech* Harcourt, Brace

Palmer, F. R. (1981) *Semantics* Cambridge University Press

Palmer, F. R. (1983) *Grammar* Penguin Books

Palmer, F. R. (1994) *Grammatical Roles and Relations* Cambridge University Press

Parker, S.T. & Gibson, K. R. (eds.) (1990) *Language and Intelligence in Monkeys and Apes* Cambridge University Press

Partridge, A. C. (1982) *A Companion to Old and Middle English Studies* Barnes and Noble

Partridge, D. & Wilks, Y. (eds.) (1990) *The Foundations of Artificial Intelligence* Cambridge University Press

Patterson, F. & Linden, E. (1981) *The Education of Koko* Holt, Rinehart & Winston

Paul, P. V. & Quigley, S. P. (1994) *Language and Deafness* Singular Publishing

Peccei, J.S. (1994) *Child Language* Routledge

Pedersen, H. (1972) *The Discovery of Language* Indiana University Press

Penelope, J. (1990) *Speaking Freely* Pergamon Press

Penfield, W. & Roberts, L. (1959) *Speech and Brain Mechanisms* Princeton University Press

Peters, A. M. (1983) *The Units of Language Acquisition* Cambridge University Press

Pfungst, O. (1911) *Clever Hans, the Horse of Mr. Von Osten* Holt

Philips, S., Steele, S. & Tanz, C. (eds.) (1987) *Language, Gender and Sex in Comparative Perspective* Cambridge University Press

Pica, T., Holliday, L., Lewis, N., Berducci, D. & Newman, J. (1991) Language learning through interaction: what role does gender play? *Studies in Second Language Acquisition* 11: 63–90.

Pinker, S. (1989) *Learnability and Cognition* MIT Press

Pinker, S. (1990) Language acquisition. In Osherson & Lasnik (eds.)

Pinker, S. (1994) *The Language Instinct* William Morrow

Pinker, S. & Bloom, P. (1990) Natural language and natural selection *Behavioral and Brain Sciences* 13: 707–27

Postman, L. & Keppel, G. (eds.) (1970) *Norms of Word Association* Academic Press

Powell, B. P. (1991) *Homer and the Origin of the Greek Alphabet* Cambridge University Press

Poyatos, F. (1993) *Paralanguage* John Benjamins

Prator, C. H. & Robinett, B. W. (1985) *Manual of American English Pronunciation* (4th edition) Holt, Rinehart & Winston

Premack, A. J. & Premack, D. (1991) Teaching language to an ape. In Wang (ed.)

Premack, D. (1986) *Gavagai!* MIT Press

Premack, D. & Premack, A. (1983) *The Mind of an Ape* Norton

Preston, D. (1989) *Sociolinguistics and Second Language Acquisition* Blackwell

Pride, J. B. & Holmes, J. (eds.) (1972) *Sociolinguistics* Penguin Books

Prillwitz, S. & Vollhaber, T. (eds.) (1990) *Current Trends in European Sign Language Research* Signum Verlag

Pullum, G. (1991) *The Great Eskimo Vocabulary Hoax* University of Chicago Press

Pullum, G. K. & Ladusaw, W. A. (1986) *Phonetic Symbol Guide* University of Chicago Press

Pulman, S. (1983) *Word, Meaning and Belief* Croom Helm

Quigley, S. P. & Paul, P. V. (1990) *Education and Deafness* Longman

Quirk, R. (1995) *Grammatical and Lexical Variation in English* Longman

Quirk, R., Greenbaum, S., Leech, G. & Svartvik, J. (1985) *A Comprehensive Grammar of the English Language* Longman

Radford, A. (1988) *Transformational Syntax* Cambridge University Press

Ramsaran, S. (ed.) (1990) *Studies in the Pronunciation of English* Routledge

Randall, B. (1991) *When is a Pig a Hog?* Prentice Hall

Raskin, V. (1985) *Semantic Mechanisms of Humor* Reidel

Raskin, V. (1986) On possible applications of script-based semantics. In Bjarkman, P. C. & Raskin, V. (eds.) *The Real World Linguist* Ablex

Raymond, E. (1991) *The New Hacker's Dictionary* MIT Press

Renfrew, C. (1987) *Archaeology and Language: The Puzzle of Indo-European Origins* Jonathan Cape

Richards, J. C., Platt, J. & Platt, H. (1992) *Longman Dictionary of Applied Linguistics* Longman

Richards, J.C. & Rodgers, T. (1986) *Approaches and Methods in Language Teaching* Cambridge University Press

Riemsdijk, H. van & Williams, E. (1986) *An Introduction to the Theory of Grammar* MIT Press

Rimpau, J. B., Gardner, R. A. & Gardner, B. T. (1989) Expression of person, place and instrument in ASL utterances of children and chimpanzees. In Gardner *et al.* (eds.)

Rivers, W. (1964) *The Psychologist and the Foreign-Language Teacher* University of Chicago Press

Roach, P. (1991) *English Phonetics and Phonology* (2nd edition) Cambridge University Press

Roberts, L. D. (1993) *How Reference Works* SUNY Press

Roberts, P. A. (1988) *West Indians and Their Language* Cambridge University Press

Robins, R. H. (1980) *General Linguistics* (3rd edition) Longman

Robinson, O. W. (1992) *Old English and Its Closest Relatives* Stanford University Press

Romaine, S. (1984) *The Language of Children and Adolescents* Blackwell

Romaine, S. (1988) *Pidgin and Creole Languages* Longman

Romaine, S. (1994a) *Language in Society* Oxford University Press

Romaine, S. (1994b) *Bilingualism* (2nd edition) Blackwell

Romaine, S. (1994c) Hawai'i Creole English as a literary language *Language in Society* 23: 527–54

Romaine, S. (ed.) (1995) *The Cambridge History of the English Language Volume 4 (1776–present day)* Cambridge University Press

Rosch, E. (1978) Principles of categorisation. In Rosch, E. & Lloyd, B. (eds.) *Cognition and Categorisation* Erlbaum

Ross, J. R. (1967) *Constraints on Variables in Syntax* Indiana University Linguistics Club

Rowden. C. (ed.) (1992) *Speech Processing* McGraw-Hill

Ruhlen, M. (1994) *The Origin of Language* John Wiley

Rumbaugh, D. M. (ed.) (1977) *Language Learning by a Chimpanzee: The LANA Project* Academic Press

Rutherford, W. (1987) *Second Language Grammar* Longman

Rymer, R. (1993) *Genie* Harper-Collins

Sacks, H. (1992) *Lectures on Conversation* (2 Volumes) Blackwell

Sacks, H., Schegloff, E. & Jefferson, G. (1974) A simplest systematics for the organization of turn-taking in conversation *Language* 50: 696–735

Salus, P. H. (ed.) (1969) *On Language: Plato to von Humboldt* Holt, Rinehart & Winston

Sampson, G. (1980) *Schools of Linguistics* Stanford University Press

Sampson, G. (1985) *Writing Systems* Stanford University Press

Sanford, A. J. & Garrod, S. C. (1981) *Understanding Written Language* Wiley

Sankoff, G. & Laberge, S. (1974) On the acquisition of native speakers by a language. In DeCamp, D. & Hancock, I. (eds.) *Pidgins and Creoles* Georgetown University Press

Sato, C. J. (1985) Linguistic inequality in Hawai'i: The post-creole dilemma. In Wolfson, N. & Manes, J. (eds.) *Language and Inequality* Mouton

Savage-Rumbaugh, E. S. (1986) *Ape Language* Columbia University Press

Savage-Rumbaugh, E. S. & Lewin, R. (1994) *Kanzi* John Wiley

Scarcella, R. C., Andersen, E. & Krashen, S. D. (eds.) (1990) *Developing Communicative Competence in a Second Language* Newbury House

Schank, R. C. (1986) *Explanation Patterns: Understanding Mechanically and Creatively* Erlbaum

Schank, R. C. & Abelson, R. (1977) *Scripts, Plans, Goals and Understanding* Erlbaum

Scherer, K. R. & Giles, H. (eds.) (1979) *Social Markers in Speech* Cambridge University Press

Schiffrin, D. (1994) *Approaches to Discourse* Blackwell

Schmandt-Besserat, D. (1991) The earliest precursor of writing. In Wang (ed.)

Schmandt-Besserat, D. (1992) *Before Writing* University of Texas Press

Scholes, R. J. (ed.) (1993) *Literacy and Language Analysis* Erlbaum

Scollon, R. & Scollon, S. W. (1995) *Intercultural Communication* Blackwell

Searle, J. (1969) *Speech Acts* Cambridge University Press

Searle, J. (1979) *Expression and Meaning* Cambridge University Press

Sebeok, T. A. & Rosenthal, R. (eds.) (1981) The Clever Hans Phenomenon: Communication with Horses, Whales, Apes and People *Annals of the New York Academy of Sciences* 364

Sebeok, T. A. & Sebeok, J. U. (eds.) (1980) *Speaking of Apes: A Critical Anthology of Two-Way Communication with Man* Plenum Press

Seinfeld, J. (1993) *SeinLanguage* Bantam Books

Selinker, L. (1992) *Rediscovering Interlanguage* Longman

Sells, P. (1985) *Lectures on Contemporary Syntactic Theories* Center for the Study of Language and Information, Stanford University

Senner, W. M. (ed.) (1989) *The Origins of Writing* University of Nebraska Press

Seyfarth, R. M. & Cheney, D. L. (1992) Meaning and mind in monkeys *Scientific American* 267 (December)

Sharwood-Smith, M. (1994) *Second Language Learning* Longman

Shatz, M. (1994) *A Toddler's Life* Oxford University Press

Shopen, T. (ed.) (1985) *Language Typology and Syntactic Description* (3 Volumes) Cambridge University Press

Skehan, P. (1989) *Individual Differences in Second Language Learning*
    Edward Arnold.
Sinclair, J. M. (ed.) (1990) *Collins COBUILD English Grammar* Harper Collins
Sinclair, J. M. (1991) *Corpus, Concordance, Collocation* Oxford University
    Press
Sinclair, J. M. & Coulthard, R. M. (1975) *Towards an Analysis of Discourse*
    Oxford University Press
Slobin, D. I. (ed.) (1985) *The Crosslinguistic Study of Language Acquisition*
    Erlbaum
Smith, F. & Miller, G. A. (eds.) (1966) *The Genesis of Language* MIT Press
Smith, G. W. (1991) *Computers and Human Language* Oxford University Press
Snowdon, C. T., Brown, C. H. & Petersen, M. R. (eds.) (1982) *Primate
    Communication* Cambridge University Press
Spears, R. A. (1990) *Forbidden American English* Passport Books
Spencer, A. (1981) *Morphological Theory* Blackwell
Sperber, D. & Wilson, D. (1986) *Relevance* Blackwell
Spolsky, B. (1988) Bilingualism. In Newmeyer (ed.)
Spolsky, B. (1989) *Conditions for Second Language Learning* Oxford
    University Press
Springer, S. & Deutsch, G. (1993) *Left Brain, Right Brain* W.H. Freeman
Stam, J. H. (1976) *Inquiries into the Origin of Language: The Fate of a Question*
    Harper & Row
Stockwell, R. P., Schachter, P. & Partee, B. H. (1973) *The Major Syntactic
    Structures of English* Holt, Rinehart & Winston
Stokoe, W. C. (1960) *Sign Language Structure* Studies in Linguistics: Occasional
    Papers 8, University of Buffalo Press
Stokoe, W. C., Casterline D. & Croneberg, C. (1965) *A Dictionary of
    American Sign Language on Linguistic Principles* Gallaudet College Press
Stringer, C. B. & Andrews, F. (1988) Genetic and fossil evidence for the origin
    of modern humans *Science* 239: 1263–8
Stubbs, M. (1983) *Discourse Analysis* Blackwell
Swisher, M. V. (1984) Signed input of hearing mothers to deaf children
    Language Learning 34: 69–85
Swain, M. (1995) Three functions of output in second language learning.
    In Cook, G. & Seidlhofer, B. (eds.) *Principles and Practice in the Study
    of Language and Learning* Oxford University Press
Swan, M. & Smith, B. (1987) *Learner English* Cambridge University Press
Swift, J. (1726) *Gulliver's Travels* (Book 4)
Tannen, D. (1984) *Conversational Style* Ablex
Tannen, D. (1986) *That's Not What I Meant* William Morrow
Tannen, D. (1990) *You Just Don't Understand* William Morrow
Tannen, D. (1993) *Gender and Conversational Interaction* Oxford
    University Press

Tannen, D. (1994) *Gender and Discourse* Oxford University Press

Tarone, E. & Yule, G. (1985) Communication strategies in East-West interactions. In L. E. Smith (ed.) *Discourse across Cultures* Pergamon Press

Tarone, E. & Yule, G. (1989) *Focus on the Language Learner* Oxford University Press

Terrace, H. S. (1979) *Nim: A Chimpanzee Who Learned Sign Language* Alfred Knopf

Thieme, P. (1958) The Indo-European Language. *Scientific American* 199: 63–74

Thomas, R. (1992) *Literacy and Orality in Ancient Greece* Cambridge University Press

Thomason, S. G. & Kaufman, T. (1988) *Language Contact, Creolization and Genetic Linguistics* University of California Press

Thorne, B. , Kramarae, C. & Henley, N. (eds.) (1983) *Language, Gender and Society* Newbury House

Tobias, P. V. (1991) The emergence of language in hominid evolution. In Desmond (ed.)

Todd, L. (1990) *Pidgins and Creoles* (2nd edition) Routledge

Tomasello, M. (1992) *First Verbs* Cambridge University Press

Trudgill, P. (1974) *The Social Differentiation of English in Norwich* Cambridge University Press

Trudgill, P. (1983) *On Dialect* Blackwell

Trudgill, P. (1986) *Dialects in Contact* Blackwell

Trudgill, P. (1990) *The Dialects of England* Blackwell

Trudgill, P. (1994) *Dialects* Routledge

Trudgill, P. & Chambers, J.K. (1991) *Dialects of English* Longman

Trudgill, P. & Hannah, J. (1994) *International English: A Guide to Varieties of Standard English* (2nd edition) Edward Arnold

Tsohatzidis, S. L. (ed.) (1990) *Meanings and Prototypes* Routledge

T.S.W. (1970) Hints on pronunciation for foreigners. In Mackay, D. (ed.) *A Flock of Words* Harcourt, Brace and World

Ullman, B. L. (1969) *Ancient Writing and its Influence* MIT Press

Umiker-Sebeok, D-J. & Sebeok, T. A. (eds.) (1987) *Monastic Sign Languages* Mouton de Gruyter

Ur, P. (1988) *Grammar Practice Activities* Cambridge University Press

Valdman, A. (ed.) (1977) *Pidgin and Creole Linguistics* Indiana University Press

Van Cleve, J.V. (ed.) (1987) *Gallaudet Encyclopedia of Deaf People and Deafness* (3 Volumes) McGraw-Hill

van Dijk, T.A. (ed.) (1985) *Handbook of Discourse Analysis* (4 Volumes) Academic Press

Viereck, W. & Bald, W.-F. (eds.) (1986) *English in Contact with Other Languages* Akademiai Kiado Budapest

Voltera, V. & Erting, C. J. (eds.) (1990) *From Gesture to Language in Hearing and Deaf Children* Springer Verlag von Frisch, K. (1962) Dialects in the language of the bees *Scientific American* 207:79–87

von Frisch, K. (1967) *The Dance Language and Orientation of Bees* Belknap Press

von Raffler-Engel, W., Wind, J. & Jonker, A. (eds.) (1991) *Studies in Language Origins* John Benjamins

Walker, C. B. (1987) *Cuneiform* University of California Press

Wallman, J. (1992) *Aping Language* Cambridge University Press

Walters, K. (1988) Dialectology. In Newmeyer (ed.)

Wang, W. S-Y. (ed.) (1991) *The Emergence of Language. Development and Evolution* W.H. Freeman

Wanner, E. & Gleitman, L. R. (eds.) (1983) *Language Acquisition. The State of the Art* Cambridge University Press

Wardhaugh, R. (1992) *An Introduction to Sociolinguistics* (2nd edition) Blackwell

Watt, W. C. (ed.) (1994) *Writing Systems and Cognition* Kluwer

Watts, R.J., Ide, S. & Ehlich, K. (eds.) (1992) *Politeness in Language* Mouton de Gruyter

Weir, R. H. (1966) Questions on the learning of phonology. In Smith & Miller (eds.)

Weisenberg, T. & McBride, K. E. (1964) *Aphasia* Hafner

Weizenbaum, J. (1976) *Computer Power and Human Reason* Freeman

Wekker, H. & Haegeman, L. (1985) *A Modern Course in English Syntax* Croom Helm

Wells, C. G. (1985) *Language Development in the Pre-school Years* Cambridge University Press

Wells, G. A. (1987) *The Origin of Language* Open Court

Whiten, A. (ed.) (1991) *Natural Theories of Mind* Blackwell

Widdowson, H. G. (1978) *Teaching Language as Communication* Oxford University Press

Widdowson, H. G. (1990) *Aspects of Language Teaching* Oxford University Press

Wierzbicka, A. (1987) *English Speech Act Verbs* Academic Press

Wierzbicka, A. (1991) *Cross-cultural Pragmatics* Mouton de Gruyter

Wilbur, R. B. (1987) *American Sign Language* Little Brown

Williams, J. M. (1975) *Origins of the English Language. A Social and Linguistic History* The Free Press

Williams, S. (ed.) (1985) *Humans and Machines* Ablex

Wilson, E. (1991) Animal communication. In Wang (ed.)

Wind, J., Chiarelli, B., Bichakjian, B. & Nosentini, A. (eds.) (1991) *Language Origins: A Multidisciplinary Approach* Kluwer

Winograd, T. (1972) *Understanding Natural Language* Academic Press

Winograd, T. (1984) Computer software for working with language *Scientific American* 251: 130–15

Winston, P. H. (1977) *Artificial Intelligence* Addison-Wesley

Wolfram, W. & Johnson, R. (1982) *Phonological Analysis: Focus on American English* Harcourt, Brace, Jovanovich

Wolfson, N. (1989) *Perspectives: Sociolinguistics and TESOL* Newbury House

Woll, B., Kyle, J. & Deuchar, M. (eds.) (1981) *Perspectives on British Sign Language and Deafness* Croom Helm

Wood, D., Wood, H., Griffiths, A. & Howarth, I. (1986) *Teaching and Talking with Deaf Children* John Wiley

Woodward, J. (1980) Some sociolinguistic aspects of French and American Sign Languages. In Lane & Grosjean (eds.)

Yannakoudakis, E. & Hutton, P. (1987) *Speech Synthesis and Recognition Systems* Ellis Horwood

Yule, G. (1996) *Pragmatics* Oxford University Press

Yule, G. & Gregory, W. (1989) Survey interviews for interactive language learning *ELT Journal* 43: 142–9

Zurif, E. B. (1990) Language and the brain. In Osherson & Lasnik (eds.)

Zwicky, A. (1982) Classical malapropisms and the creation of a mental lexicon. In Obler, L. & Menn, L. (eds.) *Exceptional Language and Linguistics* Academic Press

Index

Technical terms and page references where definitions can be found are indicated by **bold** type.

abstract 55,102,207
accent 227
acceptance 233
acoustic phonetics 41
acquisition 175–176,191
acrolect 235
acronym 68-69
action 116
active voice 89,102
adjective 88,104–107
adverb 88,105–108,208
affect 192
affective filter 192
affix 69–70,75
affricate 45, 46
age 241
agent 117
agrammatic 168
agreement 89
airstream 41
allomorph 79
allophone 55–56
alphabet 13,206
alphabetic writing 13,15
alphabetisms 68
alternate sign language 202–203
alveolar ridge 42,43,47

alveolars 43,45
alveo-palatals 43,45
ambiguity 103
Ameslan (American Sign Language) 31,34,176,202–209
Amuzgo 97
analogy 70
analytic processing 170
anaphora 131,136,140,157
Anglo-Saxons 218
angma 44
animate 115,247–248
anomia 168
antecedent 131
anterior speech cortex 163
anthropologist 246
antonyms 119–120,186
aphasia 167–169
applied linguistics 197
approximants 45,46
Arabic 13,21,45,56,65,95,214,243, 246
arbitrariness 21,22,28,32
arcuate fasciculus 164,168
Aristotle 165
arrow 104
article 88,104–105

articulation 41,58–59,152,164
articulatory parameters 205
articulatory phonetics 41
artificial intelligence 153
ASL 202–209
aspiration 55,61
assimilation 59–60
associative meaning 114–115
asterisk 87
audiolingual method 193
auditory phonetics 41
Aztec 80

babbling 178–179
Babel 2
baby talk 177
backformation 67
background knowledge 146–148
back vowels 48
Baltic 214
Balto-Slavic 214
Bantu 65
Basari 84
basilect 235
bee communication 21,23
Bell,Alexander Graham 210
Bengali 214
bidialectal 231
bilabials 42,45
bilingual 231
bilingualism 231,236
biological schedule 176
Black English Vernacular (BEV) 243
blending 66
bonobo 36
borrowing 65
bottom up 154
bound morphemes 75–76
bound stems 76
boustrophedon 15
bow-wow theory 2
braces 104
bracketed 94–95,105
brackets,round 104
brackets,curly 104
brain 5,162–172

brain stem 163
British English 49,236
British Sign Language 205
broadening 222
Broca's aphasia 168
Broca's area 163–164
Buckingham 174,265
Bulgarian 214

calque 65
caretaker speech 177–178
Carib Indians 242
category change 67
cave drawings 9
Caxton 192
Celtic 214
cerebral damage 167
characters 11
Chaucer 219
Cherokee 12
child language 175–186
chimpanzees 26,31–37
Chinese 10,11,65,199,214
Chomsky 34,37,101,177,187
Clever,Hans 34,38
clipping 66
closed class 76
closed syllable 57
coarticulation effects 58–60
coda 57–58
codification 233
cognate 215
coherence 141
cohesion 140–141
cohesive links 141,149
cohesive ties 140,142
co-hyponyms 120
coinage 64
collocation 122–123
communication strategies 197,198
communicative 19,27
communicative approaches 193–194
communicative competence 197
comparative form 77
comparative reconstruction 215–216
complementary pairs 118

completion point   143
compounding   65
comprehensible input   196,199
computer   151
conceptual meaning   114–115
conditioned response   35
conduction aphasia   168–169
conjunction   88
connotation   114
Conrad   191
consonant clusters   57–58
consonants   41–48,57–60
constancy under negation   132
constituents   93–4,104–109
context   129
continuum   230
conventional knowledge   146
conversation   142–144,149,155–156
conversational interaction   143–144
conversational style   143–144
conversion   67–68
cooing   178
co-operative principle   145
copula   243
corpus callosum   163
correction   181,184
cortex   164
co-text   129
covert prestige   240
creative construction   194
creativity   23,248
Creole   234,235
critical period   171,191
cultural transmission   24,203,246
culture   246
cuneiform   11
Cyrillic alphabet   13
Czech   65,214

Danish   214
deaf education   203–204
deep structure   102–103
deictic expressions   130
deixis   129–130,135
demotic   246

dentals   43,45,56
derivation   69
derivational morpheme   76–78,80
descriptive approach   92
de Vaucanson   151
diachronic   223
diacritic   56
dialect   227
dialect boundary   229–230
dialect continuum   230–231
dialect survey   228–229
dichotic listening   169–170
dictation systems   152
dictionary   121
diglossia   245–246
diphthong   49
diphthongization   49
direct speech act   133
discourse analysis   139–148
discreteness   24
displacement   20,21
divine source   1–2
dolphins   35
double articulation   25
double negative   221,243
drills   193
duality   25
Dutch   14,65,197,214,230

education   240
Egyptian   2,10,12,13,14
elaboration   233
elision   59–60
ELIZA   155–156
epenthesis   220
eponyms   72
errors   140,172,194
Eskimo   247,248
eth   43
ethnic background   243
experiencer   117
Ewe   111

face   134
face-saving act   134

face-threatening act   134
facial expressions   143
family tree   214
Fant   208
features   55, 115–116
female   242, 252
feminine   90, 248
filled pauses   144
fingerspelling   206
finite   101
first person   89–90
fixed reference   23
flap   47, 56
foreign language learning   193
foreigner talk   196
forensic phonetics   41
formal style   244
fossilization   195
free morpheme   75–76
free stem   76
French   14, 45, 56, 65, 66, 90, 193,
   214, 219
French Sign Language   205
fricatives   45, 46, 216
front vowels   48
function   133
functional morpheme   76, 234
functional shift   67
future   96

Gaelic   95, 96, 111, 214
Gage, Phineas   162
Gallaudet   205
Ganda   80
Gardner   31, 35
gender   89–90, 242
generate   101
generative   101
Genesis   1, 2
Genie   171–172, 173
German   45, 65, 90, 214, 220, 230
Germanic   214, 218, 224
gesture   3, 7, 27, 202
glides   47, 49
glossogenetics   4

glottals   44, 45
glottal stop   47
goal   117
gradable antonyms   118, 125
graffiti   15
grammar   87–95, 191, 249
grammar-translation method   193
grammatical competence   197
grammatical gender   90
Greek   13, 79, 89, 100, 130, 214, 215, 246
Gros Ventre   242
Groucho Marx   103
Gua   31
GUS   160

Haiti   234
Hawai'i   234, 237, 248
Hawaiian   58
Hawaiian Creole   234, 237
Hayes   31
Hebrew   2, 13, 233
Hellenic,   214
hemispheres   5, 163, 169–170
hesitation markers   144
hierarchical   95, 105, 113, 119
hieroglyphics   10
Hindi   214, 233
Hindu   1
Hmong   65, 71–72
Hockett   26
holistic processing   170
holophrastic   179, 185
homonymy   120–121, 129
homophony   120–121
Hopi   247, 248
Hungarian   65
hypocorism   67, 70
hyponymy   119–120, 185

icon   207
iconic   21, 28, 207, 210
ideogram   10, 11
idiolect   244
ill-formed   87, 101
Ilocano   81

imitation   181
immediate constituent analysis   93
implementation   233
implicature   146
inclusion   119
indirect speech act   133
Indo-European   214,223
Indo-Iranian   214
inference   131,146–148
infinite   101
infinitive   91–92
infix   69–70,81
inflectional morpheme   77–78,80–81,
   182,221,234
informal style   244
informative   20,27
innate   175,177
input   196
inscriptions   9
instrument   117
intended meaning   128
interactional   6
interdental   43
interference   195
interlanguage   195
International Phonetic Association   45
inversion   184
invisible meaning   127
Iranian   214
Irish   214
isogloss   229
Italian   65,214,216

Jamaica   .234,235
Japanese   12,58,65,95,98,194,244
jargon   245
Jespersen   1
Jones   213

Kamhmu   69–70
Kanuri   80
Kanzi   36
Kellogg   31
Kirk, Captain   91
Koasati   242

Koko   32

L1 (first language)   **190**
L2 (second language)   **190**
labeled brackets   94–95,105
labeled tree diagram   105–106
labiodentals   42–43,45
Ladefoged   45
Lana   32–33
language disabilities   163
language faculty   175,191
language function   163,194
language loyalty   243
language planning   232–233
language universals   248–249
larynx   5,41–42
lateralized   5,171,191
Latin   14,79,89–92,97,193,214,215,
   217,218,220,224
Latvian   214
learning   191
lexical morpheme   76
lexical relations   118–122
lexical rules   106–107
linguistic atlas   229
linguistic context   129
linguistic determinism   246–247
linguistic etiquette   87,91
linguistic geography   226
lipreading   203
liquids   47
Lithuanian   214
loan translation   65
localization   164–165
location   117
location (ASL)   205–206
logogram   11,12,33
Lord's Prayer   213,217
Loulis   36

machines   151–159
majority principle   216
Malapropism   166,172
male   116,242,252
manner maxim   145

Manually Coded English   204
masculine   90
Matata   26,36
mathematics   101,191
Mayan languages   233
maxims   145
meaning   114–148
Melanesian Pidgin   233
memory   156
mesolect   235
metathesis   220
metonymy   122
Middle English   218–219,224
mime   207
minimal pair   56–57
minimal set   56–57
model   151
Modern English   218,219
monolingual   232
morphemes   75–78
morphology   74–85,182
morphs   79
most natural development   216
motivation   195
motor aphasia   168
motor cortex   164
motor movements   164
movement   205–206

narrowing   222
nasalized   56,59
nasals   45,46,56,59
natural class   55
natural gender   89
natural language   151
natural-sound source   2,3
navigators   152
negative face   134
negative transfer   195
negatives   184–185
negotiated input   196,199
neologism   64
neurolinguistics   162
neuter   90
Nim Chimpsky   34,35

non-directionality   26
non-gradable antonyms   118–119
non-verbal   3,170
Norman French   218
NORMS   229
Norwegian   214
noun   88,92,104–107
noun phrase (NP)   93,104–107
nucleus   57–58
number   89

object   154,221
obligatory   104
official language   237
Old English   77,218,243
Old Norse   79,218
one-word stage   179
onomatopoeic   3,22,28
onset   57–58
open class   76
open-endedness   23
open syllable   57
optional   104,109
oral gesture theory   3,4
oralism   203,211
orientation   205,–206
output   196
overextension   185
overgeneralization   182,194
Overstreet   162
overt prestige   240

palatal   44
palate   42,43
parentheses   104
parsing   153–154
particle movement   109
parts of speech   88
passive voice   89,102,112
past tense   61,77,89
pattern recognition   155
pauses   143–144
Persian   65,214
person   89–90
person deixis   130

pharyngeals 45
pharynx 5,42,45
philology 214
Phoenicians 12,13
phone 55–56
phoneme 54–57
phonetics 40–52
phonographic writing 11
phonology 54–60,191
phonotactics 57
phrase structure rules 106–107
physical context 129
physiological adaptation 5
pictograms 10,11,17
Pidgin 233–234
place deixis 130
plan-based system 158
plural 61,77,78,79,84–85,88–90
Polish 191,214
politeness 134,137–138
polysemy 121
Portuguese 214
positive face 134
positive transfer 194
possessive 77,88
Post-Creole continuum 235
posterior speech cortex 164
PRAGMA 158
pragmatics 127–134,197
preference 150
prefix 69,80
pre-language 178–179
Premack 32
preposition 88,105–107
prepositional phrase (PP)
prescriptive approach 91–92
present tense 77,89,90
presupposition 131–132
primary sign language 203
primes 206
printing 14
processing 170
productivity 22,23,101
proficiency 190
program 154,155,156

pronoun 88–89,104–107
pronunciation 227,241
proper noun 104–107
prothesis 221
proto 214,215,224
Proto-Indo-European 214
prototype 120,124
Psammetichus 2

quality maxim 145
quantity maxim 145
questions 183–184

rapid fade 26
Rebus writing 12
reciprocity 25
recursion 101–102,107–108
reduplication 81
reference 130–131
regional dialect 228–230
register 245
relation maxim 145
resonator 5
reversive 119
right ear advantage 169–170
rime 57–58
Romanian 214
Romans 13
Rumbaugh 33
Russian 13,214,243

Sanskrit 213,214,215
Santa Claus 246
Sapir-Whorf hypothesis 247
Sarah 32–33
Savage-Rumbaugh 36
schema(ta) 147
schwa 49,59
Scottish 95,111,227
script 147–148
second person 89–90
selection 233
self-consciousness 192
semantically odd 115,124
semantic features 115–116

semantic role **116**–117,124
semantics **114**–123,154,185
semi-vowels 47
sensory aphasia 168
Sequoyah 12
sex 240,242
Shakespeare 219
shape **205**–206
Sherman and Austin 36
SHRDLU 156–157
Sierra Leone 234
Signed English **203**–204
signing 202–204
sign language **202**–209
simultaneous method 204
singular 77,89–90
Slavic 13,214
slip of the ear **167**
slip of the tongue **166**–167
social class 240–241
social dialect **240**
social identity 239
sociolinguistic competence **197**
sociolinguistics **239**–240
sound change 219–220
source **117**
Spanish 65,66,90,95,194,195,214,
220,233
specialization **25**
speech act **132**–133,136–137,142
speech community 239
speech events 142
speech recognition **152**
speech synthesis **152**
spelling reform 14
Spoonerism **166**
Standard English **227**,237
Star Trek 91
stem **75**–76
stops **45**,46,216
strategic competence **197**
structural ambiguity 102–103
structural analysis **92**
structural change 109,112
structural description 109,112

structure dependency 113
style **244**
stylistic 114
subject 154,221
suffix **69**,77
Sumerians 11
superlative 77
superordinate 120,124
surface structure **102**–103
Swahili 74,83–84,233
Swedish 214
Swift, Jonathan 30
syllabary 12
syllabic writing **12**,13
syllable 12,**57**–58,166
synchronic **223**
synonyms **118**
syntactic structure 104–109
syntax **100**–113,153–154,183–184
synthetic speech 152

Tagalog 81,84
tag question 112–113,242
task-based learning **197**
telegraphic speech **180**
tense **89**–90,96
Terrace 33–34
test frames 92
text 140–141
theme **117**
theta 43
third person 89–90
tip of the tongue **166**
time deixis **130**
Tok Pisin 233,234
tongue slips 166–167
tool using 5,7
top down **154**
trachea 41
traditional grammar 89
transactional **6**
transfer **194**
transformational rules **108**–109,112
tree diagram **105**–106
Turkish 65,82–83

turn 143
turn taking 143–144
Tuvaluan 248
two-word stage 180

understander system 155–158
unmarked 125
uvula 42,45

variation 143,223,226
velars 44,45,178
velum 42,44,46
verb 88,105–109
verb phrase 93,105–109
Viki 31
Vikings 218
vocabulary 180,188,191
vocal auditory channel 25
vocal cords 5,41–42,47
vocal tract 31,53
voice box 5
voiced 41,214

voiceless 41,214
von Frisch 23
vowels 48–49

Wales 231
Washoe 31–32,34,36
Webster 70
wedge 43
Weizenbaum 151,155
well-formed 101
Welsh 214,231
Wernicke's aphasia 168
Wernicke's area 164
windpipe 41
word order 87,204
word storage 166
world knowledge 154

Yerkish 33,36
yo-heave-ho theory 3

zero morph 79